BEING-TIME

Being-Time

A Practitioner's Guide to

Dōgen's Shōbōgenzō Uji

Shinshu Roberts

Wisdom Publications
199 Elm Street
Somerville, MA 02144 USA
www.wisdomexperience.org

Library of Congress Cataloging-in-Publication Data
Names: Roberts, Shinshu, author.
Title: Being-time: a practitioner's guide to Dōgen's Shōbōgenzō Uji / Shinshu Roberts.
Description: Somerville: Wisdom Publications, 2018. | Includes bibliographical references and index. |
Identifiers: LCCN 2017018053 (print) | LCCN 2017058164 (ebook) | ISBN 9781614291381 (ebook) | ISBN 1614291381 (ebook) | ISBN 9781614291138 (pbk.: alk. paper) | ISBN 1614291136 (pbk.: alk. paper)
Subjects: LCSH: Dōgen, 1200–1253. Shōbō genzō. | Spiritual life—Sōtōshū. | Sōtōshū—Doctrines.
Classification: LCC BQ9449.D654 (ebook) | LCC BQ9449.D654 S5337325 2018 (print) | DDC 294.3/85—dc23
LC record available at https://lccn.loc.gov/2017018053

ISBN 978-1-61429-113-8   ebook 978-1-61429-138-1

24 23 22   5 4 3

Cover design by Jess Morphew.
Interior design by Gopa & Ted2, Inc. Set in Minion Pro 10.9/15.8.

Wisdom Publications' books are printed on acid-free paper and meet the guidelines for permanence and durability of the Production Guidelines for Book Longevity of the Council on Library Resources.

Printed in the United States of America.

Please visit fscus.org.

Day and night
Night and day,
The way of Dharma as everyday life;
In each act our hearts
Resonate with the call of the sūtra.

—Eihei Dōgen[1]

Contents

Foreword

OF ALL THE many important interlocking concepts that comprise basic Buddhist teaching, none is more important than impermanence. The four noble truths—suffering, cause of suffering, end of suffering, and path—flow from it. We suffer because everything is impermanent, everything ends, loss is inevitable. This is the inescapable human condition the path is set forth to address.

But a more detailed look at Buddhist teachings on impermanence, especially Mahāyāna teachings, changes the initial impression. Impermanence, it becomes clear, doesn't mean that things last for a while then pass away: things arise and pass away *at the same time*. That is, things don't exist as we imagine they do. Much of our experience of reality is illusory. And this is why we suffer.

In effect, what these teachings are telling us is that impermanence is time itself, being itself, and that time and being are not at all as we imagine them to be, they are utterly otherwise. To really understand and fully embrace this point is to live in a radically different world—a world of awakening, inclusion, and love. Time is the lock—and the key!—to Buddhist teachings, and to our lives.

As far as I am aware, Dōgen is the only Buddhist teacher who frames the teaching on impermanence explicitly as a teaching about time. And just as for Buddha impermanence is central, so for Dōgen time is the central conception of the whole of his thought. All of Dōgen's profoundly poetic teachings flow from his seminal understanding of time, as expressed in "Uji" (Being-Time), his famous (and famously difficult) essay in his masterwork, Shōbōgenzō.

In "Uji," Dōgen teaches that time itself, being itself, is luminous awakening. It is all-inclusive, all-elusive, ultimately healing, and eternal. Clearly, there is much to ponder here. Yet "Uji" is only a few short pages in length. These pages, and this teaching, is the subject of the sturdy and detailed volume you now have in your hands.

Zen is famous for advocating direct experience and intense meditation. Traditionally—and this is still true in many Zen places—study is not only discouraged, it is forbidden. But in our Sōtō Zen tradition, following Dōgen, study is prized, not necessarily for the knowledge it provides but as an important component in spiritual practice. Shinshu Roberts, a Sōtō Zen priest of long experience, has, from the beginning of her practice, valued and prized study as a primary gate for entry into the realms of faith and illumination. This book is the fruit of her many years of practicing this.

Dōgen's works (and "Uji" is perhaps typical of them) are inspirational. But their inspiration doesn't come without some effort. Noted for the density and multifaceted nature of their presentation, Dōgen's works require serious study.

In this text Shinshu does full justice, as no other book I know of, to Dōgen's words. She offers interpretation only after careful consideration and marshaling of many sources. She offers simple everyday examples to illustrate points that seem at first abstruse. As a priest working closely with contemporary Zen students, she never loses sight of the fact that Dōgen's teachings are intended to be put into practice in daily living, not merely studied and discussed. I am truly impressed by the thoroughness, intensity, love, and faith that Shinshu has put into this book.

Allow me to suggest to the reader a way to proceed. Do not read this text as you ordinarily read, going along at a steady pace, with the assumption that you will understand what is being said. Instead, take your time. Go slow. Ponder. Read repeatedly the many quotations from Dōgen cited (not only from "Uji," but from many other related texts). Perhaps write them down. Don't try too hard to understand. Let the words seep in, echo. Be willing not to understand. Be willing to feel the uncomfortable feeling that perhaps what you think you know, even fundamentally know, about your life isn't right. Be willing to marvel at this feeling, even affirm it, and not to insist that it go away. Be amazed.

If this text causes you to doubt your most cherished concepts about your life, it will have done its work.

NORMAN FISCHER is the spiritual director of the Everyday Zen Foundation, and a former abbot of the San Francisco Zen Center. He's also the author of numerous books on Zen, religion, and writing.

Preface

I RELIED PRIMARILY upon scholarly articles, glossaries, and translation footnotes to ascertain the basic meaning of the text. Practicing with the material arose from my own exploration and reading the few practice commentaries on parts of "Uji," such as Dainin Katagiri Roshi's book *Each Moment Is the Universe*.[1]

As much as possible I have tried to grasp what Dōgen means, not what I think he might mean. When reading Dōgen, we must be careful to avoid the tendency to translate what we do not understand into something we already understand. For instance, we might be tempted to categorize everything as the doctrine of form and emptiness, or the relative and absolute. If we applied that logic to being-time, we would not see the vast scope of Dōgen's vision.

Since I do not read Japanese, I depended, in part, upon the interpretation of others. Included in this process was finding various translations of the same word or phrase in more than one fascicle of the Shōbōgenzō or another text by Dōgen, such as his collection of three hundred kōans or the Eihei Kōroku. Several of Dōgen's books have excellent translations in English.

Because Dōgen's original texts do not conform to modern textual divisions, even the scholar must make translation decisions based upon his or her understanding of the meaning the text. Dōgen did not write paragraphs or stress delineations between ideas. When we read a translation divided into paragraphs, those divisions are the translator's choice, not Dōgen's. Translators sometimes omit arcane references by translating them into a more palatable form. One such example would be transforming the phrase "one hundred grasses" into "myriad things."

Some sentences such as "Entirely worlding the entire world with the whole world is thus called penetrating exhaustively"[2] present the translator with particular challenges. In Japanese this sentence is constructed by combining the three characters *jin*, *kai*, and *gu*. Using *jin* as a root word, Dōgen combines it with *kai* and *gu* in some conventional and unlikely ways, resulting in several variations: "entirely worlding the entire world with the whole world,"[3] "To universally realize the whole Universe by using the whole Universe,"[4] or "To fully actualize the entire world with the entire world."[5]

Therefore, it is helpful to read more than one translation of a Dōgen text whenever possible. Each translator has his or her particular understanding, which will determine word choice. Some translators make the English version more accessible by interpreting and editing the text, and others stay closer to a word-by-word translation. Every translation is colored by the translator's understanding of the text and his or her imagined reader. Some translators omit any obscure references or paraphrase sentences.

Translations of the titles of the fascicles in the Shōbōgenzō vary. I have used a standard translation for the body of this book regardless of the translator's rendition found in the endnotes. You may notice the discrepancies as you look at citations for various fascicles.

I chose Waddell and Abe's translation of "Uji" because they are well respected translators of Dōgen who give an accurate reading of the complete text. Each chapter in this book roughly corresponds to a paragraph of their translation and opens with the paragraph or line of the text to be discussed. I have used the Japanese names for Dōgen's writings with the English translation in parentheses because as a reader I appreciate having access to both the Japanese and English versions of a fascicle's title.

I have deliberately tried to find supporting quotations from different fascicles of the Shōbōgenzō and other writings of Dōgen. My intention is to give the reader a broader view of Dōgen's thought by using his own words. I am also trying to illustrate that Dōgen often explains difficult ideas in various ways. There are a lot of endnotes in this book. Again, this is an attempt to give readers the resources to continue their own exploration of the text by using my source material.

In "Uji," Dōgen offers guidance for awakening. He instructs: see the Buddha's golden light in every hour of our day, cultivate doubt about your view of time and being, investigate how it is that particular being-time coexists with all being-time, and know that practice-realization is right now. He questions: What is the nature of all beings' time? Is there anything missing in your present moment? What is the nature of being-time's passage? How can this moment be an independent being-time, the preceding being-time, and the moments that come after? How is it that this moment of our practice swallows up our goal in practice? How can we expect to come to some realization when we think enlightenment is "out there" rather than "right here, right now"?

Altogether, "Uji" is a series of problems, questions, and statements about our life. As we follow Dōgen's logic, we may come to some understanding. Of course, just having an intellectual grasp of being-time does not ensure our realization, but it will help us frame the right questions and look for the right signs.

In this commentary, I begin each chapter with my understanding of the text, followed by examples of practice application. As the commentary progresses, I focus more on meaning and less on giving contemporary practice parallels. This seems to happen naturally as the text moves from an explanation of what being-time is to an exploration of how being-time expresses.

"Uji" is a series of spiraling circles coming back upon themselves. Dōgen begins the text striving to illuminate his ideas to an uninitiated audience. As he explains his various views of being-time, he moves from clarifying meaning to expressing actualization of being-time. My hope is that the reader will have made a similar journey, thereby absorbing the basic trajectory of Dōgen's teaching. By the end of the book and of "Uji," the concern is more with discussing the process of actualization rather than understanding the basic meaning of the text.

In chapters 1 and 2 of this commentary, Dōgen presents opening verses that serve as an introduction to his point of view and a summary of *uji* as being-time. Over the course of chapters 3 through 7, I examine how Dōgen lays the groundwork for our inquiry. He questions our understanding of time, and he tells us that our practice must reflect and be in accord with all being, a state that he calls "setting the self out in array and making the whole world."[6] He explains how one being-time is all being-time.

Chapters 8 through 13 introduce Dōgen's assessment of how we understand practice. Dōgen addresses the conventional idea of the spiritual path being a sequential practice leading to realization. Disabusing ourselves of this notion is of primary importance, because our preconceived ideas about enlightenment can become stumbling blocks. We want to approach our practice with an open mind, a mind of curiosity and exploration, firmly grounded in where we are right now, rather than an idea of where we think we should be.

In chapters 14 to 19, I look at how Dōgen addresses the question of each moment moving from this time to the next, while maintaining an independent presencing of just this moment. If we understand the importance of this way of experiencing our progress, we will realize the key is to be fully immersed in and fully live out our lives, just as they are. Experiencing our interconnection and interpenetrating relationship with all beings is the genesis of our happiness. Even the most mundane task becomes meaningful and fulfilling when we feel a universal connection with the totality of being.

In chapters 20 through 23, Dōgen comments on the mistaken view that realization is predicated upon sequential and causally conditioned time. The true situation is that realization is actualizing what is fully presencing in this moment, including the self. Dōgen discusses being-time's passage as the time of the whole world simultaneously presencing itself. This presencing as independent and mutual arising is the practice of all being (universal) and beings (particular) making passage as being-time.

In chapters 24 through 30, we come to the final part of Dōgen's teaching on being-time. He uses concrete examples of teachers teaching the practice of being-time. He also applies kōans associated with the phrase "for the time being."

As Dōgen reaches the end of his text on being-time, he comes full circle. Yaoshan's question of Mazu, which begins this last section, is the occasion for Yaoshan's awakening. Yaoshan's verse at the beginning of "Uji" is an expression of his understanding. The whole text has been a thorough exploration of just what it is to know and practice with time-being.

A NOTE TO THE READER

For ease of reading, diacritical marks in this book have been edited for consistency, including within quoted material.

Acknowledgments

———————————————————————————————————————◆

In 2006, I was asked by Linda Galijan to teach a seminar on Dōgen's Shōbōgenzō "Uji." Other core members of the early group were Susan O'Connell, Lee Lipp, and Cathleen Williams. Cathleen was a reader for an early draft of this book. A deep gasshō to each of these women. I would also like to thank San Francisco Zen Center for making available a meeting space for our work.

Current members Marcia Lieberman, Peter Goetz, David Zimmerman, Konin Cardenas, Julia Ten Eyck, and Daigan Gaither all helped to shape this book through our shared exploration of the meaning of "Uji."

Randy Chelsey, Sue Walter, and Hollye Hurst, students at my home temple, Ocean Gate Zen Center, also have taken this journey with me. Randy read ten pages a day of an early draft of the book, editing and offering suggestions. A herculean effort.

Professor Carl Bielefeldt was kind enough to discuss aspects of the book with me early in my process. Chodo Cross, a translator of Master Dōgen's Shōbōgenzō, generously agreed to let me quote sections of his book. A deep bow of gratitude to his cotranslator Gudo Nishijima, who died in 2014. His contribution to students of Dōgen has been immeasurable. I am also indebted to all the Dōgen scholars and translators who have made this material accessible to Western students.

Eido Frances Carney gave me the opportunity to publish an essay on "Uji" in *Receiving the Marrow: Teachings on Dōgen by Sōtō Zen Women Priests*, a book she edited and compiled. This essay was the basis for a book proposal. Thank you, Eido-san.

Norman Fischer, Gil Fronsdal, Shohaku Okumura, and Grace Schireson all wrote encouraging remarks that I included in the proposal. Deep gratitude to these four people for their help. At Wisdom, Andy Francis's editing helped me find a clearer structure for the book, and Josh Bartok brought the book home. A hearty thank-you to both Andy and Josh.

I would like to thank SUNY Press for agreeing to let me use Norman Waddell and Masao Abe's translation of "Uji" from their book of translations: *The Heart of Dōgen's Shōbōgenzō*. I am also grateful to San Francisco Zen Center for allowing me to include quotations from Shunryū Suzuki Roshi's unpublished lecture transcripts.

A deep bow to my teacher and honshi, Sojun Weitsman Roshi, who has inspired my practice since 1988. He has shown me the quiet deep practice of attending to daily life.

Finally my deepest gratitude to Daijaku Kinst, my spouse and friend, who has supported me during the writing of this book in more ways than I can list.

Introduction

APPROACHING THE STUDY OF DŌGEN

DŌGEN ZENJI founded the Sōtō School of Japanese Buddhism (thirteenth century) after returning from China, where he became a lineage holder of the Chinese Caodong (J. Sōtō) School. At this point he began a series of writings and teachings that have rocked the Zen world ever since. His ideas have gone beyond the realm of practice to become part of a larger Western philosophical discussion, and this is particularly true of his text "Uji."

"Uji" (Being-Time) is part of a larger work called Shōbōgenzō (The True Dharma Eye). Dōgen wrote "Uji" in 1240, while he was teaching at Kōshōji in Kyoto. He was forty years old.[1]

In almost all of his writings, Dōgen uses poetic wording and seemingly abstruse metaphors, which add to our difficulty in understanding his teaching. At the same time, this language encourages us to drop our quest for intellectual understanding and enter the realm of the intuitive. We often begin our journey with Dōgen through our sense that there is something we glimpse but cannot yet articulate. Based upon this feeling we return again and again to his teachings until a glimmer of understanding begins to appear. Finally we are able to take a stab at articulating his meaning.

Although parts of "Uji" appear to be repetitious, they are usually restating his thesis in order to present a more nuanced reinterpretation of the material. Dōgen's teaching in "Uji" is like the many facets of a diamond. As is true of many other chapters in the Shōbōgenzō, one can find references to most of his major ideas. For my part, I tried to briefly restate the basic premise of his thought and then offer my understanding of whatever aspect he is bringing forward. When a part of "Uji" appeared repetitious to me, I always asked myself what Dōgen's reason could be for restating an idea.

We must persevere and meet Dōgen. Meeting him includes the intellectual process of understanding the basic meaning of the text. My focus in this book is twofold: first, to explore the meaning of Dōgen's thesis in order to understand the basic flow of the text and, second, to give examples of ways to apply Dōgen's understanding to our practice. In some ways, the first task seems more difficult than the second. And of course, the second depends upon the first.

General Concerns outside the Text

Dōgen has been accused of espousing nihilistic teachings[2] because he often focuses upon the nondual aspects of practice. For this reason, caution is perhaps necessary in approaching "Uji." I find this criticism odd because the doctrine of emptiness is essentially about our sameness, not our differences. Since the use of the word *emptiness* is shorthand for "empty of inherent existence," understanding its full import means entering into a space of connection in which compassion is sure to follow. It is from this ground of interpenetration that Buddhist ethics arise. It is important to remember this while reading "Uji."[3]

One text in which Dōgen clearly states his understanding of ethical action is "Shoaku Makusa" (Not Doing Wrongs). Dōgen wrote this fascicle two months before writing "Uji"; perhaps this is not a coincidence.

In "Shoaku Makusa" (Not Doing Wrongs) Dōgen writes that the basis of not creating harm is predicated upon our interconnected nature, which is reality-itself-being-time. He writes: "Right and wrong are time; time is not right or wrong. Right or wrong are the Dharma; the Dharma is not right or wrong. When the Dharma is in balance, wrong is in balance."[4]

Right and wrong are a time of skillful or unskillful expression, but time itself is not good or bad. Right and wrong are dharmas, but a dharma's basic nature is not good or bad. Reality is unobstructed by right and wrong, because reality consists of things just as they are. Yet there is right and wrong, and as we embody the teachings we are able to express ethics based upon our shared sameness, not fixed rules of conduct. From the perspective of nonduality these rules are something added, something extra.

Again from "Shoaku Makusa" (Not Doing Wrongs):

> Know that hearing "not doing evils" is hearing the buddhas' true dharma. The [meaning of the phrase] "not doing evils" is not like what commoners first construe. Hearing this teaching as bodhi talk is hearing it like it is. Hearing it like it is means [hearing it] as expressing words of unsurpassed bodhi. Because it is already bodhi talk, it talks bodhi. As unsurpassed bodhi's speaking turns into its hearing, one moves from the aspiration for "not doing evils" toward the practice of "not doing evils." As evils become something one is unable to do, the power of one's practice suddenly appears fully. This full appearance fully appears in measure as [vast as] all the earth, all the universe, all of time, and all of dharmas.[5]

When we have fully integrated the Buddha Way, we don't need rules, shoulds, dos, and don'ts, and in this way we are unable to act unskill-fully. We are just responding to the current situation, which includes the well-being of every aspect of that situation. This is the bodhi-mind's response. It is when we insert our clinging and need to force a certain outcome that difficulties arise.

Furthermore, Dōgen clearly makes the point that we must make effort in our spiritual practice:

> Those who recognize that wrongs arise from causes and con-ditions, but do not see that these causes and conditions and they themselves are [the reality of] not committing [rights

and wrongs], are pitiful people. . . . The regret that "I have committed what was not to be committed" is also nothing other than energy arising from the effort not to commit. But to purport, in that case, that if not committing is so we might deliberately commit [wrongs], is like walking north and expecting to arrive at [the southern country of] Etsu.[6]

This quotation clearly indicates Dōgen's commitment to ethical action and his deep belief in understanding, regretting, and correcting our understanding when appropriate. The foundation of that correction must be full immersion in the present being-time of self and other.

Dōgen's primary focus in "Uji" is on the nondual aspects of being-time. For this reason, he does not discuss the karmic repercussions of our actions. He assumes that, as practitioners, we will already understand that the true nature of reality is morality itself. We cannot fully express being-time without also fully expressing morality, ethics, and the vow to benefit all beings.

"Uji" as a Journey from Conventional Understanding to Actualization

"Uji" is a full-circle journey. It begins with the old buddha Yaoshan's statement "For the time being I stand astride the highest mountain peaks. For the time being, I move on the deepest depths of the ocean floor."[7] Dōgen introduces the state of being-time through these snapshots of a moment of existence as expressed by Yaoshan. These snapshots are *uji* (being-time) summed up as "the 'time being' means time, just as it is, is being, and being is all time."[8]

Yaoshan appears again at the end of the text, this time as a confused student. He asks Mazu to clarify his understanding. Mazu says:

For the time being, I let him raise his eyebrows and blink his eyes. For the time being, I don't let him raise his eyebrows and blink his eyes. For the time being, my letting him raise his eyebrows and blink his eyes is correct. For the time being, my letting him raise his eyebrows and blink his eyes is not correct."

When Yaoshan heard this, he achieved great enlightenment. He told Mazu, "When I was at Shitou's, it was like a mosquito on an iron bull."[9]

Mazu's verses in juxtaposition to Yaoshan's opening lines are active verbal statements of being-time, pure response. "Uji" is a journey mapping how we actualize realization. Dōgen is our teacher and tour guide. In the beginning, Dōgen states "what is" by quoting Yaoshan (and adding a few verses of his own). By the time we reach the end of "Uji," Dōgen has given several examples of Zen masters who actualize and enact being-time. Yaoshan's initial dialogue with Mazu is the first of these examples.

Dōgen's primary purpose for writing "Uji" was to offer a clear approach to understanding and actualizing reality, resulting in awakening. To this end, he offers first his understanding of the relationship between being and time. From the basis of this relationship, he plots the arc of being-time in the language and progression of Buddhist practice. In "Uji," Dōgen writes that if we do not ask the right questions about the nature of our experience, we cannot actualize realization. He poses and answers questions that he would like us to ask. These questions help us clarify our muddled thoughts, encouraging us to leap beyond the intellect to enact the Buddha Way in our daily life.

Going beyond the Intellectual

Ultimately, as practitioners, we must move beyond an intellectual deconstruction of Dōgen and enter the realm of practice. We take up Dōgen's teaching in our everyday life as a kōan and ask, "How does this apply to my life?" until we gain insight into his teaching. Intellectual understanding is only a beginning. To progress, we must have a deep faith in Dōgen's understanding and its practice application.

For example, when I first encountered the concept of nonobstruction, I struggled to understand what Dōgen meant. He teaches that nothing obstructs the activity of anything else, and it seemed to me that I might take this literally. My experience was that things did obstruct other things. So how does this work? I would ask myself if the situation I was in constituted an unobstructed moment. One day, as I looked out my window during a rainstorm, I watched rain striking the branches of a tree. I wondered how rain striking a leaf constituted nonobstruction. Watching this dynamic, I realized that nonobstruction is about the practice of dropping the self-oriented mind.

The point is not about rain physically pushing or breaking a tree branch; it is that the rain does not have the *experience* of being obstructed, and the tree branch does not have the *intention* of obstructing. Neither is engaged with selfish mind. What happens is just the nature of tree and rain as one interactive entity separates as rain and branch.

Because I had faith in Dōgen's understanding, I was not trying to fit the teaching into something I already knew. Dōgen admonishes us to listen to our teachers' words "without matching them with your previous views."[10] My open inquiry resulted in a deeper understanding of what it means to drop the self. I was compelled to keep wondering until an insight came forward. I say "insight" because this practice is not about forcing an intellectual understanding. Our understanding must be organic and reflect the truth of our situation as individuals.

Dōgen's teachings do apply to our everyday life. His intention is to bring us back to our true nature within the context of daily experience. I think that the difficulty we experience with his language will bring us closer to this goal if we approach his teaching with faith, intelligence, and an open mind. Because Dōgen is not easy to understand, the difficulties we encounter with the text may free us from our preconceived ideas about practice-realization. We have to work with Dōgen and open our minds to his point of view.

I do not think that I completely understand Dōgen's Way. But I do hope that this book will help the reader to delve more deeply into a study of Dōgen's teachings and offer a direction for individual inquiry. Dōgen's vision is vast and holds the many threads of reality's presencing in a coherent whole. A friend once told me that his teacher said "no one can understand Dōgen, so you shouldn't try." I agree that it is probably impossible to completely penetrate Dōgen's mind and heart on the subject of this life. But I do not agree that we should give up working to share his vision. For me, Dōgen's writings are encouraging as well as challenging. Dōgen wrote:

> Not limited by language,
> It is ceaselessly expressed;
> So, too, the way of letters
> Can display but not exhaust it.[11]

"Uji" is a display of being-time that cannot exhaust the truth of being-time. But the beauty of Dōgen's language is that it offers so many possibilities and yet still manages to push us toward a particular understanding. His words compel us to enter into the *what* of our own experience, forcing us to go beyond concepts. He both engages the intellect and frees the intellect; he picks up reality, shows it to us, and then drops us back into the soup of life.

My approach to the text has been to have faith that his teaching is knowable and true in daily life. Dōgen's teaching can inform how I drive my car as much as it informs formal practice. How could it be otherwise? What would be the point of presenting a teaching that only applied to some rarefied situation?

ZAZEN AND EVERYDAY LIFE

There are some teachers who believe that "Uji" is a discussion of zazen. I would agree with this in the broadest sense. Actualizing our life is zazen. Zazen is presencing ourselves for the totality of our life and the life of all being. Yes, we engage in formal sitting practice in the zendo. This is *shikantaza* (just sitting), dropping body-mind as ritual practice.[12] But this practice must ground us in everyday activity and take us beyond the zendo. In "Bendōwa" (Wholehearted Practice of the Way), Dōgen writes:

> Great Teacher Śākyamuni correctly transmitted the won-
> drous method for attaining the Way, and the tathāgatas of
> the three times (past, present, and future) also all attained
> the Way through zazen. For this reason [zazen] has been
> conveyed from one person to another as the true gate.[13]

He also writes about the everyday activity of fetching water and lugging firewood ("three thousand acts in the morning" and "eight hundred acts in the evening") as mystical power in "Jinzū" (Mystical Power):

> Although we neither recognize that the three thousand acts
> in the morning are the mystical power, or sense that eight
> hundred acts in the evening are the mystical power, in them
> the mystical power is realized. Truly, those who see and
> hear the mystical power and the wondrous function of the
> buddha-tathāgatas are able without fail to attain the truth.[14]

How are we to understand these seemingly contradictory statements? On one hand, Dōgen teaches that zazen is the correctly
transmitted wondrous method for attaining the Way, and it is the
continuing expression of enlightenment. On the other hand, mystical
power (defined as everyday activity fully enacted) is also a dharma gate
to and an expression of realization.

Essentially, there is no conflict. We sit formal zazen because it is the
practice of a buddha as well as a method for attaining the Way. We also,
as buddhas, carry buckets of water, lug bundles of wood, drink tea, use
the bathroom, drive to the store, and cook meals. We interact with

our coworkers and negotiate life with our partners. All of practice-realization is fully presencing oneself with all beings to make life. This too is zazen. In "Fukanzazengi" (Universal Promotion of the Principles of Zazen), Dōgen says:

> The practice of zazen has nothing whatever to do with the four bodily attitudes of moving, standing, sitting, or lying down. . . . The zazen I speak of is not learning meditation . . . it is things as they are in suchness.[15]

Dōgen's fascicle "Uji" can be understood as the zazen of fully inhabiting this being-time. It is setting oneself in accordance with all of reality as it manifests in the particularities of our life. This is the activity of formal zazen and of zazen as everyday life. From a buddha's point of view, there is no activity that is not zazen.

The Role of the Teacher

In "Uji," Dōgen does not directly discuss the role of the teacher in a student's development. Yet the many references in "Uji" to kōans and quotations of student-teacher dialogues indicate the importance of this most intimate relationship. In other writings, he makes it very clear that our spiritual development, clarification, and verification are predicated upon the student-teacher relationship. In "Gakudō Yōjin-shū" (Guidelines for Studying the Way), Dōgen states: "To understand dharma and attain the way can only be the result of studying with a teacher."[16]

Nevertheless, because of the nondualistic emphasis on being-time in this text, it might be possible to assume that one can attain realization and verification without a teacher. In the fascicle "Menju" (Face-to-Face Transmission), Dōgen tells the story of the Zen monk Shoko who believed Zen ancestor Unmon had posthumously affirmed his awakening. Shoko announces to the assembly that he has received transmission from Master Unmon. Dōgen questions this assertion in no uncertain terms: "Does Great Master Unmon personally see you, or not? If Great Master Unmon does not see you, it might be impossible for you to succeed Great Master Unmon." And Dōgen continues, "You do not see a master, do not know a patriarch, do not know yourself, and do not see yourself, at all. And there is no master who sees you."[17]

Now on a roll, Dōgen becomes even more emphatic,

> You are an utterly witless and stupid man who has never seen the face of the sun and the face of the moon in the Buddha's state of true. You talk of succeeding to Unmon even though it is already more than a hundred years since Great Master Unmon entered nirvāṇa—is it by virtue of some momentous ability that you can succeed to Unmon? You are less reliable than a three-year-old child![18]

Clearly Dōgen believed that direct transmission could only happen between a student and teacher who have met and seen each other in the flesh.

The Ecology of Being-Time

Practice-realization in Dōgen's understanding includes the totality of all being-time and all beings' time. It is the universal multidimensional enactment of reality. From the standpoint of our being-time, it is experiencing our life with all beings without obstruction. When we fully embrace this vision, we will respond to our particular situation in such a way that we include everyone and everything. This will have a radical impact on the ways in which we understand our relationship to all beings. We will cease to use other things and beings as tools for our comfort or even our continued existence, as we envision it. Hee-Jin Kim writes:

> Dōgen never lost sight of the larger picture in which human and nonhuman beings engaged in an ongoing communion

through their respective languages/expressions. Farfetched as it may seem, this was his vision of the universe in which all beings—living and nonliving—engage in a shared salvific project, through their "vast, giddy karmic consciousnesses."[19]

This "vast, giddy karmic consciousnesses" is just the particular effort of each being and time expressed. This community of the world cannot be denied and is essential to our realization. Nothing is left out. From this view, we cannot continue to abuse self, others, or the earth. Although Dōgen's teachings do not explicitly make comment upon our misuse of resources, he does reiterate many times that we are not different, better, or more important than grasses, trees, rocks, and tiles.[20]

Connecting with and understanding the nature of all being-time could not be more relevant to our situation as world citizens. Realization itself is not divorced from everyday life, nor is it divorced from our connection with all of earth's denizens. This is the Bodhisattva Path as Dōgen envisioned it. A bodhisattva's vow is to save all beings. All beings are the entire universe and each particular thing. To "save" is to reintegrate oneself with all of being-time: each and every one and each and every thing throughout time and space. How could we think this is not relevant to our own situation?

Dōgen's vision is the enactment of this shared salvific endeavor. We are not the only ones engaged in the Bodhisattva Way. The whole universe has vowed to save all beings. It should be our aim to incorporate this truth and manifest the Bodhisattva Way as our life. The premise of my understanding of "Uji" is that Dōgen's intention is to provide us with a foundational understanding of relational reality, thereby enabling us to go beyond words and enact each moment infused with the bodhisattva vow of benefiting all beings.

Uji (Being-Time)

An old Buddha said:

For the time being, I stand astride the highest mountain peaks.

For the time being, I move on the deepest depths of the ocean floor.

For the time being, I'm three heads and eight arms.

For the time being, I'm eight feet or sixteen feet.

For the time being, I'm a staff or a whisk.

For the time being, I'm a pillar or a lantern.

For the time being, I'm Mr. Chang or Mr. Li.

For the time being, I'm the great earth and heavens above.

THE "TIME BEING" MEANS TIME, just as it is, is being, and being is all time.

The sixteen-foot golden Buddha-body is time; because it is time, it has time's glorious golden radiance. You must learn to see this glorious radiance in the twelve hours of your day. The [demonic asura with] three heads and eight arms is time; because it is time, it can be in no way different from the twelve hours of your day. Although you never measure the length or brevity of the twelve hours, their swiftness or slowness, you still call them the twelve hours. As evidence of their going and coming is obvious, you do not come to doubt them. But even though you do not have doubts about them, that is not to say you know them. Since a sentient being's doubtings of the many and various things unknown to him are naturally vague and indefinite, the course his doubtings take will probably not bring them to coincide with this present doubt. Nonetheless, the doubts themselves are, after all, none other than time.

We set the self out in array and make that the whole world. We must see all the various things of the whole world as so many times. These things do not get in each other's way any more than various times get in each other's way. Because of this, there is an arising of the religious mind at the same time, and it is the arising of time of the same mind. So it is with practice and attainment of the Way. We set our self in array, and we see that. Such is the fundamental reason of the Way—that our self is time.

Since such is its fundamental reason, we must study and learn that myriad phenomena and numberless grasses [things] exist over the entire earth, and each of the grasses and each of the forms exists as the entire earth. These comings and goings are the commencement of Buddhist practice. When you have arrived within this field of suchness, it is a single grass, a single form. The forms are understood and not understood, the grasses are grasped and not grasped.

As the time right now is all there ever is, each being-time is without exception entire time. A grass-being and a form-being are both times. Entire being, the entire world, exists in the time of each and every now. Just reflect: right now, is there an entire being or an entire world missing from your present time, or not?

In spite of this, a person holds various views at the time he is unenlightened and has yet to learn the Buddha's Dharma. Hearing the words "the time being," he thinks that at one time the old Buddha became a creature with three heads and eight arms, and that at another time he became a sixteen-foot Buddha. He imagines it is like crossing a river or a mountain: the river and mountain may still exist, but I have now left them behind, and at the present time I reside in a splendid vermilion palace. To him, the mountain or river and I are as distant from one another as heaven from earth.

But the true state of things is not found in this one direction alone. At the time the mountain was being climbed and the river being crossed, I was there [in time]. The *time* has to *be* in me. Inasmuch as I am there, it cannot be that time passes away.

As long as time is not a modality of going and coming, that time on the mountain is the immediate present—right *now*—of "the time being" (being-time). Yet as long as time takes upon itself a modality of going and coming, the being in me in the immediate now of "the time being" is being-time. So does not the time climbing the mountain or crossing the river swallow up the time of the splendid vermilion palace? Does not that time spit out this time?

The creature with three heads and eight arms is yesterday's time. The sixteen-foot Buddha is today's time. Nonetheless, the nature of the truth of this yesterday and today lies in the time when you go directly into the mountains and look at the myriad peaks around you—hence there is no passing away. So even that three-headed, eight-armed creature makes a passage as my being-time. Although it might seem as if it were somewhere else far away, it is the time right now. The sixteen-foot Buddha-body also makes a passage as my being-time. Although it might seem as if it were somewhere else over there, it is the time right now.

Hence, pine trees are time. So are bamboos. You should not come to understand that time is only flying past. You should not only learn that flying past is the virtue inherent in time. If time were to give itself to merely flying past, it would have to leave gaps. You fail to experience the passage of being-time and hear the utterance of its truth, because you learn only that time is something that goes past.

The essential point is: every entire being in the entire world is each time an [independent] time, even while it makes a continuous series. Inasmuch as they are being-time, they are my being-time.

Being-time has the virtue of seriatim passage. It passes from today to tomorrow, passes from today to yesterday, passes from yesterday to today, passes from today to today, passes from tomorrow to tomorrow, this because passing seriatim is a virtue of time. Past time and present time do not overlap or pile up in a row—and yet Qingyuan is time, Huangbo is time. Mazu and Shitou are times too. Since self and other are both times, practice and realization are times. "Entering the mud, entering the water" is time as well.

Although the views the ordinary, unenlightened person now holds and the conditions that cause them are what the unenlightened person sees, it is not the unenlightened person's Dharma; it is only the Dharma temporarily causing him [to see that way]. Since he learns that this time, this being, is not the Dharma, he supposes the sixteen-foot golden Buddha-body is not himself. His attempts to escape by saying, "I am not the sixteen-foot golden Buddha-body" are, as such, portions of being-time as well. It is the "Look! Look!" of "those who have not confirmed this yet."

The horses and sheep now arrayed throughout the world are each dharma stages dwelling in their suchness and moving endlessly up and down. Rats are time. So are tigers. Sentient beings are time, buddhas are as well. This time realizes the entire world by being a creature with three heads and eight arms, and realizes the entire world by being a sixteen-foot golden body.

Entirely worlding the entire world with the whole world is thus called *penetrating exhaustively*. To immediately manifest the bodying of the tall golden Buddha with the body of the tall golden Buddha as the arising of the religious mind, as practice, as enlightenment, as nirvāṇa—that is being, that is time. One does nothing but penetrate exhaustively entire time as entire being. There is nothing remaining left over. Because any dharma left over is as such a leftover dharma, even the being-time of a partial exhaustive penetration is an exhaustive penetration of a partial being-time. Even a form [of understanding] that appears to be blundering is being. On a still broader plane, the times before and after one immediately manifests the blunder are both, along with it, dwelling positions of being-time. The sharp, vital quick of dharmas dwelling in their dharma-positions is itself being-time. You must not by your own maneuvering make it into nothingness; you must not force it into being.

You reckon time only as something that does nothing but pass by. You do not understand it as something not yet arrived. Although our various understandings are time, there is no chance for them to be drawn in by time. There has never yet been anyone who supposed time to be coming and going who has penetrated to see it as being-time dwelling in its dharma-position. What chance is there, then, for a time to arrive when you will break through the barrier [into total emancipation]? Even if someone did know that dwelling-position, who would be able truly to give an utterance that preserved what he had thus gained? And even were someone able to utter such an utterance at will, he could still not avoid groping to make his original face immediately present.

Left entirely to the being-time of the unenlightened, both enlightenment and nirvāṇa would be being-time that was nothing more than an aspect of going-and-coming. [But] no nets or cages remain for long—all is the immediate presencing here and now of being-time. The deva kings and deva multitude actually presencing to the left and right are even now being-time that put forth my total exertion. And everywhere else in the universe the hosts of being-times in water and on earth are now immediately manifesting themselves in the full power that I exert. Entities of every manner and kind being time in the realms of darkness and light are all the immediate manifestation of my full exertion, all my full exertion making a passage. One must learn in practice that unless it is one's self exerting itself right now, not a single dharma or thing can either immediately manifest itself or make a passage.

You must not construe this passing to be like a squall of wind and rain moving from place to place. The entire world is not changeless and immoveable, nor unprogressing and unregressing—the whole world is passing seriatim. Passing seriatim is like spring, for example, with all of its many and varied signs. That is passing seriatim. You should learn in practice that passing takes place without anything extraneous. For example, springtime's passage invariably passes through spring. The passage is not spring, but as it is the springtime's passage, passing attains the Way now in the time of spring. All of this you must give careful and repeated examination.

If, in speaking of a "passage," you imagine that the place of passage lies somewhere outside, and the dharma of the one doing the passage moves toward the east [like the spring] through 100,000 worlds over 100,000 kalpas of time, that is a result of not giving total devotion to the single-minded practice of the Buddha Way.

Once Yaoshan Hongdao, at the direction of Wuji Dashi, went to Zen master Mazu with a question. "I believe I have a fair grasp of the three vehicles and the teaching of the twelve divisions, but what about the meaning of the First Patriarch's coming from the west?"
Mazu said:
For the time being, I let him raise his eyebrows and
blink his eyes.
For the time being, I don't let him raise his eyebrows and
blink his eyes.
For the time being, my letting him raise his eyebrows
and blink his eyes is correct.
For the time being, my letting him raise his eyebrows
and blink his eyes is not correct.
When Yaoshan heard this, he achieved great enlightenment. He told Mazu, "When I was at Shitous, it was like a mosquito on an iron bull."

What Mazu utters is not the same as other men. Here eyebrows and eyes must be mountains and seas, because mountains and seas are eyebrows and eyes. Within this "letting him raise," you should see mountains. Within this "letting him blink," you should essentiate the sea. "Correct" enters into intimate terms with "him." "Him" is ushered in by "letting." "Not correct" is not "not letting him," and "not letting him" is not "not correct." All of them are equally being-time.

Mountains are time, and seas are time. If they were not time, there would be no mountains and seas. So you must not say there is no time in the immediate now of mountains and seas. If time is destroyed, mountains and seas are destroyed. If time is indestructible, mountains and seas are indestructible. Within this true dharma, the morning star appears, the Tathāgata appears, eye-pupils appear, the holding up of the flower appears. This is time. If it were not time, things would be not-so.

> Zen master Guixing of Shexian, a Dharma descendant of Linji and direct Dharma heir of Shoushan, once instructed the assembly of monks:
>> For the time being, the mind reaches but the word does not.
>> For the time being, the word reaches but the mind does not.
>> For the time being, the mind and word both reach.
>> For the time being, neither mind nor word reach.

Mind and the word are equally being-time. Their reaching and not-reaching alike are being-time. Even when the time of their reaching is not yet over, the time of their not-reaching has arrived. The mind is a donkey, the word a horse, making the horse a word and the donkey the mind. "Reaching" is not coming; "not-reaching" is not yet. This is how being-time is.

Reaching is impeded by reaching and not impeded by not-reaching. Not-reaching is impeded by not-reaching and not impeded by reaching. The mind impedes the mind and sees the mind, word impedes word and sees word, impeding impedes itself and sees itself. Impeding impedes impeding—that is time. Although impeding is employed by other dharmas, there has never yet been impeding that impedes another dharma. The entire world, exhaustively, with no thing or time left out, is impeding. I encounter a man. A man encounters a man. I encounter myself. Going forth encounters going forth. If they do not obtain the time, it cannot be thus.

Moreover, the mind is the time of the immediately present ultimate Dharma. The word is the time of the key to higher attainment. Reaching is the time of the body of total emancipation. Not-reaching is the time "you are one with this and apart from this." You should attest and affirm thus. You should being-time thus.

We have seen above how the respected elders have both spoken. Yet is there not something even further to utter?

We should say:

> Half-reaching of mind and word is also being-time.
> Half not-reaching of mind and word is also being-time.

Your investigation must go on like this.

> Letting him raise his eyebrows and blink his eyes is a half being-time.
> Letting him raise his eyebrows and blink his eyes is a "Wrong!" being-time.

> Not letting him raise his eyebrows and blink his eyes is a half being-time.

> Not letting him raise his eyebrows and blink his eyes is a "Wrong!" "Wrong!" being-time.

Such investigations continuing in thoroughgoing practice—reaching here and not reaching there—that is the time of being-time.

· · · · ·

Norman Waddell and Masao Abe, trans., from *The Heart of Dōgen's Shōbō-genzō* (New York: State University of New York Press, 2002), pp. 48-58. The colophon, which is omitted in Waddell and Abe's translation, reads:
Treasury of the True Dharma Eye
Being Time
Book 20
First winter day, the first year of *Ninji* (seventh stem, first branch)

[October 17, 1240], written at Kosho Horinji. Copied during the summer retreat, the tenth stem, fourth branch year of *Kangen* [1243].

Translated by Carl Bielefeldt, "Treasury of the True Dharma Eye, *Shōbōgenzō* Book 20, Being-Time, *Uji*," *Sōtō Zen Journal Dharma Eye: News of the Sōtō Zen Buddhist Teachings and Practice,* no. 30, (September 2012), 22.

Uji Is Being-Time 1

The title of "Uji" translated as "Being-Time" essentially contains the totality of the text. Unpacking the meaning of this hyphenated word opens a vast interconnecting vista of practice. The two characters *u-ji* (有時) are usually translated as *arutoki* or "for the time being." Dōgen separates the two characters (*u* meaning being, and *ji* meaning time) and reassembles them as the one word *uji*, often translated in English as being-time or existence-time.[1] As Hee-Jin Kim writes:

> Dōgen . . . transforms such an everyday phrase as *arutoki* ("at a certain time," "sometimes," "there is a time," "once") into one of the most important notions in his Zen—*uji* ("existence-time"). This metamorphosis is executed by way of changing its two components—the *aru* and the *toki*—into *u* ("existence," "being") and *ji* ("time," "occasion"), respectively, and recombining them as *uji* so that it unmistakably signals the nondual intimacy of existence and time.[2]

This new word *uji* becomes a shorthand for bundling all aspects of reality into one word/thought: being-time. Being-time embraces many of the key teachings found in Dōgen's writing. Among several words or phrases found in "Uji" which express these teachings are dharma position (*jū-hōi*): the fully embodied totality of myriad things/beings as a moment of being time; continuous practice (*gyōji*): the completely realized activity and effort of each being's-time as all being-time; fully expressing the Way (*dōtoku*): the enlightened expression of practice-realization; manifesting ultimate reality (*genjōkōan*): the totality of the actualization of the fundamental point; penetrating exhaustively (*gūjin*): complete expression of a moment; practice-realization (*shōjō no shu*); this very mind is Buddha (*sokushin zebutsu*); and buddha-nature (*busshō*): the totality of life's activity; among others. Dōgen's descriptions of practice, expression, mind, and reality are also designations of actualized being-time. These words are a rich mosaic illuminating our being-time, each aimed at helping us find deep awakening as we express our rich, intimate life.

> An old Buddha[3] said:
> For the time being, I stand astride the highest mountain peaks.
> For the time being, I move on the deepest depths of the ocean floor.
> For the time being, I'm three heads and eight arms.
> For the time being, I'm eight feet or sixteen feet.
> For the time being, I'm a staff or a whisk.
> For the time being, I'm a pillar or a lantern.
> For the time being, I'm Mr. Chang or Mr. Li.
> For the time being, I'm the great earth and heavens above.[4]

"Uji" begins with four couplets introducing the meaning of the text. The first two lines are attributed to Zen master Yaoshan Weiyen, from a text called the *Jingde chuandeng lu* (Jingde era Record of the Transmission of the Lamp), a series of stories about Zen masters compiled in 1004 by Daoyuan.[5] The rest are thought to be Dōgen's own composition.

There are two important elements in these opening verses: the repeated phrase "for the time being" and the unique moments, things, or events that it modifies. The individual moments, things, or events are called *jū-hōi* or "dharma positions." A dharma position is a singular moment, state of being, or occurrence that has no fixed duration and about which we intuitively understand something of its particularity. Standing on the highest mountain peak, moving along the

ocean floor, being a wrathful deity with three heads and eight arms
or a golden buddha of eight or sixteen feet, a staff, a whisk, a pillar, a
lantern, Mr. Chang, Mr. Li, the great earth, and the heavens above are
all dharma positions.

In short, the four couplets opening the text depict unique, particular
situations that are illustrative of being-time's totality. Dōgen's examples and their metaphoric meaning encompass reality as both particular and universal.

BEING-TIME

The translations of *uji* as "for the time being," "sometimes," "at a certain time," or "once" can be read as a kind of throwaway line, especially
in English.[6] Our tendency may be to skip over these words and move on
to what seems to be the meat of each sentence. But for Dōgen, "for the
time being" is the whole basis for his discussion of time's relationship
to being.

In conventional use, "for the time being" seems to indicate a specifically limited demarcation of time, as in "at the moment" or "just for
now." Dōgen's use of the phrase, however, has a deeper meaning than
"at this time." Reading the two characters that comprise the phrase as
the compound term *uji*, rather than as an idiomatic phrase, yields the
more universal reading "being-time."

Grammatically, the characters *u* and *ji* do not indicate singular
or plural.[7] We can read the compound "being-time" to mean either
a being's time, a time's being, or all being-time. Understanding the
multiplicity of meanings within the phrase "for the time being" reveals
new depths in Dōgen's opening lines. For Dōgen, "for the time being"
encompasses all states of being-time. Rereading the opening line in
light of this understanding, we find several meanings within each
situation: "a particular time being stands on the highest mountain
peak," "the time when one stands on the highest mountain peak," "all
being(s)-time(s) stand on the highest peak," or "all time's being and/or

all beings' time is now standing on the highest peak." We can read the remaining lines in the same ways. No single thing and no moment of time is left out of this very moment of being-time.

DHARMA POSITION AS ALL BEING-TIME

We can't really penetrate what Dōgen means by being-time if we don't understand the unique particular moments, things, or events, called dharma positions or dharma stages. A dharma position, understood as a unique independent moment, also has multiple aspects, which, when taken together, are being-time. Without understanding the encompassing nature of a dharma position as a being-time and all being-time, we mistakenly experience unique particular moments like the Buddhist parable of the blind men examining an elephant. One man said the ears were like a basket, another said the tusk was a plow's blade, and a third thought the foot to be a pillar—you get the idea. Since the examiners were blind, not one of them was able to see the whole of the elephant, so they grasped what they could and compared it to something they already knew, not understanding that each thing they touched was a part of a larger unseen whole.

A dharma position is a moment, thing, or event of being-time that is also definable as transitive and impermanent. A person is a dharma position. Since nothing ever stays the same and all things are in flux due to their interactive, interpenetrating nature, it would be folly to say that a dharma position or a moment of being-time begins here and ends there. Dharma positions are not finite in this sense, nor are they sequential way stations along a continuum of past, present, and future. Although Dōgen does not deny the conventional, everyday sense of time as a horizontal line of sequential events that we experience as past, present, and future, in "Uji" Dōgen is concerned with the nondual nature of time and being as expressed in the presencing moment. From the point of view of practice, a linear view of time can impede realization.

A dharma position has a past, present, and future, but it is freed from being defined by that past, present, or future. Each dharma position is particular and independent. We are aware of past experience and future desires when actualizing our enlightened mind, but such ideas do not obstruct our ability to respond fully to the totality of each situation as it is. This nonobstructive awareness is important because the independent nature of a dharma position allows us to choose how we will respond to them. We are not caught up in some fatalistic, predetermined course of action. Dōgen writes in "Hotsu-Bodaishin" (Establishment of the Bodhi-Mind):

> In general, establishment of the mind and attainment of the truth rely upon the instantaneous arising and vanishing of all things. If [all things] did not arise and vanish instantaneously, bad done in the previous instant could not depart. If bad done in the previous instant had not yet departed, good in the next instant could not be realized in the present.[8]

From the perspective of nonduality, past, present, and future are present in this moment, yet at the same time each moment must have the freedom to express its individual flavor. In the example above, Dōgen is describing how we are not trapped by unskillful behavior. This "instantaneous arising and vanishing" is the dharma position as fluid and all-inclusive. At the same time it is an independent dharma position. Dōgen famously expresses this idea in the "Genjōkōan" (Manifesting Suchness), where he writes about the nature of firewood:

> Firewood becomes ash; it can never go back to being firewood. Nevertheless, we should not take the view that ash is its future and the firewood is its past. Remember, firewood abides in the place of firewood in the Dharma. It has a past and it has a future. Although it has a past and a future, the past and the future are cut off. Ash exists in the place of ash in the Dharma. It has a past and it has a future.[9]

Here we have what appear to be two opposing ideas: the future of fire-wood is ash and the past of ash is firewood, and yet the past and future of firewood and ash are cut off from what seems like their natural pro-gression. Each statement is equally true and important to our under-standing of a dharma position or a being-time. We do have a past and future, but we are not bound by a fossilized past or future. We use our past experiences and future desires as tools for discernment. If we can engage with the present moment in this way, we are freed to respond to this moment unobstructed by motivations that might hinder a skillful response.

A dharma position holds all being-time—a being's time and time's being—in this very moment. This is the complete nonduality of things, existence, and time. A particular being-time expresses two states. First, there is the universal state of all being-time. This is the inclusive nature of everything taken as a whole. Second, a being's time is a particular event, person, or thing, which is expressed as an independent dharma position. Simultaneously, a dharma position is both universal being-time and a particular being-time. Everything is present at the same time without hindering the universal and particular nature of any other. This is also true of time's-being.

When we include everything in our understanding, we are more cognizant of the intrinsic value of each thing, and we are more aware of the place each being or event has in relationship to us. We don't exclude anything, recognizing that everything is already present. Accepting things as they are is predicated upon knowing that the present includes all those things we want and those things we don't want. We cannot reject anything merely because it causes us discomfort or does not fit our idea of how it should be. Our suffering arises from this overlay of likes and dislikes, but truthfully there is nothing obstructing the fully realized moment because nothing is excluded and all things arise simultaneously.

Furthermore, everything interpenetrates everything else and is all other beings and times, within a particular dharma position. This idea is articulated in the Huayan[10] phrase "to know one thing is to know all things." If you understand this foundational truth about a thing's essential nature, you will also understand the basic truth of all things. Our interconnecting, interpenetrating, unobstructed nature is the basis for intelligent empathy resulting in compassionate and wise action.

Since a dharma position is interconnecting, interpenetrating, impermanent, and fleeting, it functions within the context of all other dharma positions. In concert, these dharmas practice together and make the world. From this perspective Dōgen writes in "Zenki" (All Functions), "life is what I am making it, and I am what life is making me . . . life is the self and self is life."[11] Lest we get too anthropocentric in our views, he also writes in "Uji" "each grass and each form itself is the entire earth . . . each moment is all being, is the entire world."[12]

Included in each moment is the entire world and the individual being-time-ness of each being making the world. Dōgen calls this all-inclusive activity *gyōji* or continuous practice. Continuous practice is the practice-realization of the Buddhist ancestors, and it also includes the continuous practice of all other beings: trees, rocks, insects, etc. It is the wholehearted effort and total presencing of each being in the ten directions within the context of each dharma position or being-time. Dōgen writes in "Gyōji" (Continuous Practice):

> The working of this activity-unremitting upholds the self and the other. Its import is such that through one's activity-unremitting the entire earth as well as the whole heaven of the ten directions share in its working. Even if others are unaware of it, and you may be unaware of it, that is the way it is.[13]

When does this practice happen? It happens within a particular dharma position as one, all, and everything as it is right now. As Dōgen writes in "Gyōji" (Continuous Practice), "The time when continuous practice is manifested is what we call 'now.'"[14]

In addition, there is the issue of how a dharma position transitions from this moment to the next in a nonsequential model. Dōgen also addresses this in "Uji." This passage is not sequential nor is it strictly nondual. In general, while not denying cause and effect, Dōgen avoids characterizing reality as sequential in any way. If all being-time is essential for each being-time, then there cannot be one thing that we can say is a first cause. Passage or transition happens within the context of this moment's movement in concert with all being.

For example, an ear of corn must be born from a corn seed. But that seed (and the resulting cornstalk) is as dependent on water, air, earth, and the totality of the universe for its life as it is upon the seed. In this way, the corn is beholden to all of existence for its appearance. Myriad events are necessary for a life. From this view, how can we distinguish one cause separately from all causes or one time separated from all time?

In Buddhist practice, transformation happens through our focus on this moment as direct experience and our response informed by the Buddhadharma. To practice with a sequential expectation of spiritual attainment, such as delusion transforming into enlightenment via a particular activity, is false. Practice unfolds in the context of all of reality coming forth at this very being-time, which creates a flow of activity not delineated by sharp boundaries of before and after, then and now.

Masao Abe discusses this by saying:

> Each and every time (for example, yesterday), because it is simultaneously the manifestation of the total dynamism of all times while abiding in its own dharma-stage, cannot be correctly seen as passing into another time (for example, today). The relationship of one time and another time must be seen not as a matter of passing away, but as *passageless-passage* (*kyōryaku*).[15]

Dōgen does not deny that change is happening, but he emphasizes that it does not happen the way we think it does. How things do happen and the importance of this view to our understanding of practice as realization are part of Dōgen's discussion of being-time as Buddhist practice in "Uji."

LINE-BY-LINE READING

Again, the opening verses are presentations of being-time as dharma positions. The occasion of the verses themselves are being-time. They are the being-time of Dōgen, Yaoshan, the reader, and all beings. As soon as we read these words the connection comes forward:

> For the time being, I stand astride the highest mountain peaks.
> For the time being, I move on the deepest depths of the ocean floor.

The top of Mount Everest as the world's highest peak and the deepest point of the ocean in the Mariana Trench seem very far apart. Since the verses are written in couplets, it is understandable that we would interpret them as being in opposition to and separate from each other. They seem to be linear in time and position, an idea further strengthened by the phrase "for the time being," as if this were just a temporary state, definable in a dualistic scheme.

Nevertheless, from the viewpoint of being-time, although they may appear to be different, they are not. Perhaps we think the highest peak is some rarefied place and the deepest ocean is mysterious and unknowable, but both of these states are within the realm of our experience. Nothing is left out. The mountains are our world, and the oceans are our world. When we stand on the highest peak, it is just this moment, and when we stand on the ocean floor, it is just this moment.

Dōgen associates both dharma positions with realization. He writes in "Kai-in-zanmai" (Ocean Seal Samādhi):

Encountering the buddha face . . . is nothing other than fully
recognizing myriad things as myriad things. Because myriad things are all-inclusive, you do not merely stand atop the
highest peak or travel along the bottom of the deepest ocean.
Being all-inclusive is just like this; letting go is just like this.[16]

Both the mountain peak and the ocean floor are the territory of realization. "The buddha face" is our life seeing the true nature of "myriad
things." Even if you are on the mountaintop or at the bottom of the
ocean, the myriad things, times, beings, and events are never absent
in your present now. Actualizing this place includes the peak and the
ocean floor, and at the same time it has the independent nature of making oneself present for the "right now" of either state without holding
on to anything.

For the time being, I'm three heads and eight arms.
For the time being, I'm eight feet or sixteen feet.

We again seem to have two ends of the spectrum. There is the being
with three heads and eight arms: the demon of delusion. Opposed to
this image is the golden body of the buddha, often described as sixteen
feet or eight feet tall. If we look more closely at Dōgen's teaching on
these two apparent opposites, we find that he writes later in "Uji":

So even that three-headed, eight-armed creature makes a
passage as my being-time. Although it might seem as if it
were somewhere else far away, it is the time right now. The
sixteen-foot Buddha-body also makes a passage as my being-
time. Although it might seem as if it were somewhere else
over there, it is the time right now.[17]

The "right now" of our experience holds both realization and delusion. From the perspective of nonduality, both must be included in

our understanding. When we are responding with our buddha-mind, where does the demon mind go? When we are responding with delusion, where does our realized mind go? Or we could ask, "when we respond skillfully to a situation, where does our selfish mind go, and when we respond unskillfully, where does our compassionate mind go?" Both are present, although we generally experience either one or the other.

Hee-Jin Kim writes, "The relationship between delusion and enlightenment is such that one is not the simple negation or absence of the other, nor does one precede or succeed the other."[18] If both were not present, we could not respond so readily with one or the other. One aspect comes forth and the other aspect is hidden, yet both are still part of the other's appearance. The world of myriad things is all of being-time fully presencing itself. This world has no labels, although there is delusion and enlightenment. We should not say, "Oh, I'm enlightened, so everything I do is okay." Nor should we say, "Oh, I'm so unskillful, I will never be compassionate or wise."

When we realize the nondual nature of a dharma position or particular being-time, we can include everything and avoid getting caught in a constricting story about our current situation. Making up a defining story line takes us further away from the true state of our experience. For example, we may find ourselves wanting to deny our own unskillfulness (the three-headed demon) because it doesn't fit our idea of a Buddhist practitioner. Denying our difficulties will only draw them forward, often when we least expect or want them to arise.

It is only when we accept and investigate our experience as flawed human beings that we begin to exhibit wisdom and recognize the totality of our life.

Dōgen writes in "Sesshin Sesshō" (Speaking of Mind, Speaking of Essence):

> From the time we establish the bodhi-mind and direct ourselves toward training in the way of Buddha, we sincerely

practice difficult practices; and at that time, though we keep practicing, in a hundred efforts we never hit the target once. Nevertheless, sometimes following good counselors and sometime following the sūtras, we gradually become able to hit the target. One hit of the target now is by virtue of hundreds of misses in the past; it is one maturation of hundreds of misses.[19]

We will never hit the target if we refuse to realize our arrows are missing. Missing the target is not about being a good or a bad person; it is just our sincere effort to hit the target of skillful means. Our human life, the arrow, and the target are not different. Missing and hitting are not opposites, as long as we are sincerely present for our life as it unfolds within the being-time of self and others practicing together. Including both is the key concept here. If we only think of this moment as a reflection of our individual needs, then we miss the mark. We must include the totality of both self and other; then act in accord. This is the basis of sincerely shooting the arrow. In this way our ideas about having three heads and eight arms or standing sixteen feet tall will not obstruct our actualization of the Way.

> For the time being, I'm a staff or a whisk.
> For the time being, I'm a pillar or a lantern.

The staff and whisk are symbols or tools of the realized teacher. The outdoor pillar and stone lantern represent the monastic structure and garden respectively. Pillars and lanterns are a metaphor for monastic training. These objects point to our spiritual training or the path we follow in order to actualize our understanding. The everyday interpretation would be that "at a certain time" we are a teacher, and "at a certain time" we are students. In this way of thinking, "for the time being" I am this or that. But being-time is larger than our definition of our experience and our quantification of spiritual progress. At the time of being a student, the teacher is already present. At the time of being a teacher, the student is also present. There is the dharma position of student and the dharma position of teacher, distinct states, but simultaneously present within each other's position. The key to skillful response is seeing and acting from the appropriate position.

Dōgen writes extensively about equating the four objects—a staff, a whisk, an outdoor pillar, and a stone lantern—with realization.[20] The staff, whisk, outdoor pillar, and stone lantern may be understood in the same dynamic relationship as Dōgen's well-known paring of practice-realization (*shushō-ittō*). Conventionally, we understand practice as the stone lantern and outdoor pillar, and realization as the whisk and staff: we think of practice as before and realization as after. In truth, realization is fully expressed in practice. Even as we endeavor to learn practice, we are exhibiting the mind of realization. Our efforts to understand and enact realization are driven by realization. In this way, the pillar and lantern do not represent steps along the path to attainment of the whisk and staff, but are already fully engaged with actualizing the Way.

On one hand there is practice, as expressed in the quotation in the previous section, about shooting an arrow at a target. On the other hand there is realization—hitting the target. But when we look at the totality of the activity of making the effort to hit the target or enact realization, this can only come from the mind of realization. It is realization, fully present, that is the foundation of our sincere effort. Dōgen expresses this when he writes in "Bendōwa" (Wholehearted Practice of the Way):

> To suppose that practice and realization are not one is nothing but a heretical view; in buddha-dharma they are inseparable. Because practice of the present moment is practice realization, the practice of beginner's mind is in itself the entire original realization. Therefore, when we give instructions for practicing we say that you should not

have any expectation for realization outside of practice, since this is the immediate original realization. Because this is the realization of practice, there is no boundary in the realization. Because this is the practice of realization, there is no beginning in practice.[21]

We are not waiting for realization to arrive, as it is manifest in the now of being-time. Being fully present ourselves, here and now, in company with others, is realization. The whisk-staff representing realization and the pillar-lantern representing Dharma training are not so far apart. They are all speaking the truth of realization as it is actualized in practice. This practice is in and of itself realization.

> For the time being, I'm Mr. Chang or Mr. Li.
> For the time being, I'm the great earth and heavens above.

Mr. Chang or Mr. Li is the same as saying "every Tom, Dick, or Harry" in English. Yet, as common as we are, when we look into the night sky, do we also recall that we too are made of stars? The true nature of our life is that we are not separate, we inter-are (as the Venerable Thich Nhat Hanh would say). We know from scientific study that the carbon from the Big Bang is also in us and in all things. We know from observation that in this very moment we are dependent upon heaven, earth, and everything in between for our very life. We cannot live without air and water. We are dependent upon and enmeshed with all being for all time, at this moment. Yet we persist in thinking there is a disconnect between ourselves and others. What a trick our senses play on us! This great life of the cosmos is just the everyday life of the common person.

PRACTICING WITH BEING-TIME

The verses opening this fascicle present particular dharma positions, being-times, or individual moments. These moments are examples of particular events: standing on a mountain, holding a whisk, viewing the temple pillars, or being an ordinary person. None of these situations obstructs the complete expression of the other examples given. Each situation is an opportunity to fully enact our being-time, as it is right now. If our worldview is a being-time that entertains all possibilities, this enables us to let go of our attachment to any particular ideas about our situation and thereby actualize the totality of the moment. Our being-time's moment must include all being(s)-time(s). When this inclusivity is actualized, we are fully present with whatever is happening in its totality and we respond. This response is unobstructed. It alleviates suffering.

I am walking on the sidewalk; next to me is a bike lane in the street. Approaching me on the sidewalk is a person on a bicycle. Without thinking and without judgment I step into the bike path and let the bicyclist pass me on the sidewalk. My response is immediate and without thought. I don't feel angry or have some idea of how it is supposed to be. I just respond to what is, at that moment. There is the being-time of a bicycle and the being-time of a person walking. Each is a particular manifestation of two being-times sharing and expressing their mutual unique fully realized being-times as one being-time.

Things Just as They Are

> The "time being" means time, just as it is, is being, and being is all
> time.

THIS SENTENCE CLARIFIES Dōgen's intention that the phrase "for the
time being" (*arutoki*) means "being-time" (*u-ji*).[1] Now, it is quite clear
that he is not referring to an idiomatic phrase but, rather, to a new word
that expresses his understanding.

When Dōgen equates time and being, he shifts our erroneous notions
of time from time outside the person to time as the person. The dharma
position "person" is time. This being-time also includes everything
at this time. A person, our person, does not exist or function outside
the maṇḍala of all beings, things, and the being-time of each thing or
person. Furthermore, our person is not separate from what we perceive
as the other, while simultaneously we and all beings are unique.

Using Dōgen's understanding of the unique embodiment of a particular being-time combined with its universal aspect, we can, for example, reinterpret the Buddha's well-known proclamation "I alone am the
World-Honored One." From the perspective of *uji* we see that the Buddha was not speaking of an isolated self. His "I" includes all being(s)-
time(s). This inclusive "I" becomes an expression of the bodhisattva's
vow. "Beings are numberless, I vow to save them" is a commitment to
awaken at this moment with all beings, enacting the moment's truth
or salvation. Śākyamuni's "I" is an expression of the simultaneity of
his and all beings' actualization as this being-time. "I" and "saving all
beings" are the moment of one's realization that reveals the activity of

all of reality, thereby saving all beings in concert with all being-time. The bodhisattva's ardor to awaken with all beings happens within the context of the activity of each being's time. This is the practice of the statement "the 'time being' means time, just as it is, is being, and being is all time."

The sixteen-foot golden Buddha-body is time; because it is time, it has time's glorious golden radiance. You must learn to see this glorious radiance in the twelve hours[1] of your day. The [demonic asura with] three heads and eight arms is time; because it is time, it can be in no way different from the twelve hours of your day.

EVERYTHING AS BEING-TIME, IS RADIANT: both buddhas and demons. Time's glorious golden radiance is the attribute of all things, even though we may find this image counterintuitive. Dōgen wrote in "Kōmyō" (Radiant Brightness), "The brightness that is utterly clear is the hundred weeds."[2]

Golden radiance is our true state as being-time. Even if we are not manifesting this golden radiance of the Dharma, we are this golden radiance. Even if we become caught by our clinging and wrong views and we are floundering, still there is the golden radiance. In "Kōmyō" (Radiant Brightness) Dōgen writes of the self's radiance:

> Who, then, was even aware of the radiant light of the self? Even though people had been carrying the radiant light within their heads and encountering it all the time, they still did not practice it as their own eyeballs. Thus, they did not clarify the shape and function of radiant light. Because they avoided encountering the radiant light, their radiant light was missing radiant light. Although missing is itself radiant light, they were immersed in missing.[3]

Although our true nature is radiant light, we do not see it, we do not practice it. Even so, Dōgen characterizes this blindness as "missing is itself radiant light." This does not mean that it is acceptable to engage in unskillful or immoral actions. Dōgen is speaking of golden radiance as the fundamental state of being-time, a state that is deeper than right and wrong. When we abide in that state as our true nature, we naturally respond skillfully. In the fascicle "Shoaku Makusa" (Not Doing Wrongs), Dōgen explains it this way:

> There is a great difference between the buddha way and the worldly realm in what is called unwholesome action, wholesome action, or neutral action. Wholesome action and unwholesome action are time, although time is neither wholesome action nor unwholesome action. Wholesome action and unwholesome action are dharma, although dharma is neither wholesome action nor unwholesome action. As dharma is all-inclusive, unwholesome action is all-inclusive. As dharma is all-inclusive, wholesome action is all-inclusive.[4]

Foundational, nonsequential reality must include everything both wholesome and unwholesome. Dōgen never denies that we can engage in actions that cause suffering. But, in the essential realm of reality itself, it is radiant being-time. All being-time includes the being-time of wholesome and the being-time of unwholesome. This essential being-time is the golden radiance of our day. It is our job as practitioners to wake up to this truth. When we learn to see the hours of our day as glorious radiance, we will naturally respond ethically and skillfully.

Our twenty-four hours are the twenty-four hours of brightness in our everyday life. We are not talking about some special place or state in which practice occurs. We are talking about the practice of washing our clothes, buying groceries, and relating to our coworkers. This practice of golden radiance is our twenty-four hours, not someone else's. It is our being-time. This is the being-time of every concrete thing.

This radiant light can be spoken of as the continuous effort and teaching of all things. Dōgen writes in "Bendōwa" (Wholehearted Practice of the Way) that when we can enter into and express this golden radiance we and all beings practice together expounding the Dharma:

> In stillness, mind and object merge in realization and go beyond enlightenment. Thus, in the state of receptive samādhi, . . . you engage the vast buddha activity, the extremely profound and subtle buddha transformation. Grasses, trees, and lands that are embraced by this way of transformation together radiate a great light and endlessly expound the inconceivable, profound dharma.[5]

INCLUDING MISTAKES

"The [demonic asura with] three heads and eight arms is time; because it is time, it can be in no way different from the twelve hours of your day." Buddha-nature/being-time must include all the different aspects of our life. It cannot exclude the parts we don't like, the parts we call delusion. When we think about our life as Buddhist practitioners, we want to think that spiritual life does not include mistakes. But it is these very mistakes that are the foundation of our wisdom. Where does our wisdom come from if not in learning from our mistakes?

When I first began to practice, I really wanted to be the *doan*, a person who hits the bells, keeps time during meditation, and does other functions associated with the ritual in a temple. But what came with that job, for me, was anxiety about making mistakes. And of course, there were many opportunities to make mistakes. This was difficult, because I wanted to be perfect. I was smart enough to know that how I hit the bells said something about who I was, but I was not mature enough in practice to let go of the ego involvement of needing to be perfect. This is a stage of practice. Our involvement with looking good gets in the way of our ability just to meet the moment without adding something extra. That something extra, in this case, was my desire to look good, to be perfect. Of course, this "mistake" was actually what I was learning about. It was my practice.

Our wisdom is always present, even in the midst of our delusion. It is wisdom that stretches our mind and helps us to explore further, even in the middle of our discomfort and mistakes. This is our sixteen-foot Buddha bathed in a golden radiance that stands in the very body of our being-time. This golden radiance is never absent, even as we struggle. Golden radiance is not a god who stands next to us, or a spirit that waits to develop within us. It is who we are, as are all beings, at this moment. This does not absolve us from the responsibility of enacting our wisdom. The enactment is the vow and goal of our practice. As we practice, we are embodying the golden radiance of our everyday life and effort.

There is no other time than this time-being to enact our realization. We are not waiting for another time to actualize our understanding, our compassion, and our wisdom. If we are waiting, we are (as Dōgen said above) "avoiding encountering our radiant light." Waiting is catering to our selfishness. If we do not apologize when we know we are wrong, we are denying ourselves the opportunity to let the golden radiance of the moment come forth. Sometimes practice is hard, and we have to drop our defensiveness and desire to be right. Yet golden radiance is always present regardless of the kind of action in which we decide to engage.

The truth of being-time or golden radiance is something deeper than the labels we attach to our experience. If we label our experience as delusion (three heads and eight arms) or realization (sixteen-foot golden Buddha-body), we are not getting at the truth of our being-time. It is helpful to know when we are being unskillful or when we have done something helpful, but the reality of our experience is deeper than the labels we put on it.

Sequential time (past, present, future) can be instructive as a way to talk about our experience. But it is not productive when we become trapped by our desires or goals. Like sequential time, labeling our experience as good and bad can hinder us from experiencing and responding to our life just as it is. If we are judging our encounters as good or bad, we are also saying yes and no. This binary thinking is often the source of suffering for ourselves and others. We want to let our mind open and directly experience life, allowing us to drop extraneous dualistic thinking. In this way our discerning mind operates as a tool helping us to make decisions rather than as a cloud that blocks the golden radiance of our life as practice-realization.

Present Doubt

4

Although you never measure the length or brevity of the twelve hours, their swiftness or slowness, you still call them the twelve hours. As evidence of their going and coming is obvious, you do not come to doubt them. But even though you do not have doubts about them, that is not to say you know them. Since a sentient being's doubtings of the many and various things unknown to him are naturally vague and indefinite, the course his doubtings take will probably not bring them to coincide with this present doubt. Nonetheless, the doubts themselves are, after all, none other than time.

BY AND LARGE, we don't analyze our understanding of time. We measure time against our activity. We say, "Oh, time is flying by," "There isn't enough time," "I'm behind or ahead of schedule," or "I've got time on my hands," etc. Our relationship to this thing called time is being ahead or behind, not having enough or having too much of it. We quantify time. We measure time. We are caught by clock time. This is the twelve—or twenty-four as we would state it—hours of our day.

We accept clock time and its artifices, such as daylight saving time or time zones, because we use clock time as a way to negotiate the business of our day. We don't usually doubt the nature of time, or if we do, it is to ponder the physics of time. Dōgen's concern is time-being and practice. For this reason he wrote, "Even though you do not have doubts about them [the twenty-four hours of your day], that is not to say you know them." From Dōgen's perspective we are essentially clueless about our relationship to time, and this understanding is at the heart of his attempt to clarify and define questions about existence and time, which are fundamental to awakening.

DOUBTING TIME

Unfortunately, we are often in the dark about how to investigate the nature of our experience. That is why Dōgen says, "Since a sentient being's doubting, of the many and various things unknown to him are naturally vague and indefinite, the course his doubtings take will probably not bring them to coincide with this present doubt." Here, Dōgen makes a very important observation: doubt is essential to actualizing understanding. Truly productive doubt must bring us to a point in which we drop our intellect and enter the realm of actualization. Before we can attain a mental state of spontaneous response, we may need to wander in the fields of intellectual investigation. Such investigation lays the foundation for stepping off the hundred-foot pole.[1]

"Uji" is Dōgen's attempt to present the teachings through a certain kind of logic. Dōgen combines intellectual understanding with a poetic sensibility in order to invite us to enter a new paradigm of practice. People learn in different ways, but however we may pass through this process, it begins with a question. The question is critical. Our tendency is to define our experience, not open it to further ambiguity. In this case, Dōgen wants us to expand our view by doubting what we think we know about being and time. Until we understand our true nature in relationship to time, we will not deeply penetrate the importance of thoroughly engaging the present moment. From Dōgen's point of view, if we deeply investigate the nature of being-time within a specific context, we will completely penetrate the true nature of each and all being-time. In Zen, this deeper investigation or doubting is referred to as "great doubt." Great doubt is doubt that brings us face-to-face with life just as it is without our conceptual overlay. Zen master Hakuin wrote,

To all intents and purposes, the study of Zen makes as its essential the resolution of the ball of great doubt. That is why it is said: "At the bottom of great doubt lies great awakening. If you doubt fully you will awaken fully." [2]

We often need help in our understanding of the cultivation of great doubt. In the dialogue below between Shunryū Suzuki Roshi and a student, the student is asking the wrong question. The student's doubt will not lead to a deeper understanding, but will only reinforce his or her misconceptions and judgments about practice:

> The student asked: "What can you say to my doubt about whether my zazen is true zazen, my practice is true practice, and my effort is right effort—that type of thing?" Shunryū Suzuki Roshi replied, "Don't doubt your practice. . . . If you think too much about your practice, you will lose your practice. Okay. So don't think too much, or don't try *too* hard. Take your time . . . Okay?"[3]

Here is a clear example of the student thinking too hard and analyzing the practice too much in the wrong way. He or she has doubts, they seem like reasonable doubts, but they are not helpful doubts. This student is judging the quality of his or her experience. Shunryū Suzuki Roshi's response is don't worry too much, just do the practice without judgment. Sometimes we don't know where to direct our attention. This is also Dōgen's point, and it is another reason we seek the advice and guidance of a teacher. In "Uji," it is Dōgen's intention to guide us step by step through our investigation.

CULTIVATING DOUBT

As we make this exploration with Dōgen, cultivate doubt. Ask yourself, "what is it?" and "how does this apply to my life?" If you wonder about life's golden radiance, then keep asking yourself, "what is it?" or "Can I see golden radiance as my life?" Over and over again in "Uji," Dōgen presents questions. We must apply Dōgen's teachings to our everyday life in order to benefit from his wisdom. Dōgen did not write "Uji" for our intellectual edification. His intention is to offer us guidance in how to participate fully in the Bodhisattva Way. The doubts we have, the kōans we create, should bring us closer to actualizing the Buddhadharma in every moment of our ordinary day.

What does it mean to live just this moment? Who is this sixteen-foot Buddha and the three-headed demon? How can entire being-time be my being-time? Can I accept, understand, and enact my day as a radiant buddha? How does Dōgen's teaching inform my life? These are the kinds of questions you might ask yourself. Not in the abstract, but in the here-and-now. As the text goes on, Dōgen will frame these questions and guide our inquiry.

Embodying the World   5

We set the self out in array and make the whole world. We must see all the various things of the whole world as so many times. These things do not get in each other's way any more than various times get in each other's way. Because of this, there is an arising of the religious mind at the same time, and it is the arising of time of the same mind. So it is with practice and attainment of the Way. We set our self out in array, and we see that. Such is the fundamental reason of the Way—that our self is time.

SETTING ONESELF IN ARRAY means that we place or set ourselves in accord with something, someone, an event, or an interaction. In this case, Dōgen writes that when we are in array with the world, the world will come forth and "make" itself, or reveal itself, to us, as we reveal ourselves to or with it. This revelation can only happen within the context of our specific situation. In "Yuibutsu Yobutsu" (Only a Buddha and a Buddha), Dōgen makes a similar statement when he offers this quotation:

> An ancient buddha said, "Mountains, rivers, and earth are born at the same moment with each person. All buddhas, of the past, present, and future are practicing together with each person."[1]

Each moment reveals itself or is born with all of that moment's presencing, hence "mountains, rivers, and earth are born at the same moment with each person." This is to "make the world" or to fully penetrate the is-ness of the totality of our life. (More on this in chapter 26.)

Another way to express "we set the self out in array" is a translation that removes the pronoun "we." This reading is helpful because of our tendency to view effort in practice as solely our own. Now the sentence, as translated by Kim, reads, "The self arrays itself and embodies the whole world."[2]

Kim notes in his book *Flowers of Emptiness* that "self" is the translation of the Japanese word *ware*. He writes *ware* has two possible interpretations in this context: (1) self/being and (2) time/impermanence.[3] Following Kim's lead we can understand "to set the self in array" is to fully occupy the moment (time) of one's existence (being). Setting time in array is to fully occupy the fluctuating impermanence of the present moment as embodied in one's person. Since a being-time includes the individual's unique being-time and simultaneously the arising of all being(s)-times(s), this becomes the totality of all being at that moment practicing together. To set the self out in array includes both the universal (time as interpenetrating/interconnected impermanence presencing) and the individual (our particular/independent experience) interacting without any obstruction.

All things or beings are manifesting at this moment, and our response must incorporate and be incorporated by the totality of that activity. The moment "made" is a moment inclusive of all being, while simultaneously embodying the particular moment's arising. We make each moment and each moment makes us. It is a reciprocal and unobstructed event. To include everything in each moment is to array oneself with right now. It is the totality of a moment being born with us as we are born with it.

For example, when driving our car, we incorporate and respond to the totality of our experience, thereby establishing our experience in concert with others. When we first learn to drive, it seems very difficult to remember everything we were taught about maneuvering the car. Our focus is almost exclusively on our effort. As we become more experienced, driving becomes second nature and we forget the self. In this respect, the more successfully we engage in the here-and-now of driving, without excessive thinking, the more likely we are to arrive at our destination without mishap or dismay to our fellow drivers. Yet driving does require learning. We must make an effort to acquire a new set of skills. When this effort becomes second nature, we could easily say driving drives itself, meaning we are incorporating the totality of the road's activity, other drivers' activity, our activity, the weather's activity, and so on. How we experience our driving and how the totality of the moment of driving arises are the moment's making. In a very similar way, all beings make the world.[4] Simultaneously we are making this world with the world. Both are arising together. Whether this activity is in the stage of being self-conscious or without thought, there is never a time when all the elements of our situation are not coming forward to meet us.

Unhindered Confirmation and Effort

In the "Genjōkōan" (Manifesting Suchness), Dōgen writes: "Practice that confirms things by taking the self to them is illusion; for things to come forward and practice and confirm the self is enlightenment."[5] When we want to control a situation, our small self is charging ahead. This small self gives us a false confirmation of our actions. Conversely, when we allow things to come forward and practice with us, this is the confirmation of the arrayed self. In a sense we can say that the world is made or born with us in that moment. By being sensitive to the needs of all things presencing, we are confirmed by the whole. Returning to the example of driving our car, we are aligning ourselves with all the other cars, drivers, rules of the road, weather, road conditions, etc., that might arise. The enlightened driver would be the driver who is able to negotiate all the elements present while including but not imposing her own agenda. This is to conduct oneself in a way that does not push the self forward inappropriately. When we drive aggressively (this includes

driving too quickly or too slowly), we are not in accord. We are imposing our own agenda at the expense of the needs of the situation. This
is delusion. It is not a matter of whether you arrive without having an
accident; it is the how of your interactions that determines realization.
This how is what makes the world your world. Your world may be a
world of suffering or a world of equanimity. When we are able to conduct ourselves in this inclusive way, the self is confirmed.[6]

Thus when we array the self, we are able to manifest the true self—
the self of enlightened response. The self of enlightened response is able
to reflect, hold, and embody all aspects of its situation. It is the self that
orders and ranks itself (in the best possible way) with true reality: the
world arising at this time-being. Each of us and all things are like a
hologram in which each part is also the whole.

If we are upset with someone and can still be the self that not only
holds itself but also the other, then this is the means by which we are
able to embody the totality of the situation. To hold both self and other
means experiencing the nonduality of self and other. This is not a practice of discounting our needs in order to appease another. The self's
needs are included as part of the totality of a situation. Part of practice
maturity has to do with our ability to discern what is appropriate.
Actualizing bodhisattva precepts[7] becomes the enactment of setting
oneself out in array and making the world.

Unobstructed Being-Time

When Dōgen writes, "We must see all the various things of the world
as so many times. These things do not get in each other's way any
more than various times get in each other's way,"[8] he is setting up the
simultaneity between time of the arising of the thought to practice
and the actualizing of the time of practice. This idea is presented in
the next sentence of the text: "Because of this, there is an arising of
the religious mind at the same time, and it is the arising of time of the
same mind." This concurrent activity carries both the specific time of

a mind awakening as the same time of the awakened mind. More on this later.

He is also continuing the theme of all being-time arising at the same time as our being-time. Beings, things, and events do not exist in time: beings, things, and events are times. When we think of a moment of time as nondual, it is easy to imagine that it does not hinder any other time. But when we think of each being-time as a particularity, we might think those various moments, beings, or events could not exist simultaneously without becoming a problem. The simultaneity of being-time means each being-time is independent and interpenetrating without obstruction.

THINGS DO NOT GET IN THE WAY

Dōgen writes: "Things do not get in each other's way any more than various times get in each other's way." Let's look at this sentence backward: When you are thinking about moments of time, do they hinder each other? Does a moment's happening keep another moment from happening? We can only experience the moment we are experiencing, yet simultaneously this very moment is being experienced by every being, person, and thing in this universe. And nothing stops anyone from being in the time that is his or her experience. Our time right now is not a problem for the person in New York or Sydney, Australia. We rarely think about it, but when we do, we see that we do not obstruct each other. Observing this, we accept the idea of one being's time not preventing the simultaneity of another being's time. But when we think about things, we tend to think of things as occupying space, which presents a problem. Dōgen isn't talking about solid things occupying the same space. He is teaching us to think about our experience of separateness versus our interdependent nature.

Time and being are different aspects of the same thing. What you experience with time, you also experience with being. If we view the world from the nondual perspective of one process acting, there is no separation. The reason things, persons, and beings get in our way is because we understand ourselves to be separate and disconnected from the other. This view results in suffering caused by trying to make the world reflect what we think it should be versus allowing things to come forward and share our experience. The more we believe we are separate from another person, the more conflict arises when we are confronted with that person's view. We have a difficult time incorporating the idea that we are the same being-time as the person who does not agree with us. Hence we think that someone holding a different idea than ours has no kinship with us. We might even think that this other person is a threat. This kind of thinking is polarizing and makes it difficult for us to work together. In such instances, we are aware of our uniqueness but not our sameness. Do not mistake this as a practice of passivity. This teaching is not about allowing yourself to be run over by someone. We should set boundaries; the question is how we set boundaries. Are we punitive or intelligently compassionate? Our ability to be skillful is, in large part, dependent upon our understanding of our shared experience as human beings.

A student told me about a coworker with whom cooperation was difficult. It occurred to that student to try letting go of his previous ideas about the coworker and just listen and be open to the interaction. This curiosity and nonjudgmental attitude completely changed their interactions. The difficult coworker relaxed and became more open himself. He was friendlier. By accepting and listening to his coworker, the Zen student shifted the dynamic of the interaction. Freedom came from including the other person. The student said, "I just listened and didn't think about problems. It was very easy, relaxed, and liberating." Once we stop the story about what is happening and allow ourselves to be present, we have a better chance of diffusing suffering. Our mind finds equanimity, and our equanimity allows us to meet the situation with skill and compassion. When we are rigid in our notions about what can and cannot be present simultaneously, we experience what Dōgen calls "getting in each other's way."

A sequential view of process also results in the inability to hold two seemingly conflicting thoughts at the same time. For example, we think we can't be enlightened and deluded at the same time. But in truth, we contain both enlightenment and delusion, because reality is not hindered by our realization or our delusion. Reality is more fundamental than the ideas we have about things or experiences. Time-being as both a universal and a unique moment contains all being-times. From this perspective there is nothing left out of a moment. Each present moment is beyond realization and delusion, because each moment is more than either.

PRACTICE-REALIZATION

Dōgen continues:

> Because of this, there is an arising of the religious mind at the same time, and it is the arising of time of the same mind. So it is with practice and attainment of the Way. We set our self out in array, and we see that. Such is the fundamental reason of the Way—that our self is time.

Now we come to the critical question of spiritual progress and being-time. In a sequential timeline, practice begins with the arising of the way-seeking mind. In this model of practice, we engage in spiritual activities, and at some point in the future we attain realization. But this is not Dōgen's teaching. He instructed that expressing our intention to practice is simultaneously the expression of our realization. Thus, the arising of the way-seeking mind is the same as the time of the way-seeking mind. They are not separate events. Dōgen writes in "Busshō" (Buddha-Nature):

> With respect to the saying "If the time arrives," there are those, both past and present, who would interpret it to mean

that one must wait for a time in the future for the Buddha-nature to present itself, and that, if one is diligent in one's training, one will naturally be aware at such a time of the Buddha-nature's manifestation. Until that time comes, however, the Buddha-nature will never present itself, even though one seeks the Dharma from a mentor or endeavors to enact the Way. Those who think this way will only reenter the dusty world and watch the Milky Way in vain [for the manifestation of the Buddha-nature].[9]

Way-seeking mind arises simultaneously with way-seeking time. This is practice-realization. That time and being arise simultaneously is an important concept for understanding practice. We are not waiting for some future time to enact realization, as that time is our present moment. Everything we need is already present. This is a fundamentally different understanding than thinking we are now deficient and need to attain something outside of our current being-time in order to enact realization. The time of our delusion does not obstruct the time of our realization. Our practice is not in order to attain realization. Practice itself is the actualization of realization. Dōgen writes in "Bendōwa" (Wholehearted Practice of the Way), "If practice and enlightenment were two things, as it appears to an ordinary person, each could be recognized separately."[10]

To say the arising of way-seeking mind is the same time as way-seeking mind is just like the wave and ocean example. It is not an either-or situation. Both are true at the same time, and both are facilitating the production of the other. We are way-seeking mind right this moment, and way-seeking mind is also this moment. When we are expressing the arising of way-seeking mind, the time of way-seeking mind is also present.

Practice arises in this moment, and realization arises in this moment. I engage in spiritual practice, and that practice in and of itself is realization. But when I relate to them as one or the other, then I want to label my activity as practice or as realization. Yet they are always, like wave and ocean, happening together and dependent upon each other for their actualization. There can be no wave without the ocean and no ocean without the wave. It is the nature of ocean to manifest sometimes as ocean and sometimes as wave, and no matter which we are seeing, the one does not obstruct the other. Practice and realization are both the same event and cannot obstruct each other. They are both simultaneously present, helping each other manifest. This is why it is necessary to practice. Realization does not manifest outside of its actualization. The fact that we are buddha-nature does not mean we will act according to that nature. Expressing buddha-nature (realization) is dependent upon practice, which is the enactment of our true nature.

We can view practice as a dharma position's independent aspect. In this way we say practice can be broken down into aspiration for practice, training, etc., but simultaneously nothing is missing. Practice is a unique moment, and it is also expressed realization. Realization is the aspect of the dharma position in which every aspect is already present.

To separate practice and realization is to think that when we are practicing we are not actualizing buddha-mind. We think we are practicing to develop some capacity for this mind. This kind of thinking creates problems because it is predicated upon preconceived ideas about enlightenment. Rather, practice and realization are simultaneously present, helping each other manifest. They are each other manifesting, and they are the manifestation of actualization itself.

In Eihei Kōroku (Dōgen's Extensive Record), Dōgen gives the example of zazen as practice enacting realization:

> The principle of zazen in other schools is to wait for enlightenment. For example, [their practice] is like having crossed over a great ocean on a raft, thinking that upon crossing the ocean one should discard the raft. The zazen of our buddha

ancestors is not like this, but is simply Buddha's practice. We could say that the situation of Buddha's house is the oneness in which the essence, practice, and expounding are one and the same.[11]

Now we gain a deeper understanding of the importance of being-time. Time is the medium in which our being is manifest. This medium is not different from this being. If we think of time as a separate entity from our self, then we are going to place ourselves within that structure sequentially. We will think practice is one time and realization is another time. Or we will be discouraged if we are waiting for our practice to result in a certain outcome. When we approach our life realizing that practice and realization do not obstruct each other, we are more likely to find ease and to acknowledge the confirmation of our effort by all being. Big mind is always present. We don't have to wait for a time in which it can appear. Realizing this simultaneity is crucial for awakening. This is the activity of practice-realization.

The self setting itself out in array is the self of big mind. It is the self that can hold seemingly contradictory views simultaneously. It is the self that arises both as all being-time and the self that independently occupies each moment. This self-being-time is impermanence; it is the temporal aspect of our particular presencing. It is the interpenetration and impermanence of the constant interaction and flux of reality. It is impermanence realized.

This mind sees itself and, in seeing itself, sees the whole universe as itself. This is the self that is totally penetrating the world as it is and being verified by the world. In this way, the self is fully being in the time of right now and in the time of the whole world. Time does not carry us along. We are time itself. Time resides within the essential nature of our being. When we set our self out in array, we see that our true nature is the interpenetrating activity of all being and time. Realizing such, we respond to each situation with compassion and insight. The welfare of others is our welfare. Our empathy for others is real and personal. Our wisdom is a sword that cuts through the delusion of thinking we are separate. This moment of being is also the time of response. We set the self in array, and we respond as buddhas.

The One Hundred Grasses Exist   6

Since such is its fundamental reason, we must study and learn that myriad phenomena and numberless grasses [things] exist over the entire earth, and each of the grasses and each of the forms exists as the entire earth. These comings and goings are the commencement of Buddhist practice. When you have arrived within this field of suchness, it is a single grass, a single form. The forms are understood and not understood, the grasses are grasped and not grasped.

THIS FUNDAMENTAL REASON is the self setting itself in array as the whole-world-being-time. Dōgen perhaps most clearly states this in "Genjōkōan" (Manifesting Suchness): "To forget the self is to be experienced by the myriad dharmas. To be experienced by the myriad dharmas is to let our own body-and-mind, and the body-and-mind of the external world, drop away."[1] This dropping away is enacting our (and all beings') true state of impermanence, interbeing, and cooperation. We do not lose our self-identity, rather we drop clinging to a particular self-identity and take our true place as and with all being(s)—this is dropping body-mind (shinjin-datsuraku). Dropping body-mind enacts our kinship with all beings. This is setting the self in array. We are myriad phenomena, and we are the entire earth. This is not an abstraction; it is the basis for the bodhisattva's altruistic path. Dainin Katagiri Roshi addressed this when he said:

In the human world we see things as separate from us. In Buddha's world all things come together and melt into one.

So, very naturally, if we set ourselves out in array in Buddha's world, we can see all other beings. Then we know that we must live with others in peace and harmony because we are intimately related, with no gap between. This is Buddha's world.[2]

This is the fundamental reason for our practice. This is the enactment of the bodhisattva's vow. The bodhisattva strives to enact this understanding as response and knows it is not enough to just understand with our mind. Intellectual understanding is important, but we must go beyond thinking about reality to enacting reality. This is enlightened response. This enlightened response is the being-time or present moment of setting the self out in array.

HUAYAN SCHOOL: MUTUAL IDENTITY AND MUTUAL PENETRATION

While "we must study and learn that myriad phenomena and numberless grasses exist over the entire earth" would seem self-evident, we do not understand that "each of the grasses and each of the forms exists as the entire earth." Realizing this relationship is key to Dōgen's understanding of the simultaneity of practice as realized response. He wrote in "Genjōkōan" (Manifesting Suchness), "If a person practices and realizes the Buddha Way, when he attains one dharma he penetrates completely that one dharma; when he encounters one practice, he practices that one practice."[3] This one dharma and one practice involve learning that each grass is the entire earth. Dōgen extols us to study and learn that everything (the one hundred grasses) is the entire world as it manifests as particularity.

The seventh-century Chinese Huayan School[4] called this teaching, "to know one thing is to know all things." In order to understand Dōgen's comment that each grass or form is the entire earth, two Huayan concepts are key: mutual identity and mutual penetration.

Mutual identity is the observation that all things share the qualities or processes of (1) having no inherent existence separate from all being, (2) being subject to and the result of causal relationships, and (3) being impermanent. When seen from this perspective of nonduality, there is no difference between one thing and the next. Is there anything in this world that has a separate inherent existence? Is there anything that does not arise from causes and conditions? Is there anything that is not impermanence?[5] If these three states are our criteria for defining the basic nature of all beings, then we must say that all beings are the same. If you know the truth of grasses' impermanence, you will know the truth of your own impermanence, interconnection, and interpenetrating intimacy with all beings. Essentially all being-time is a process, rather than unrelated events banging up against each other. Being-time is dynamic, not a fixed thing. This is how we can talk about reality when we view it from the perspective of nonduality.

Mutual penetration posits that if all beings share mutual identity they also physically penetrate or commingle with each other. Taking the idea further, it can be said that seen from a being's independent aspect, that being cannot be isolated and is embedded in a codependent relationship of function and existence. Mutual penetration is not an abstract concept. If you are sitting in a room with a group of people, you are all sharing the same air. As soon as you breathe in, your inhalation includes gases from another's exhalation. That air becomes incorporated into your body on a cellular level. In a very real way you have become part of another person, as they are with you.

The scope of mutual identity and mutual penetration applies to all of time and space, in each moment. Everything arises simultaneously. All the forms and all the grasses are dependent upon each other and arise together to make up the earth. In the way of mutual interpenetration and mutual identity, the grasses and myriad things exist as the entire earth. Usually when we think of causal relationships, we think of them as sequential: this caused that and that caused this. Viewing this process as a multidimensional holistic event is a more accurate model that includes the simultaneity of causal, interpenetrating, interconnected, and unobstructed being-time.

Huayan uses the image of a net to illustrate this teaching. Imagine a net with jewels at every intersection within the net. Each jewel reflects all the other jewels. This jeweled net is everything, without end. This is Indra's Net. Fazang's[6] "The Golden Lion" describes Indra's Net as:

> The infinite interpenetration [of all things], the unimpeded identity [of all things], . . . [is] shown in the symbol of the net of Indra. When these concepts are manifested [in the mind of the Bodhisattva], then when one of the many obstacles is overcome, all are overcome, and one acquires the destruction of [moral and intellectual faults . . .] . . . In practicing the virtues, when one is perfected, all are perfected, and with regard to reality, when one [part] is revealed, everything is revealed. All things are endowed with universality and particularity, beginning and end are the same, and when one first arouses the aspiration for enlightenment [*bodhicittotpāda*], one also becomes perfectly enlightened. . . . the goal is inherent in causal practice.[7]

The actual state of the world is that things do not obstruct each other. The particularity of each being or thing does not get in the way of the universal sameness of each being or thing. At the same time that each grass and form exists as a particular being, they simultaneously exist as the entire earth. Let's return to the example of the wave and ocean. The wave is the particular, and the ocean the universal. When we see or conceptualize wave, then it is just one wave. At the same time, it is also the ocean. If you truly know the nature of the wave, you understand the nature of ocean or water. Depending upon our view, we see water, or wave, or ocean. Or we might see the atoms that make up water if we were scientists, or we see a medium to surf on or swim in if we like water sports, or we see undrinkable salt water if we are thirsty, and so on. No matter what we see or think it is, it is always simultaneously all of the other aspects. All of the aspects are always the one ocean or one water. Because the ocean and wave are essentially the same thing, they must, by definition, not obstruct each other. The perspective of obstruction is one of delusion. Dōgen writes in "Hokke Ten Hokke" (Dharma Blossoms Turn Dharma Blossoms):

> When you see a speck of dust, it is not that you do not see the world of phenomena. When you realize the world of phenomena, it is not that you do not realize a speck of dust. When buddhas realize the world of phenomena, they do not keep you from realization. Wholesomeness is manifest in the beginning, middle, and end. Thus, realization is reality right now. Even shocks, doubts, fears, and frights are none other than right now.[8]

COMING AND GOING HAS NO BEGINNING, MIDDLE, OR END

Now Dōgen, returning to the question of practice, writes, "These coming and goings are the commencement of Buddhist practice."[9] Numberless grasses, in the state of unobstructed mutual interpenetration and identity, are the activity of coming and going. Dōgen wrote that coming and going is the real activity of a buddha-mind,[10] is a real human body,[11] engaged in the activity of actualized truth through engaging problems[12] and the instruction of the buddhas.[13] Coming and going is the activity of practice-realization as our present experience. It is that aspect of the dharma position that is making a passage as this moment expressed. It is impermanence connecting, becoming, and verifying the actualized moment.

Our Buddhist practice is learning that the coming and going of our life is life itself, is the place and time of practice-realization expressed. Life expressed happens at this time, and for this reason it should not be understood as a linear progression. Furthermore, from the standpoint of nonduality, mutual identity, and interpenetration, there is no beginning, middle, or end. The activity of practice becomes present practice as realization, not practice for a future realization. Dōgen writes in "Sesshin Sesshō" (Speaking of Mind, Speaking of Essence):

> The way of the buddha is the way of the buddha at the time of the first production of the thought; it is the way of the buddha at the time of attaining true enlightenment. It is the way of the buddha throughout beginning, middle, and end.[14]

Therefore our effort in practice must be directed to each moment of the twenty-four hours of the glorious radiance of our day.

This Field of Suchness

Returning to "Uji," Dōgen continues, "When we have set ourselves out in array we arrive at this field of suchness." In this field there is the form of Buddha's Way, expressed fully in one grass or as one grass at this time. It is a single thing completely expressing itself and all being through its activity. To arrive is to actualize our understanding, thereby realizing suchness.

Dōgen writes in "Shoaku Makusa" (Not Doing Wrongs):

> Someone who has come to know a single particle knows the whole Universe, and someone who has penetrated one real dharma has penetrated the myriad dharmas. Someone who has not penetrated the myriad dharmas has not penetrated one real dharma. When students of penetration penetrate to the end, they see the myriad dharmas and they see single real dharmas; therefore, people who are learning of a single particle are inevitably learning of the whole universe.[15]

Dainin Katagiri Roshi translates this section of "Uji" as "When you reach this state you *are* the one grass; one form . . ."[16] What would our life be if we truly were cognizant of our grass-ness? As humans we tend to feel that we can always use the grass or other form-beings for our convenience, comfort, or nurturance. When we deeply understand that we are not different from the grass, that we might be exactly the same as the grass, then surely our relationship with this earth will change.

This is true for people as well. We feel separate and cannot understand that we are connected. In this world we are surrounded by much prejudice and violence born from a deep ignorance of our sameness. To understand the truth of mutual identity and mutual interpenetration is not an abstract philosophical idea, it is the dharma gate of compassion and wisdom. As quoted from Fazang earlier, "When these concepts are manifested [in the mind of the Bodhisattva] . . . one acquires the destruction of [moral and intellectual faults]."[17]

Having fully integrated ourselves with our life, as it is now, is the place of arrival, and that place or field is a fully expressed moment. This is *inmo no denchi* (the field of suchness), reality itself actualized within the context of a specific place or moment of being-time.[18] Practice-realization is not an abstract concept, it is each and every moment of our life, right now.

UNDERSTANDING, NOT UNDERSTANDING, GRASPING, NOT GRASPING

Dōgen continues, "The forms are understood and not understood, the grasses are grasped and not grasped." In this state of setting the self in array, we may understand or not understand, we may grasp reality or not grasp it. Dōgen writes in "Shin Fukatoku" (Mind Cannot Be Grasped) that in the activity of our "living and dying, coming and going" we should understand that nothing can be grasped; only lived. He asks:

> If [someone] says "What is the state of 'past mind cannot be grasped'?" we should say "Living and dying, coming and going." . . . "What is the state of 'present mind cannot be grasped'?" we should say "Living and dying, coming and going." . . . "What is the state of 'future mind cannot be grasped'?" we should say "Living and dying, coming and going." In sum, there is buddha-mind as fences, walls, tiles, and pebbles, and all the buddhas of the three times experience this as "it cannot be grasped." There are only fences, walls, tiles, and pebbles, which are the buddha-mind itself, and the buddhas experience this in the three times as "it cannot be grasped."[19]

This coming and going which cannot be grasped is the particular and universal presencing itself moment after moment. They are, as Dainin Katagiri Roshi has said, coming and going at superspeed. Katagiri elaborates:

> We are connected and simultaneously we are going back and forth. It's not exactly going back and forth; it is coming and going at superspeed. This is the real state of existence of all sentient beings.[20]

We perceive a moment as one thing. That is our focus. Yet, this individual moment never loses the aspect of including everything. Katagiri writes, "real practice is done simultaneously in the realm of the twelve hours of your day and the realm of timelessness."[21] This coming and going at superspeed is not this or that. Katagiri Roshi's use of the word "superspeed" gives us an image of simultaneous arising. He helps us rethink how we might negotiate our life and how we might go beyond the binary concepts of this or that, coming or going. "Superspeed" is responding to what is. This is the moment Dōgen calls "it cannot be grasped."

Is this a wave or the ocean? Superspeed we see first as one then as the other, then the totality of both. This awareness is not intellectual; it is an open response to what is happening right now. We are practicing with the totality of the universe in this one single moment of washing the dishes or talking with our neighbor. What is it? What is right for this moment? And the next?

Sometimes, we just respond, the intuition of "it cannot be grasped." Sometimes we have to think about it. Sometimes we totally miss the mark. Here it comes, superspeed, what to do? The foundation of this practice is one grass, is setting the self out in array, is just our coming and going, living and dying—in this moment and the next. This is the intimacy of living in this world, as this world, with all beings.

♦

As the time right now is all there ever is, each being-time is without exception entire time. A grass-being and a form-being are both times. Entire being, the entire world, exists in the time of each and every now. Just reflect: right now, is there an entire being or an entire world missing from your present time, or not?

IN THE PREVIOUS SECTION, Dōgen wrote that the hundred grasses (all phenomena) exist over the entire earth and exist as the entire earth. To understand the true nature of a single form is to understand all of reality. This paragraph is the same teaching from the perspective of time. A present moment is all there is, and each particular time is entire time. Just as one being's existence is the entire earth, so that being's time is entire time.

There is no experience of time that we can have that is not grounded in the present moment. Our minds are constructing or remembering events in this moment, even if we feel that we are actually experiencing past or future. Present time is really all there is. Our mind defines our experience as past (a memory that can only be recalled in the present moment), as present (which can only be defined to ourselves at this time), and as future (a present moment thought about something that might happen). All of this mental activity is in the present being-time.

This is not to say that we do not have a past, but our conscious experience of our past can only happen in the now. Fazang writes this about time:

Regarding the harmonizing mergence of one moment with the aeons . . . since a single moment has no substance of its own, it becomes interchangeable with the great aeons. Because the great aeons have no substance, they also embrace the single moment. Since both the single moment and the great aeons have no substance, all the marks of the long and the short are merged into [a great harmony], . . . all the Buddhas and sentient beings, and all things and events in the past, present, and future come into view simultaneously. Why is this so? . . . [Since time is inseparable from events,] if one moment becomes non-obstructive, all dharmas will [automatically] become harmoniously merged. That is why all things and events in the three times vividly appear within one moment . . .[1]

Shohaku Okumura points out in his book *Realizing Genjokoan*[2] that the present moment we think we are experiencing cannot be thought about or defined at the time of its happening. He surmises that time does not exist in the way we think it does; therefore, we cannot grasp it. We cannot fix or conceptualize the present moment as it is happening. Our being-time is always morphing into the next moment. Yet, this present now is a particular now that we experience, and simultaneously it is the inclusive now of our entire world, which includes all past, present, and future. This is the intersection of all of being-time with right now.

As you read this book, this moment contains all the moments and events, known and unknown, that have ever been or will be. The causal connections of your present moment contain all the causal connections possible. This book you hold is paper and that paper was a tree, and that tree depended upon the sun, rain, soil, and the whole universe throughout time in order to grow. This moment of reading is being-time spread throughout the 360 degrees of time and space. Like the grass-being, your being-time includes entire time, and in this way, the time right now is all there ever is.

Is There Anything Missing?

If each moment includes everything, then we should not feel that something is lacking. Yet we do. So far Dōgen has presented a concise explanation of the totality of being-time. Now Dōgen wants to get our attention away from the intellectual and plunk us down into our present experience. A question like "is something missing from your present experience?" may seem rhetorical, but do not pass over it, because it is really a gateway for deepening practice. Earlier in "Uji," Dōgen prodded us to investigate the nature of our doubt about time, telling us we do not know how to focus our investigation. Now, he points directly to the inquiry we need to make. Is there anything missing "from your present time"? Having discussed the Huayan's mutual identity and mutual penetration, we intellectually know the answer to Dōgen's question must be no—there is nothing missing. Yet we cannot leave it at that.

While writing this section of the book, I got the flu. I lay in bed with a headache asking myself, "Is there anything missing?" If the answer is no, then why do I wish my headache would go away? If I let go of the idea that I don't want a headache, is it any different? There cannot be a time when something is missing, yet we all know what it is to feel that indeed something is missing. We want our situation to be different than what is; we do not want to suffer. We resist accepting our situation. Yet, Dōgen teaches that everything is present right now. This moment, the place of awakening, also includes the things we don't want. If we can include everything, it's not such a big problem. Realization must be inclusive of our feeling that something is missing.

Dōgen begins "Genjōkōan" (Manifesting Suchness) with four lines. He writes:

> When all dharmas are seen as the Buddha-Dharma, then there is delusion and realization, there is practice, there is life and there is death, there are buddhas and there are ordinary beings. When the myriad dharmas are each not of the self, there is no delusion, and no realization, no buddhas and no ordinary beings, no life and no death. The Buddha's truth is originally transcendent over abundance and scarcity, and so there is life and death, there is delusion and realization, there are beings and buddhas. And though it is like this, it is only that flowers, while loved, fall; and weeds, while hated, flourish.[3]

In the first sentence, I am completely caught in the dichotomy of headache-nonheadache. Life is a series of this and that. I am not a buddha because I have a headache or because I wish I didn't have a headache. Yet, Dōgen writes that delusion as well as enlightenment are Buddhadharma. In the second sentence, there cannot be a headache. I live in the realm of the absolute where there is no difference between headache and no headache. Yet, if they are the same, what is it I'm calling a headache?

In the third sentence, there is the place of this and that and going beyond this and that which is the true state of life and death, delusion and realization, buddhas and ancestors. In Buddha's truth, I go beyond headache and just experience what is. But Dōgen adds the last line regarding flowers and weeds. This is the human condition. I have a headache, I wish it were different; I hope it will pass. I get caught, and I work on letting go in the midst of my desire. This situation of desire and practice does not interfere with intimacy and response. This state includes everything: delusion, realization, life, death, and even a headache.

Including the suffering is key to actualizing our compassion and wisdom, since we don't live in a state of nonduality where everything appears the same and we have no likes or dislikes. Knowing one thing is knowing all things. This knowing has to include flowers falling, head-aches, loss, intense love, and deep aversion. Nothing can be rejected or ignored. We need to understand that whether we are open to including the totality of our experience, the totality is present anyway. This is the hundred grasses making the world and each grass existing as the world. Each experience I have is embedded in the totality of existence.

Our daily life and our spiritual life are the same life. We must explore Dōgen's teachings as they apply to the life we are living. Try it for your-self. Find your own truth in Dōgen's question. Keep returning. Our sincere inquiry brings Dōgen alive to stand with us in our exploration of his teaching. If we understand that everything is part of our present experience, as the dynamic coming and going of the Buddha Way, then we can enter the dharma gate of being-time. Is there anything missing? Flowers fall and weeds spread. Yet, in the midst of this—or because of this—we continue to practice the Bodhisattva Path.

In spite of this, a person holds various views at the time he is unenlightened, and has yet to learn the Buddha's Dharma. Hearing the
words "the time being," he thinks that at one time the old Buddha
became a creature with three heads and eight arms, and that at
another time he became a sixteen-foot Buddha. He imagines it as
like crossing a river or a mountain; the river and mountain may still
exist, but I have now left them behind, and at the present time I reside
in a splendid vermilion palace. To him, the mountain or river and I
are as distant from one another as heaven from earth.

IN THIS PASSAGE, Dōgen explains that we think of spiritual awakening
as happening in sequential time: past is delusion, present is working on
getting rid of delusion, and future is attaining realization. He writes
that we imagine our spiritual development to be like crossing a river or
climbing a mountain. Once we've gotten over the stream and climbed
the mountain, we will have arrived somewhere that no longer includes
where we have been. This is a spiritual journey, right? We're crossing
rivers, we're climbing mountains, and we're doing all these kinds of
activities that we imagine to be a journey from delusion to realization.
Dōgen says we then think, "But I have now left them behind." We make
up an imaginary progress. We believe that in the past we were in delusion but right now we are somewhere along a continuum of practice
leading to enlightenment.[1] This erroneous model is based upon our
initial misunderstanding of how one addresses the spiritual journey
as a continuous sequence. We think that we cannot get to realization

from our present delusion because realization resides in a different time than our current being-time.

For example, your criteria for spiritual progress might be that you can sit a seven-day sesshin, or maybe you can sit zazen for twenty-five days straight. You think, "I must be three-quarters of the way to enlightenment." Maybe you can dry towels with your body heat. You must be 90 percent along the way. You have an idea about the nature of this continuum from delusion to enlightenment. Concurrent with this kind of thinking is the notion that once we are enlightened we can't go back to delusion. Mistakes are behind us, and perfection is in front of us.

When you view your practice in this way, you think, "Oh, well, I left behind all those mistakes because I'm here on the path to enlightenment." You have arrived at the vermilion palace, the place of imagined enlightenment.[2] When we view practice as a means to attain realization, we tend to view our previous stage as behind us, and our attainment as not yet arrived. In this view, the mountain or the river is completely different from the place you are right now. Your struggles, the difficulties that you had, are something in the past, and they are not currently in your present situation. This is Dōgen's description of how we get caught when we frame our spiritual path as steps-and-stages. But don't just apply this teaching to spiritual practice; clinging to this way of thinking is always a problem regardless of the situation.

Steven Heine likens this belief in sequential time to creating a gulf between oneself and one's experience. Being caught in thinking of time as three sequential time periods—past, present, and future—we "obliterate the immediacy and comprehensive totality of the here-and-now."[3] We are cutting ourselves off from our own life as well as the life of all being(s). Ultimately this is deeply disturbing and destructive. We adhere to this notion of time out of a kind of anxiety to protect the self. The desire to define realization as something outside of ourselves, only attainable at some future date and better than our current ordinary life, will only take us further from our true experience. Yet we persist in this kind of fantasy about enlightenment. Our practice must continuously bring us closer to who we are in accordance with all of reality, not who we are as an idea about reality.

Dōgen may be making a little play on words when he writes, "To him, the mountain or river and I are as distant from one another as heaven from earth." Usually this expression is used to indicate a problem with our understanding: the gap is as great as heaven is from the earth. To understand that delusion is something to be discarded and enlightenment something to be picked up is really missing the point. We think delusion and enlightenment are as distant as heaven and earth, but actually it is our understanding that is as distant as heaven is from earth. There truly is no distance at all.

As we strive to close this imaginary gap between our situation and a seemingly distant place of enlightenment, we project upon the teachings our ideas of how to practice in order to attain this desired state. Our striving may have the opposite effect of what we most desire. For example, in practice we sometimes misunderstand how to best use our energy. We think our effort must be harsh, and we push ourselves too hard. The result is that we end up creating an aversion to practice. Our attempt to do our best actually backfires, and we end up creating a chasm in our practice instead of a bridge. We do not trust our body-mind to find the way by relaxing into the practice without leaning into the gale-force wind of our expectations.

It is this kind of misunderstanding that causes people to avoid meditation. They physically burn themselves out, or they constantly tell themselves that they "think too much" and their effort is therefore futile, resulting in the feeling that practice activity and enlightenment are as distant as heaven from earth. We think that the time of the river and the time of the mountain are separate from each other. We view them as stages along our path. Yet heaven and earth are not separate and the way back is only a matter of hearing and understanding. The time of the river and the time of the mountain are not disconnected.

It is all here, in us and of us, all the time. We must come back to what is unfolding right now.

We are afraid to plant ourselves firmly in the present moment, perhaps because we sense that to live fully in this moment is to experience the profound impermanence and changing nature of our life. We want to fix and control our understanding. We want to see a clear beginning, middle, and end to our spiritual path. We don't like surprises. Contrary to our intention, this kind of logic often traps us and leads us further and further from the freedom we seek. As we try to fix and quantify our experience, we find ourselves walled off from our life as it is unfolding.

Perhaps we are afraid that if we face our current situation, we will discover that we are the delusional three-headed and eight-armed demon we fear. When we perceive our practice as off the mark, we think that we are far away from the Buddha. Yet this is not so. Dōgen addresses this issue in his fascicle "Kattō" (Twining Vines) when he writes that practitioners think the way to advance in practice is to cut off their problems rather than working through their problems. He calls working through "cutting the complicated with the complicated."[4] In this way we use our problems as teaching tools to transform selfish and delusional practice into realized skillful response. It is only when we address our current situation without trying to cut off or repress our difficulties that we will be able to fully address and transform our practice. This can only happen where we are, not where we wish we were.

BIFURCATING TIME-BEING

A way to explore our tendency to define our practice experience as good (buddha) or bad (delusion) is to ask: where is the Buddha (good person) when we are a three-headed creature (unskillful person)? Where is the three-headed creature when we are a sixteen-foot Buddha?

When we begin our studies we may think, "Oh, I'm in delusion and I'm deluded about the nature of reality, and if I do the right kind of training, I'm going to become a buddha." When we are in delusion, we think we are a demon, and when we think we have attained some knowledge, we are closer to being a buddha.

The good buddha and the bad delusional person are not two beings. When we are skillful, we are skillful. When we are off the mark, we are off the mark. Yet in our unskillfulness our essential nature is still the same. This foundational is-ness of things just as they are means we do not have to cut off or run away from our problems. Our problems are the soil in which our wisdom will grow. This is the good news. We don't have to worry about finding the vermilion palace. Heaven and earth are united.

But the true state of things is not found in this one direction alone. At the time the mountain was being climbed and the river being crossed, I was there [in time]. The *time* has to *be* in me. Inasmuch as I am there, it cannot be that time passes away.

THE FIRST LINE of this passage disabuses us of any ideas we might have that time is just about leaving the past, occupying the present, and anticipating the future. Dōgen writes: "The true state of things is not to be found in one direction alone." As we have discussed, our true situation is not grounded in sequential time. Dōgen does not negate the presence of conventional time. There is no problem with using sequential time to get to work, plan a vacation, or meet a friend for dinner. The problem occurs when you develop concretized ideas about what has happened in the past and what will happen in the future in relation to your present moment.

If we only understand our life to be a series of discrete sequential moments passing by, we do not see the virtue and intimacy of each moment's interconnection and impermanence. Impermanence can be understood not just as fleeting stability, but as an expression of process and interconnection. It is when we embrace the impermanence of being-time that we drop our egocentric self and fully participate in the total activity of all beings' time because we can now perceive ourselves as part of the whole.

This complete engagement is freedom. Engaging with an open mind is inclusive, skillful response. When we are totally engaged with each moment, we stop pitting ourselves against something we perceive as outside and in need of control. This is the intimacy of no-self.

OUR BEING-TIME IS ALL BEING-TIME

Experiencing our present moment is experiencing our life. Our life includes "the time the mountain was being climbed and the river being crossed." We are simultaneously being all the individual being-times that we have known along the way. The elements of all the being-times we meet make up each being-time. In other words, this moment in time holds all the other moments and times of our experience, including past, present, and future. Wherever we are, it includes the time of the mountain and the time of the river; it is still "in us" and not something that has left us.

In the example given, Dōgen is speaking of our practice. The mountain may represent a monastic practice period, and the river might be a meeting with a teacher. What is important in the example is that this spiritual journey is more than our sequential conceptualization. Our experience may appear sequential, but that is not the full experience. The meeting with the teacher is already present in the moment of the monastery.

EACH MOMENT INCLUDES ALL BEING-TIME

Although the totality of being-time is usually not experienced consciously, since our focus is on the activity of this moment, it is still present. Each moment of our experience is part of a network of interconnected and interpenetrating being-times which includes past (time of climbing the mountain and crossing the river) as present. Each moment is Indra's Net. This is the truth of mutual interconnection and interpenetration, and this is why the time of climbing the mountain and crossing the stream is in each step.

Dōgen writes, "It cannot be that time passes away." Each present moment holds all being-time. Another expression used to talk about the present moment is the eternal now. As we ground ourselves in experience, our reality, this reality, this life, right at this moment, there is nothing else but this moment, and that is the eternal now. Each moment is this impermanent moment, eternally renewing itself as this moment. Eternal does not mean unchanging; it means that this impermanent moment goes on endlessly. In this way, we come to understand that time cannot pass away. It is the eternal presencing of all being-time. Again, it is not a moment that divorces us from interconnecting relations; rather, it is a moment that includes the totality of all existence and will be the genesis of our ethical enlightened response.

In the example given of climbing mountains and crossing rivers, each aspect of the journey is present in each moment or step of that journey. The time of the mountain and the time of the river are also part of a person's being-time. Imagine you are actually walking through mountain ranges and crossing rivers. Can you feel the time of the mountains and rivers is also your being-time? You and the mountain are having a particular experience of being-time that includes the being-time of each other, and simultaneously, the particular being-time of each individual expression of that moment. Our experience is not one-sided; it's just that as human beings, we tend to think about things exclusively from our perspective, not from the perspective of a mountain or other beings. In actuality, we make up the mountain's being-time just as much as the mountain's being-time makes up ours.

Living Includes the Present

If the mountains we have climbed and the streams we've crossed are still part of our present circumstances, this expanded view of time and being will prevent us from concretizing the past. The past as present is fluid. What happens when we have a negative response to a situation or person in the past? If we understand the past as having no living connection to the present, we hold on to our perception of what occurred.

We define the experience we're having now based on something that may or may not have happened in the past. This is human nature. It's very difficult to avoid being caught by an interpretation of our past. Later in this section, Dōgen integrates this idea of past time and present time merging and reforming as pure response.

Bringing forth the time of the mountains and rivers as our present time allows us to incorporate the whole of our experience. We can use the past as a tool to help us, not as a fixed view defining our experience. Did I learn from a mistake in the past or am I still carrying it with me? If my past dominates my experience of the present, I am limiting my life. Yet, if I completely discount the past, I am also limiting my life. This is a pitfall of understanding our experience only from the perspective of sequential time.

Another way to understand the interconnected simultaneity of being-time is from an environmental point of view. What we do locally makes a difference globally. What's happening in China makes a difference to us in the United States. The situation in which we misuse fossil fuels affects other people, animals, the earth, and the environment. These interconnected personal and global events become a real part of our awareness. Once this awareness develops, the teaching transforms us. This understanding will strengthen and guide the aspiration to respond to each situation anew, with ethical and skillful responses. This is actualization of practice-realization. This is the mind of buddha.

Every once in a while we go out into the woods and we take a big deep breath of air and hear the leaves rustling in the trees, and we have this complete, holistic experience of being of this world. We say, "Oh, wow. I'm a human being in the world. I'm part of the universe. I can feel the time of a tree as my being-time." It's a great experience. But most of the time, we're saying to ourselves, "I've got to get somewhere. I've got to do this thing or that thing." Time seems to obstruct our ability to get enough done. Or we feel a person is getting in our way. The sense we had of unobstructed connection when standing in the woods is gone.

Open inclusiveness gets lost. Dōgen teaches us to stay grounded in the being-time of our life at just this moment.

When we can hold both the three-headed, eight-armed self-centered me and still express the sixteen-foot Buddha of our true nature, we are able to incorporate the whole of the journey. The true vermilion palace is just the time-being of where we are right now. This right now includes everything and lacks nothing. It is the gateway to unobstructed practice. You are here; you are fully present right now. Your being and your time are also the being-time of everything, and everything is interpenetrating as your being-time. In this moment, this dharma position, there is just this, which is simultaneously all being-time.

Whose Time Is It Anyway?

10

As long as time is not a modality of going and coming, that time on the mountain is the immediate present—right *now*—of "the time being" (being-time). Yet as long as time takes upon itself a modality of going and coming, the being in me in the immediate now of the "time being" is being-time. So does not the time climbing the mountain or crossing the river swallow up the time of the splendid vermilion palace? Does not that time spit out this time?

WHEN BEING-TIME is viewed from its nonsequential aspect, the time we climb the mountain or cross the river is "the immediate present" of our current situation. What we would conventionally call past is present in this moment. Even when being-time is viewed from its sequential aspect, it is still being-time, right now. Because this is so, the "past"—climbing the mountain, crossing the river—transforms our idea of the goal—the vermilion palace. Dōgen does not deny sequential time's existence, but he does question how we perceive that time. In this section of "Uji," Dōgen explains how the relationship between nonsequential and sequential being-time transforms our experience.

Earlier in the text Dōgen articulates a problem that we often have in practice: We tend to hold oppositional views. We think we can only be enlightened or in delusion. For this reason, we view practice as a progression from delusion to realization. This movement appears sequential and gradual. We tend to make judgments about our progress based upon various notions we have about the teachings. We are inclined to interpret what we hear or read through the lens of these fixed ideas, regardless of the intention of the original teaching. To be able to drop our preconceived ideas is a sign of practice maturity.

Included in these erroneous ideas about spiritual progress is the notion that enlightenment is a place or state of mind reached once. Upon our reaching realization, everything else falls away and we are born anew, divorced from all previous delusional states forever. As Dōgen writes, "The true state of things is not found in this one direction alone . . ."[1] The antidote to this kind of thinking is to realize that being-time can only be experienced and actualized in this moment.

When we drop the model of time as sequential, all aspects of our path are present in this moment, and we are free to respond or set ourself in array with the totality of that moment. Each moment makes up our current experience, including all previous and future experience, and at the same time our current experience has its own life, separate from a past experience or a possible future.

A concrete example of this is the moon. In Zen, the moon is often used as a metaphor for realization. It is also a good image because the moon's phases happen in a sequential manner—coming and going— yet the moon is never not full—the immediate present. Dōgen writes in "Tsuki" (The Moon), "Round and pointed are not concerned with the cycle of coming and going. The moon is beyond coming and going."[2] Whether we perceive the moon as full or in a phase, the moon itself is just the moon. Its true nature is not the view we see based upon the earth's shadow upon it. What we see is a portion of the moon, yet we know that the moon itself does not diminish or grow. In each phase of the moon, all phases of the moon are always present and yet, to our eye, there is just the phase we see, independent of the other views. The moon's phases are not a problem; they come and go as the days progress. The problem arises when we think sequential time is time's totality. We forget that the moon is always full.

When Dōgen writes, "the time on the mountain is the immediate present," he is referring to the previous paragraph in which he said, "at the time the mountain was being climbed and the river being crossed, I was there [in time]."[3] He was both climbing the mountain and crossing the river. He finishes the paragraph with, "Inasmuch as I am there, it cannot be that time passes away."[4] How do we experience this?

If we look at the night sky, we are awestruck by the vastness of a starry night, and we forget the self. Forgetting the self has a quality of stopping time. Time does not pass away, nor is it coming and going. We are experiencing the eternal now. We see the incredible vista of the night sky and at that moment, we are completely one with everything in front of us. We have dropped our "I" or the sense that we are separate. We directly experience the awe of being completely present with everything.

We have been told by astrophysicists that when we look into the night sky and see a star, we are seeing the star's light from a distant time simultaneously with the time of our present now. The distance light travels from a star in one year is called a light-year. Depending upon the distance the star is from the earth, we will be seeing light that has traveled for thousands of years.

We see an uncountable number of stars all projecting their own time continuum, which we experience as now. Although this is true, the time of the stars and the time of our being are part of the whole of that moment. We make the moment as the moment is making us. We with all of reality share the function of making the whole, and in that way each part is the same as the whole. Yet, each aspect—a person, a star—has its own past and future particularity. At the same time there is just this one moment being enacted as right now, an interconnected, totally functioning universal whole.

THE BEING IN ME IS THE NOW OF TIME

We have the experience of our being-time moving—coming and going—yet at the same time it is still the time of right now. No matter what we think is happening, reality itself, which always includes us, is present, completely unobstructed. We have the simultaneity of time taking upon itself going and coming—the sequence of past, present, and future—and the immediacy of being-time as now.

Dōgen cannot let us get caught in one side or the other. We are being asked to hold both views simultaneously. Both have their function and place, both are necessary for the whole to manifest. Our tendency is to feel most comfortable viewing our experience as sequential. Yet, Dōgen writes in "Sangai Yuishin" (The Triple World Is Only the Mind) that although there is the sequential time of the father preceding the time of the child, something more is required to essentiate being-time's full expression. He writes:

> The state in the moment of the present is beyond the father being former and the child being latter, beyond the child being former and the father being latter. . . . It is beyond the forms of leaving and coming, beyond the scale of large and small, and beyond discussion of old and young.[5]

Grasping this nondual aspect of being-time is critical for enacting the spiritual path.

Swallowing Up and Spitting Out Time

Next Dōgen asks, "So does not the time of climbing the mountain or crossing the river swallow up the time of the splendid vermilion palace? Does not that time spit out this time?"

It is in each step that practice is actualized. Realized practice is the dynamic action response arising from our total immersion in this moment's arising. Therefore, we can only enact our understanding in each moment. Each moment includes everything making up the whole of our experience. We cannot respond to a situation with realization without including every element of that situation as it arises now.

When our response includes everything, then the particular being-time is fully expressed—this is realization.

In this inclusive way, each step swallows up the vermilion palace; it swallows up the ideas we have about practice and enlightenment. Our experience is the experience of this moment, not the experience of some future event. The present moment, while made up of climbing the mountain and crossing the river, is swallowing up our climbing and crossing. The present moment has incorporated any ideas or conceptualizations we might have, thereby grounding us in the present.

In turn, when we spit out the present moment "as it is," it becomes the transformational moment from delusion to practice-realization. In the fascicle "Jinzū" (Mystical Power), this swallowing up and spitting out[6] is the everyday enactment of an appropriate response. Appropriate response can only happen when we are fully present for what appears. What Dōgen calls the mystical power of practice-realization is the self setting itself out in array in our daily activity. Dōgen quotes layman Ho-on, "The mystical power and wondrous function, carrying water and lugging firewood."[7] It is nothing special, just our response to what is needed.

When we are going about our business, and we realize that we have to shop for food, we respond by going to the supermarket. If we go to the supermarket looking for a fight because we had a rude clerk the last time we were there, we are inappropriately including a past that will obstruct our current experience. If we go to the market incorporating the past and just responding to what is happening right now, then we go with an unobstructed mind. This unobstructed mind swallows up the previous experience and spits out the present moment. If that clerk is not present or in a good mood, we respond to that. We don't need to harbor ill will toward that person even though we have not forgotten what came before.

It is simple to understand, but may be difficult to actualize. This swallowing up and spitting out comprise the action of dropping the self. It is not an intellectual activity: dropping the self is just being totally present this moment. We are able to reside in equipoise between holding what has happened and is still presencing and letting go as we fully respond to what is.

To swallow something has two connotations, one of which is to make something disappear. In this way the goal of the vermilion palace disappears in the time of now. Swallowing also leads to digestion. When you digest something, you chew it up and swallow it. When you spit it out, you regurgitate it. The original substance is no longer recognizable as what it was, yet it has not completely disappeared. There is this constant reciprocity going on, things are happening simultaneously; the swallowing, the chewing, and the spitting out is all happening in each moment.

Upon arriving, there is swallowing up and spitting out every step that you've taken. This place includes and is the result of each individual step. This place is direct response.[8] The swallowing up and spitting out make up a process of grounding oneself in the here-and-now. It involves active participation. Viewed as no-self, spitting out is dropping the self. Viewed from the perspective of preconceived ideas, spitting out is active participation in being-time. Spitting out is going beyond fixed notions of past, present, and future, thereby becoming firmly rooted in the very is-ness of being-time. It includes and goes beyond conventional time. Each moment of our life's journey, or in this particular example our spiritual path, incorporates or swallows the totality of a being-time and manifests or "spits out" an independent present moment.

FINDING THE VERMILION PALACE

Often we carry an idea of enlightenment that leaves no room for mistakes and focuses solely on perfection. We imagine that perfection will take all the struggles out of life, and we are attracted to this idea of ease. In this way we spend our time striving for an impossible view of enlightenment, a situation that Dōgen likens to attempting to live in the vermilion palace.

If we are grounded in the moment, the striving for perfection gets lost. The moment swallows up our idea of enlightenment, because what we are attending and responding to is right now. We forget about this thing called perfection, and we just live our life with the tools that we have in that moment.

There is no vermilion palace.[9] Dōgen writes in "Yuibutsu Yobutsu" (Only a Buddha and a Buddha), "Realization inevitably differs from your expectation."[10] No matter what your idea of enlightenment may be, it is just an idea. Dōgen admonishes us to stay focused on what is in front of us and avoid getting caught up in some idea about the future. This is our mandate as practitioners, as people. We must let go of our preconceived ideas about enlightenment.

Each moment swallows up the vermilion palace. By the time we get to the moment we thought was going to be the moment of arrival, it is just another moment, another step. That step spits out every step that's happened before it. That arrival includes everything that preceded it. Take up Dōgen's question as a kōan: "So does not the time climbing the mountain or crossing the river swallow up the time of the splendid vermilion palace? Does not that time spit out this time?"

What Is Today's Time?   11

The creature with three heads and eight arms is yesterday's time. The sixteen-foot Buddha is today's time. Nonetheless, the nature of the truth of this yesterday and today lies in the time when you go directly into the mountains and look at the myriad peaks around you—hence there is no passing away. So even that three-headed, eight-armed creature makes a passage as my being-time. Although it might seem as if it were somewhere else far away, it is the time right now. The sixteen-foot Buddha-body also makes a passage as my being-time. Although it might seem as if it were somewhere else over there, it is the time right now.

WHEN WE THINK about having attained some wisdom, we think delusion is yesterday's time and our current wisdom is today's time. Nevertheless, Dōgen writes, "The nature of the truth of this yesterday and today lies in the time when you go directly into the mountains." Going directly into the mountains is a way of talking about true realization or making yourself totally present for what is happening, without labeling the experience as delusion or enlightenment. Yesterday (delusion) and today (enlightenment) represent a sequential model of practice as progressing from delusion to enlightenment.

Going directly into the mountains is being present for your life just as it is. When you go directly into the mountains, you stand on the ridge line and see the myriad peaks around you. Your view is panoramic. This 360-degree view is a view that includes the sixteen-foot Buddha and the three-headed eight-armed creature and goes beyond both. You understand that each moment contains both delusion and realization, yet your immediate experience is beyond labeling various being-times as this or that, delusion or realization. You are immediately manifesting, with all beings, this present time.

No Passing Away

While both the three-headed eight-armed demon and the sixteen-foot Buddha are present, the true expression of reality is more than either of these. Reality includes everything, as the interpenetrating expression of codependent arising of all beings, which is called buddha-nature. Buddha-nature is always fully present. Our ideas about sixteen-foot Buddhas and eight-armed demons come and go, but buddha-nature, just as it is, is always abiding. "Hence," Dōgen says, "there is no passing away." So we are present for what is actually happening: going directly into the mountains. Everything that came before and everything that is happening now are included. As such, they cannot pass away. All these different activities are happening simultaneously, interpenetrating in this moment.

This eternal now is impermanence. It is an independent moment expressed. It is interpenetrating time expressed. Your actions are not exempt from karmic repercussions, because everything is still in a state of codependency. Yet, the moment can be freely expressed unobstructed by past demons or future buddhas.

Delusion Is Included

Even delusion is part of being-time.[1] Delusion and enlightenment are both right here, right now in this moment, and it's not a problem. Even though it seems like realization is "over there," we must perceive its presence in the midst of our confusion. When we can include everything and just be this moment, without attachment to our own view, we are fully engaged and free.

Imagine a multidimensional 360-degree circle as the present moment. You enter into the circle from one of the many degrees. This is what we can conventionally call your present moment or independent dharma position. The question becomes, how will we exit that circle of possible responses? If we are being driven by our preconceived ideas, we have a very narrow exit band. If we can include everything—our needs and those of all beings present—then we have a much wider band in which to exit that moment. The possibilities will be defined by the needs of a given situation, not by our misconceptions about a situation. Hence we are more likely to respond skillfully. When all possible 360 degrees of response are present, you are not being forced into a particular response based upon erroneous ideas or past actions. This is what it means to go directly into the mountains and see the total vista of your circumstances.

For example, you're having a difficult interaction with a sibling with whom you have had unpleasant experiences in the past. These concretized past moments severely narrow the scope of how you are going to respond to that brother or sister. If you could truly be present with this person, you might notice that this brother or sister is frightened or suffering in some way. Or you remember the hardships this person experienced in childhood too. Suddenly you feel compassion rather than aversion. You may notice something about him or her that might also be true for you as well. You might feel empathy that then creates a more open and spacious response.

STANDING IN THE MOUNTAINS

Standing on the mountain of the present moment, we realize that being-time includes everything. It includes peace and war, calmness amid chaos. It includes realization in delusion, compassion in the midst of anger. All of these aspects of experience are present. Our actualized inclusive response is not obstructed by our self-centered views; this is realization. When we respond in an inclusive way, our realized self is in charge of our actions. This realized self does not need to banish delusion. In fact, our wisdom is a result of the problems created by delusion. It is like the grain of sand necessary to make a pearl. The oyster transforms the irritant of the sand into a beautiful object, but this could not happen without that particle of sand.

In the *Vimalakīrti Sūtra,* the bodhisattvas from the Land of the Host of Fragrances make a visit to our world. They have a condescending attitude about us because of all our problems. In their world everything is wonderful or, in their case, everything smells great! Vimalakīrti describes us as having the minds of monkeys and being stubborn and uncontrollable like elephants and horses.[2] The bodhisattvas from the Land of the Host of Fragrances are appalled and wonder about the level of our practice. Vimalakīrti responds that we have excellent qualities that enhance our practice, which a perfect place like the Land of the Host of Fragrances is lacking. Vimalakīrti tells the visiting bodhisattvas that the poor give us a chance to practice generosity; sinners repent through their attraction to the precepts; the impatient are attracted to patience; the lazy look to right effort; lacking mental stability, we seek meditation; and when acting foolishly, we seek wisdom.[3]

All of these states that we wish would disappear are the grains of sand from which to build wisdom's pearl, which is both practice and realization. Our true nature, buddha-nature, nudges us to respond to difficulties and seek their remedy. We do not find wisdom, compassion, and skillful means in a vacuum. Through the passage of our demons, we find the willingness to go deeper into the nature of our experience. This widening circle of inclusiveness is the sixteen-foot Buddha-body. Entering the realm of the time right now is transformation enacted through swallowing and bringing forth with each step along the path. It is not rejecting this (demon) or picking up that (buddha), but just this moment of seeing.

Learning Intimacy

Hence, pine trees are time. So are bamboos. You should not come to understand that time is only flying past. You should not only learn that flying past is the virtue inherent in time. If time were to give itself to merely flying past, it would have to leave gaps. You fail to experience the passage of being-time and hear the utterance of its truth, because you learn only that time is something that goes past.

ALL OF EXISTENCE is included in each being-time, not just our particular perception of self or other as persons. Just as it is said that to know one thing is to know all things, we can also say that to know one time is to know the nature of all time. This is expressed as the particularity of life. Pine trees, bamboo, rivers, and mountains are all being-time.

Dōgen never underestimates the virtue of rocks, tiles, and trees. The natural world, which in Western culture we often classify as outside the realm of intelligence or sentience, is part of Dōgen's understanding of awakening. He writes that all dharmas are "real form" in the fascicle "Shohō Jissō" (All Dharmas Are Real Form):

> The realization of the Buddhist patriarchs is perfectly realized real form. Real form is all *dharmas*. All *dharmas* are forms as they are, natures as they are, body as it is, the mind as it is, the world as it is, clouds and rain as they are, walking, standing, sitting, and lying down, as they are; sorrow and joy, movement and stillness, as they are; a staff and a whisk, as they are . . . succession of the Dharma and affirmation, as

they are; learning in practice and pursuing the truth, as they
are; the constancy of pines and the integrity of bamboos, as
they are.[1]

Dōgen's reference to pine trees and bamboos places us in the realm of
the being-time of everything, not just the human realm. We cannot
enact our realization without the participation of all dharmas. This
sensibility toward bamboos, pines, a staff, a whisk, clouds, and rain
being actively present causes us to realize that there is a vivid world
dynamically unfolding around and with us.

Several of Dōgen's references to bamboo are in conjunction with
the enlightenment experience of Zen master Chikan, who awakens at
the sound of a pebble hitting bamboo.[2] Chikan's enlightenment is not
an individual effort to awaken, but the totality of Chikan, bamboo,
and pebble awakening. It includes the being-time of all beings, the
activity of myriad things coming forth and making passage. Chikan
awakens as he meets vivid real form right-here-and-now. He realizes
the intimacy of all being as his life. This intimacy cannot happen if you
think of time as outside your own being. Therefore, Dōgen continues,
"You should not come to understand that time is only flying past. You
should not only learn that flying past is the virtue inherent in time."
To understand that time has another aspect other than flying past is
to say that we must ground ourselves in what is happening right now.

We may think time is outside of us, flying by, but this is an illusion.
Universal time resides within each of us and is experienced by each
being (even if we are not aware of it). There is the time of the pine tree,
the bamboo, a sixteen-foot Buddha, a three-headed and eight-armed
creature, which are interpenetrating, unobstructed, and simultaneous. Through this dynamic interbeing time-and-being are expressing
impermanence's passage. This is the interconnected experience of
bamboo, a pebble, and Chikan's awakening as time. This awakening
is an example of integrated experience. When we experience another
being's time as our immediate being-time, the gap that prevents us

from experiencing the intimacy of all being-time is closed. In this way
we connect with each activity as the perfectly realized real form. This
is what happened when Chikan heard the pebble strike the bamboo.

Dōgen tells this story in the fascicles "Gyōji" (Continuous Practice)[3]
and "Keisei-Sanshiki" (Sounds of the Valley, Forms of the Mountain).[4]
Chikan was studying with Master Dai-i at his monastery. Master Dai-i
asked Chikan, "You are sharp and bright, and you have wide understanding. Without quoting from any text or commentary, speak a
phrase for me in the state you had before your parents were born."
Chikan was stumped. He tried to express his understanding with
words, but he couldn't.

In frustration he burned his books and gave up intellectual study of
the Dharma. Instead he began to aid his fellow monks by serving meals.
This must have been a major transition in his practice. In all probability
his teacher Dai-i had a pivotal role in his decision to shift from intellectual study to a path of service. This transition can be understood as
dropping the practice of interpreting the world through the lens of his
intellect and moving to a more inclusive body-mind–centered practice
through serving others.

Although Chikan spent years in this capacity, nothing much seemed
to be happening. Finally, he felt that he had to take a different tack.
Obviously he was having a difficult time, but he had not given up his
effort. After several years, he left the main monastery and moved to a
hermitage in the mountains, a major transition that would have again
involved consultation with Dai-i.

We should not see these various modes of practice as failure. Each
activity would have had an impact and contributed to his eventual
awakening. Dōgen says Chikan planted a bamboo outside his hut "and
made it his friend"[5] in the intimate activity of engaging with life. Dōgen
wrote in "Gyōji" (Continuous Practice), "One day [Chikan] happened
to be sweeping the path when a pebble flew up and struck bamboo; it
made a sound which led him suddenly to awaken to the state of truth."[6]
Master Chikan turned to face in the direction of Dai-i-zan Mountain

(Zen Master Dai-i's monastery) and addressed his understanding to his master Dai-i:

> At a single stroke I lost recognition.
> No longer need I practice self-discipline.
> [I am] manifesting behavior of the way of the ancients,
> Never falling into despondency,
> There is no trace anywhere.

Later, Master Dai-i verified Chikan's awakening by responding, "This disciple is complete."[7] Chikan's realization came about because he gave up on his ideas about how realization would present itself. He completely immersed himself in his life as it was unfolding around and with him. His attention was placed on the activities of sweeping and other tasks at his hermitage and he no longer actively sought enlightenment. This mind of no-self opened the mind that includes everything.

CLOSING THE GAP

Before his realization, Chikan was clearly caught in an intellectual trap. He was not grounded in his present experience, he was off somewhere in his head trying to figure out the right answer to Master Dai-i's question. He was caught in the experience of time as flying past, in a way that divorced him from the immediacy of his situation. Chikan would never be able to answer Dai-i's question without settling into his life as it was.

Finally, in frustration, he stopped intellectualizing. Sometimes we have to stop our activity when it is fruitless. Obviously, he wasn't sure what to do, but in Buddhism we have the example of past masters and teachers who have stopped extraneous activity and sat down, literally and metaphorically, to fully occupy their lives as this moment arising. He didn't know exactly how to do this, but he never abandoned

LEARNING INTIMACY · 111

the Way. He stuck to his effort, but redirected it to the daily tasks of serving other monks, and later of tending his garden. As Dōgen says, he made friends with the bamboo. In the moment of the sound of the pebble, he understood that time does not fly by. He was grounded in his life, just as it is, perfectly unobstructed by his ideas about what that might be. Furthermore, he closed the gap that had kept him from the intimacy of direct experience. His intimacy was so complete that there was no longer a gap between him and myriad things coming forth to meet him.

When we find ourselves falling into the gap of the missed present moment, we lose connection. We are not experiencing the actuality of our being-time. We often feel that something is missing. Living being-time as the actualizing moment closes the gap. For this reason Dōgen writes, "You fail to experience the passage of being-time and hear the utterance of its truth, because you learn only that time is something that goes past."

Minding the Gap

Realizing and examining habitual ways of thinking help us wake up and hear the Dharma of our life. Being-time, as it is expressed in this moment, in this body, is speaking right now. Chikan offers a good example of how we awaken to our experience. Each one of us has our own path in this matter, and sometimes it takes us a while to figure out how we should proceed. This is one way that a teacher, a specific teaching, and training are of paramount importance. We must make an effort, and that effort should lead us toward, not further away from, understanding. Without help we often don't know how to direct our effort.

Dōgen discusses this aspect of Chikan's awakening in Zuimonki (Record of Things Heard):

Ponder the fact that someone realized the Way by hearing the sound of bamboo. . . . How could it be possible to differentiate smart bamboo trees from dull ones, or deluded ones from enlightened ones? . . . Stones often strike bamboo yet not everyone who hears the sound clarifies the Way. Only through the virtue of long study and continuous practice, with the assistance of diligent effort in the Way, does one realize the Way or clarify the Mind. This did not occur because the sound of the bamboo was especially wonderful. . . . Although the sound of bamboo is marvelous, it does not sound of itself; it cries out with the help of a piece of tile. . . . Practicing the Way is also like this. The Way is inherent in each of us; still our gaining the Way depends upon the help of co-practitioners. Though each person is brilliant, our practicing in the Way still needs the power of other people. . . . Therefore, while unifying your mind and concentrating your aspiration, practice and seek the Way together.[8]

CLOSING THE GAP IS INTIMATE PRACTICE

A student asked me to give a modern example of intimacy. How do we think about this gap and how do we ground ourselves in the moment and not experience time as flying by? Traditionally we do this through zazen. Zazen is a direct experience of being-time. When we meditate, fully presencing ourselves, we are experiencing our life as gapless intimacy. In this moment, we are sitting with the ancestors: buddhas actualizing buddhas. In zazen this is our total activity. We sit down and allow the intimacy of the arrayed self to come forward and meet the moment. Zazen is, ideally, that unobstructed moment of intimacy. Yet, we must not think zazen is the only expression of intimacy. Each moment holds this intimacy, without gaps or snares.

In our life off the cushion, how do we think about intimacy? Intimacy can be likened to a close relationship. We hear people say, "I love my friends, but I don't always understand or agree with them." This is a way that we express our understanding of intimacy. In our immediate relationships, most of us never stop being open to the intimacy or love that we have for each other. Even when our situation is difficult, we maintain a sense of connection. We stay open to the possibility of healing. Although we may get caught in our ideas about the difficulties, we are still being present as best we can.

In our Buddhist understanding, this connection is true of all beings. All beings are kindred. I think we have an innate understanding of this. We cannot let go. We keep practicing and making effort. That effort in itself is intimacy. When we isolate ourselves, we suffer. Our world becomes about us in opposition to the other. Closing the gap and reestablishing intimacy creates generosity and connection. When things are hard, intimacy will make it easier. When we are feeling judgmental, remembering our intimacy with all beings will create space and wisdom.

One day while sweeping his garden, Chikan woke up upon hearing the bamboo's voice and experienced complete accord with being-time. None of the struggles in his life were wasted. In the midst of endeavoring to ground ourselves in being-time, we are already family. This is our original face before our parents were born. The next time you are feeling annoyed at someone, remember that we share this common ground. How does that change the interaction? Can we keep coming back and closing the gap? Can we find the intimacy of this moment and "experience the passage of being-time and hear the utterance of its truth"?

The essential point is: every entire being in the entire world is each time an independent time, even while it makes a continuous series. Inasmuch as they are being-time, they are my being-time.

HOW CAN A MOMENT be independent, dependent, and interpenetrating all at the same time? We are so prone to understanding our experience as sequential that we have a difficult time including what we think of as contradictory ideas. If the present moment did not have the aspect of independence, we would be caught in some kind of fatalistic cycle we could not escape. We would always be returning to our habitual responses dictated by past experience and future desires. This repetitive cycle is the situation of being caught by patterns that block our ability to respond inclusively to the moment.

It is the standalone characteristic of a being-time that allows us to respond to the needs of each situation, without being caught by previous or future events. Unfettered by our ideas about our experience, we can fully engage the present. This independence was critical for Chikan's awakening. Chikan had to occupy his own unique position in order for him to experience the awakening intimacy of a pebble striking bamboo. The resulting sound closed the gap between Chikan and all the elements of his experience. Yet, this could not have happened unless Chikan was independent in his interconnection.

When we are a student, our job is to be a student. If we are constantly trying to be a teacher, we won't be open to learning. Yet, within the moment of being a student is the moment of being a teacher. In the moment of being a student there is the time before student and after student. In the opening verses of "Uji," the juxtaposition of seeming opposites points to this idea. You are an independent being-time and its opposite. Standing on the highest mountain includes the ocean bottom, and it also includes everything in between. The verses at the beginning of "Uji," taken as a whole, include many, many scenarios of being-time. We can read the verses as couplets that seem to offer contradictory situations. We can also view the verses as one thought denoting a range of independent, connected, and interpenetrating being-times.

This is an important point: while we are not separate from all beings-times, we are still unique individuals. While we are interpenetrating with all being-time, we are still singular independent entities. Chikan's awakening happened within the context of many unique dharma positions interacting and presencing with each other, thereby awakening with each other. We understand this conventionally. What we often miss is that enlightenment is not merging with all being-times, rather it is the unique practice of each being expressing and making the world, with the world as one activity.

Nonsequential Continuous Series

Dōgen does not deny that each moment is part of a continuum or a continuous series of moments. Although not strictly sequential, this continuous series is an aspect of our particular before and after. In Buddhism, we are taught that everything is codependent and causally based. This model is often presented as X causes Y, with X as the primary cause and Y the result. If we don't think of our experience as sequential, cause and effect includes everything. This more inclusive model goes beyond primary causal sequences. One might say that all causal relationships become the whole causal relationship. What I am calling the whole causal relationship is the concurrence of each particular moment of being-time, including its before and after and all of the various being-times arising at the same time. This multiplicity of individual dharma positions' expression brings about change, but because of the holistic, interpenetrating quality of each being-time as simultaneously all being-time, change cannot be said to happen in a straight line of cause and effect.

While Chikan's awakening included a before and after, there was just this moment of its arising, completely free from before and after. His realization also included the being-time of pine trees and bamboos. It included the being-time of his teacher and all beings simultaneously.

Think of it this way: You are having a conversation with someone. In that moment the before and after of your life is present as is your relationship with this person. At the same time, you can respond independently from any history or desires you might have. At exactly the same time, all being-time is being expressed simultaneously. At that moment, each person, each rock, everything in the sea, and so on, is experiencing their independent moment of being-time. Furthermore, it isn't just the present in this being-time, but also "all befores and all afters." This unobstructed coexistence of expression creates a kind of passage from one moment to the next. In this way we, along with all beings, are the world worlding the world.[1]

ALL BEING-TIME IS CONNECTED THROUGH CONTINUOUS PRACTICE

We share activity and responsibility with all beings as we continuously create this world. In "Gyōji" (Continuous Practice), Dōgen writes:

> Because of this continuous practice, there are sun, moon, and stars. Because of this continuous practice, there are earth, sky, and heart within and body without. . . . Conditional arising is continuous practice. . . . The time when continuous practice is manifested is what we call "now."[2]

Because our being-time is the being-time of all beings, we enter into a shared reality and responsibility. My continuous practice and the continuous practice of all beings are not different, just as my being-time and the being-time of all beings are not different. In "Gyōji," "Busshō," and "Uji," among other fascicles, Dōgen unites realized activity and being-time as one actualized unit.

We cannot escape the interpenetrating effects of our actions. This effort can only be actualized in the now of our being-time. Realizing this interlocking and interconnected simultaneity of activity and responsibility within the present moment is a key element of practice. Dōgen writes: "One must learn in practice that unless it is one's self exerting itself right now, not a single dharma or thing can either immediately manifest itself or make a passage."[3] This is a theme that Dōgen returns to over and over. We are not separate from the simultaneity of arising being-times. To see the world only from the side of our need and desire is delusional. But when we can allow everything to come forward, present itself, and respond inclusively, that is realization.

Furthermore, we want to avoid getting trapped in trying to manipulate and force this actualization. We don't always know what is happening. Again, quoting from "Gyōji" (Continuous Practice), "When the continuous practice which manifests itself is truly continuous practice, you may be unaware of what circumstances are behind it . . ."[4] We can only present our understanding as it arises within the context of our present situation. Our practice is to focus on the needs of a situation without inappropriately abandoning our own needs. In this way, we can look at our circumstances and include the circumstances of others.

We enact this teaching by realizing our shared continuous practice, which is not hindered by our problems. Each moment is a fresh moment that we can enact to the best of our ability. Each moment is another birth of continuous practice. This is living being-time. This is the shared being-time between ourselves and all beings. Again, this is not abstract. It must be enacted while we wait in line at the supermarket or drive to work. We do not need extraordinary circumstances to actualize our realization.

Being-time has the virtue of seriatim passage [j. *kyōryaku*].[1] It passes from today to tomorrow, passes from today to yesterday, passes from yesterday to today, passes from today to today, passes from tomorrow to tomorrow, this because passing seriatim is a virtue of time. Past time and present time do not overlap or pile up in a row—and yet Qingyuan is time, Huangbo is time. Mazu and Shitou are times too. Since self and other are both times, practice and realization are times. "Entering the mud, entering the water" is time as well.

DŌGEN DOES NOT DENY that time has the quality of sequential passage, but his understanding of its passage is not sequential. He writes that today becomes tomorrow, as well as yesterday. Or today can be yesterday becoming today, which can just skip to becoming tomorrow. In other words, Dōgen's understanding of passage cannot be explained by sequential time. Joan Stambaugh writes about time: "Since it is not a static container or a rapid stream flowing inexorably by—since, more precisely, it is nothing by itself separate from being—it is to be found right in the middle of all beings."[2] Each independent time is also yesterday, today, and tomorrow all making passage as this time. Passage is not sequential in the way we think it might be, nor is it chaotic.

By naming specific individuals and events, Dōgen indicates passage through the independent aspect of dharmas. Time is not separate from being; time and being are two sides of one event. Dharmas are both a being-time and all being-time, as embodied in each being-time. A person is empty of a fixed identity and universal, yet simultaneously functions as a particular being-time. The problem arises when we try to fix these states as sequential and separate. Passage is life as process, not a life fixed and explicated.

Interpenetrating continuous practice or passage is being-time's virtue. Virtue is a buddha's golden radiance, and it is the goodness and compassion of each being's individual and continuous passage. This is because Dōgen's description of being-time's passage as virtue is based upon the idea that the interconnection of all things is the engine of altruistic response. Virtue is inherent in the structure of each being's true nature. A being-time becomes the totality of life living life at the juncture of time and being as this particular moment. It is the moment's total expression (self and all being simultaneously) that is passage; it is not time's passage alone. This passage of mutual and interpenetrating events or moments happens even when we try to force it into a particular shape. It is the forcing that is suffering. Forcing arises when we misunderstand the nature of being-time or impermanence, thereby thinking we can impede or control its passage or transformation.

How We Perceive Being-Time's Passage

If time cannot be understood as a progression from past to present to future, what is it we experience as time? Time is our experience of a being-time's impermanence. Nevertheless we often can't see passage as it is happening in each moment. Perhaps this is so because we cannot perceive subtle change through our senses. When we do notice a being-time's passage, we understand it not as many simultaneous events' passage, but as one fixed moment of recognized change, such as "I am now old." We look at ourselves in the mirror and notice we look older or have become old. How did that happen? We imagine it happens over time, when we are not looking. Somehow it piles up, it accumulates, and then we see it. We exclaim, "Oh no, I have gray hair;

I have wrinkles!" We perceive transformation as gradual (piling up) or sudden (without precedent), yet transformation is enacted as the mutual interdependence of all things and each thing expressed in each and every interpenetrating moment.

Shohaku Okumura writes, "There is always some gap between the actual experience of the present moment and our thoughts about the present moment and how we define it; the present moment is ungrasp-able even though it is the only actual moment of experience."[3] Before we can define a moment to ourselves, that moment is gone.

To compound matters we think that a moment defined is encapsulated. This is not true, as there is really no moment to capture. In the case of old age, we are making comparisons to a previous time when we were younger. From Dōgen's point of universally inclusive being-time, old age is a label and perhaps not a useful one. The actuality of our situation is the fluidity of "just this" as passage. Okumura continues with this thought when he writes, "There is nothing, no actual unit of time. . . . The present does not exist and therefore *time itself* does not really exist."[4] Time is the continuous interactions, processes, or changes during the passage of the various aspects of being-time that can only be expressed in this moment, within the context of a particular dharma position.

Although we think of time as something separate from our own being, it resides in each particularity. When we speak of all being-time, that time is still particular to all being. And all being-time is still found in the particularity of each being-time. Finding our center of response at the intersection of time and being is important because this is how being-time interacts and expresses as the world, our world, making itself. Since we are part of this process, we must pay attention and actualize this moment's passage with all beings as our being-time. If we think practice can wait until the right time arrives, the time will never arrive. The time is now, being is now, continuously making the world. There is no beginning of this moment, nor is there an end. Everything is continuously simultaneously presencing.

TIME DOES NOT PILE UP IN A ROW

We might think that time is piling up or overlapping. We learn from Western psychology and Buddhist karmic theory that our experience is predicated upon past actions that define and determine our present situation. In this way, time seems to pile up and create a predetermined or habitual response. This overlapping and piling up seems to indicate a linear timeline, which can make us feel like victims of time's passage, instead of active participants in each moment.

Dōgen discusses the problems associated with events piling up in his fascicle "Dai Shugyō" (Great Practice). The topic is the kōan "Hyakujō and the Fox."[5] In the story a teacher is reborn over and over as a wild fox because he told a student that after enlightenment a person was not subject to cause and effect. In the kōan the old "fox" teacher is telling Master Hyakujō what has happened to him and asking for some relief from his condition. Hyakujō responds, "Do not be unclear about cause and effect."[6]

What Hyakujō warns against is misunderstanding karma as a piling up or cascade of events that trap us. Dōgen comments, "The meaning of ... not being ignorant of cause and effect, is that because great practice is transcendent cause-and-effect itself, it gets rid of a body of a wild fox."[7]

What is transcended is not responsibility for one's misdeeds; rather it is the model of sequential piling up of one's actions in such a way that one is forced to react unskillfully in the future. Dōgen's "great practice" is the bodhisattva practice of incorporating and responding to the whole of our situation, thereby deeply seeing cause and effect. As soon as we return to the totality of this moment's complete expression, we are not caught by anything. Even though we are still subject to the repercussions of our past actions, we are free to respond skillfully in the present moment.

If we have been rude to someone in the past and that person is wary of us, our total participation in this moment of meeting that person will not necessarily take away the karma of our past meeting. What it will do is free us to respond skillfully in this situation. Since we are not caught by "piled up" or overlapping experiences, we are freed to enact the new paradigm of "great practice."

Another example: If you are playing baseball and you drop the ball, you don't let your mistakes "pile up." You must forget dropping the ball and be present for the next opportunity to catch the ball. Holding on to a past mistake will often hinder your ability to respond skillfully in the present, although you still file away your mistake and make adjustments. From the point of view of practice this would translate to making a mistake, acknowledging the mistake, atoning for that mistake, and moving on from the mistake.

In the fascicle "Yuibutsu Yobutsu" (Only a Buddha and a Buddha), Dōgen points out that our understanding of self can become a fixed idea of accumulated traits or experiences. He observes, for example, that spring, autumn, and ourselves are independent moments that are not the results of being piled up.[8] He writes, "This means that we cannot see the four elements and five aggregates[9] of the present as our self and we cannot trace them as someone else."[10] The self is both independent and the totality of all being-time. We are no-self and a particular self at the same time, caught by neither and more than both. In the case of practice-realization, we are not waiting for a particular set of experiences to line up or pile up, thereby creating the circumstances for realization. Realization is present in each moment. Realization is each moment. It is true that we may progress in our practice, but realization is not predicated upon a particular set of circumstances, since it is actualized being-time: a response to our current circumstances.

In concrete terms, this means we must engage and fulfill our understanding of practice in each moment, not putting it off. A student once said, "I know what is skillful, but I don't want to do it right now." This kind of procrastination usually arises when our small self is trying to avoid facing a situation that will cause us to look at our own faults. Dōgen wrote in Zuimonki (Record of Things Heard), "Just cast aside all affairs and devote yourself to the practice of the Way only. Do not have expectations of any later time [to practice]."[11]

QINGYUAN, HUANGBO, MAZU, AND SHITOU ARE TIME

Qingyuan, Huangbo, Mazu, and Shitou are all Tang dynasty Chinese Zen masters. Steven Heine explains this passage:

> By virtue of *kyōryaku* [passage], the lives of former Zen masters are not to be added up backwards in terms of chronological sequence, but are to be understood as interpenetrating occasions of the spontaneous manifestations and continuing transmission of being-time.[12]

Our activities have a life that is not bound by sequential time. Each expression of the Zen master is in response to a particular situation, yet it is embedded in the interpenetration and continuous transmission of the teachings. In "Busshō" (Buddha-Nature), Dōgen writes: "Buddhas such as Kāśyapa and Śākyamuni inherited the capacity that the Fourth and Fifth Patriarchs' utterances *mu-buddha-nature* have to totally restrict [ordinary understanding of buddha-nature]."[13] From the standpoint of sequential time what Daoxin and Hongren (the fourth and fifth ancestors) understood could not be the inheritance of Kāśyapa and Śākyamuni, because Kāśyapa and Śākyamuni lived hundreds of years before the fourth and fifth Zen ancestors. Yet, the mutually interpenetrating passage of being-time is not restricted by notions of time passing from past to present to future in the way we imagine.

Mu-buddha-nature[14] was not a phrase that Śākyamuni Buddha, the founder of Buddhism, used to describe the nature of reality. Nevertheless, the is-ness of mu-buddha-nature was fully present in the time of Śākyamuni. In that way, what the fourth and fifth ancestors transmitted was also the "inheritance of Kāśyapa and Śākyamuni." Dōgen makes a similar statement in "Den-e" (Transmission of the Robe):

> A kaṣāya[15] [buddha's robe] transmitted by buddha ancestors is authentically transmitted from buddha to buddha without fail. . . . In authentically transforming the past, present, and future, a kashaya is transmitted from past to present, from present to future, from present to past, from past to past, from present to present, from future to future, from future to present, from future to past. It is authentic transmission only between buddha and buddha.[16]

Here, again, Dōgen writes about a nonsequential transmission of the particular being-time of the kaṣāya as all being-time. What is transmitted is each person's understanding of mu-buddha-nature or being-time, which is more than the sequential boundaries of either self or time.

MOVING A MOMENT ALONG: ENTERING THE MUD AND WATER

What exactly does this passage of "Uji" say about the relationship between a single dharma position and the passage of time? Dōgen puts his emphasis on the action and response of this moment,[17] which he calls practice-realization or entering the mud and water. Universal interpenetrating dynamism moves each moment along as enacted by the simultaneity of a particular independent being, self, or moment, and the moment's entirety. In plain English this refers to the interactions of our daily lives.

We greet each moment as it is. We don't add the preconceived ideas and the fixations we cling to as we try to define and control each experience. We have to let all that go and just be present with the one hundred grasses. This is total dynamic functioning or making the world. When we meet each person, moment, or particularity, we are not thinking of our life as a succession of piled-up moments. We engage each encounter afresh, not being pulled around by the past or future. Total presencing is so important for practice-realization that zazen is considered the primary dharma gate for its enactment. We sit because this dharma gate gives us a chance of directly experiencing the universality of this dualistic life. Zazen is the nonintellectual foundational activity of Sōtō Zen.

We also enact our understanding in every action of daily life by entering the mud and water. A bodhisattva's arena, like the often given example of the lotus in muddy water, is the place out of which wisdom and altruism are born. We practice realization in the messiness of daily life. Returning to an earlier example, driving our car may be just such a moment of wondrous function.

If we can go so far as to call our driving enlightened, then that driving must include the arising of compassion and selflessness as the situation requires. Ultimately our driving includes everything throughout time and space. Yet, we can't drive thinking about the nondual aspects of each thing we meet. Nor can we let our gripes about other drivers dominate our perspective. Rather we just meet each thing and respond within the context of a shared situation.

This meeting, this skillful means, wisdom, and compassion, may manifest as letting someone into a line of traffic, forgiving another driver's mistakes, or avoiding an accident. It means we can share the road when a stoplight is broken or a car is stalled. I cannot cite all the possibilities for enlightened driving, but we know when we are in its presence, especially if we are the recipient of such enlightened passage. This is our everyday experience of practicing "entering the mud, entering the water." Bodhisattva practice is not predicated upon a special religious environment; it is this moment as it is. This is the being-time of practice-realization. Entering the mud and entering the water are the activity of a bodhisattva entering his or her daily life. It is getting down in the trenches and helping ourselves and others realize the Way. This is passage as everyday occurrence.

Although the views the ordinary, unenlightened person now holds and the conditions that cause them are what the unenlightened person sees, it is not the unenlightened person's Dharma; it is only the Dharma temporarily causing him [to see that way]. Since he learns that this time, this being, is not the Dharma, he supposes the sixteen-foot golden Buddha-body is not himself. His attempts to escape by saying "I am not the sixteen-foot golden Buddha-body" are, as such, portions of being-time as well. It is the "Look! Look!" of "those who have not confirmed this yet."

Being-time, while not understood by "the unenlightened person," is still the basic truth or Dharma of that person's life. Although we are unenlightened, due to various causes and conditions,[1] we are still essentially the true nature of Dharma.[2] Dharma is reality actualizing and from this perspective cannot be said to be unenlightened or enlightened.

While a person caught by delusion understands life in a way that is unenlightened, that does not mean that this person's life is not reality fully presencing. Since the circumstance of our delusion is still reality manifesting, Dōgen writes that the Dharma as causal conditions temporarily leads a person to understand his or her life in a way that is not in accord with all being.

Because reality's true nature is constantly renewed in the impermanence of this very moment arising, our state as an ordinary person and a buddha is also renewed moment after moment. Sometimes we are the three-headed demon caught in our delusion. Sometimes we are a sixteen-foot Buddha. Sometimes we are in a state that goes beyond both, just expressing the totality of our present moment.

Dōgen writes in "Hosshō" (Dharma Nature): "All phenomena and dharma nature go beyond arguments about whether they are the same or different. . . . What is not past, present, and future, not permanent or impermanent, not form, perception, feeling, inclination, and discernment, is dharma nature."[3] Dharma is beyond the duality of enlightenment and unenlightenment; it is beyond our notions of self. Interpreting the world from the perspective of oppositional labels will only lead us farther from the deep subtlety of our actual situation.

Insisting on labeling our experience and others as being in delusion or enlightenment is just a desire to concretize our experience. Saying that we are this or that is attachment to self. If we say, "I am a buddha (good person)," then we are putting forth a fixed idea of a buddha and perhaps bolstering an egoistic self-centered view. If we say, "I am a demon (bad person)," then we are defining ourselves in a negative way, which is also a form of self-clinging. Both views, delusion or enlightenment, are still the groping of the ordinary mind. What is required is a shift in our perception from self-centeredness to inclusion. Our practice is to meet each moment sincerely, making our best effort to include all the factors present. We strive to engage in a kind of active listening that goes beyond the self and other.

WE CANNOT ESCAPE

Dōgen's comment that we try to escape may be admonishing us not to shirk our responsibilities as bodhisattvas. We say, "Oh, don't include me, I'm a lost cause. I couldn't possibly be a buddha." This is not helpful. "Look! Look!" Dōgen cries. Take a closer look at your true nature and you will discover the Dharma is already you.

Furthermore, when Dōgen writes in "Busshō" (Buddha-Nature), "If you wish to know the buddha-nature, you must realize that it is nothing other than temporal conditions themselves,"[4] he is saying that being-time, all being, and our own selves are expressing buddha-nature right now. This is what "Look! Look!" means. If we have not confirmed that our being-time right now, warts and all, is being-time, is a sixteen-foot Buddha-body, and is a three-headed demon, then we haven't really seen our true circumstances. This deep looking is how we will discover the truth of our situation. Seeing only occurs within the context of a vibrant intimate situation, which includes everything.

The question is not "Am I a buddha?" or "Am I a demon?" The question is "How do I engage in practice-realization? How do I make my best effort in this situation, this being-time?" To say, "I am not buddha, I am not ready" is to put off practice. "I am not ready" is the path of waiting for something to happen in the future. Practice-realization is predicated upon the teaching that this very moment is it. If we internalize this truth, then we are acutely aware of the immediacy and transiency of our situation. Indeed, to say "I am not the sixteen-foot golden Buddha-body" is to refuse to be responsible for our life. We are absolving ourselves from taking up the responsibility of the Bodhisattva Path. We might think this alleviates our suffering because we are not requiring ourselves to do the work of dropping the self at this time. But what other time is there? This kind of thinking is setting time outside of our own being.

Do not put off responding skillfully because you want to defend an idea you have about yourself. If you know that what you are doing is not helpful, but you don't make the effort to rectify the situation, this is a missed opportunity. If we wait for some other time when conditions will be better and our small self will be left intact, then we are wasting time. We should not try to escape the present moment by thinking we are waiting for the right time to exert effort in practice. Dōgen reminds us of this teaching in Zuimonki (Record of Things Heard): "Students of the Way, you should not postpone beginning to practice the Way. Just do not spend this day or even this moment in vain. Practice diligently day by day, moment by moment."[5]

Nevertheless, we get caught, saying, "I am not the sixteen-foot Buddha-body," and we forget that this too is still part of suchness. Dōgen writes in this paragraph that our attempts to deny our buddha-nature "are, as such, portions of being-time as well." Later in "Uji" he writes,

> One does nothing but penetrate exhaustively entire time as entire being. There is nothing remaining left over. Because any dharma left over is as such a leftover dharma, even the being-time of a partial exhaustive penetration is an exhaustive penetration of a partial being-time.[6]

There cannot be half a being-time. Each moment is a fully expressed being-time, even if we miss the mark. (More on this in chapter 19.)

Dōgen ends this paragraph of the core text with an example in the form of a kōan. He writes, "It is the 'Look! Look!' of 'those who have not confirmed this yet.'" Dōgen is referring to the opening lines of a kōan by the Chinese Zen master Linji. Here's how the story goes: The master, taking the high seat in the hall, said, "On your lump of red flesh is a true man without rank who is always going in and out of the face of every one of you. Those who have not yet confirmed this, look, look!"[7]

Linji and Dōgen agree that there is a sincere person steeped in the Dharma, although that person may be an ordinary, unenlightened person who is unaware. Yet, as Linji said, "It [the Dharma] is always going in and out of the face of every one of you."[8] We will, even caught in delusion and selfishness, show sparks of realization. We cannot say we are not a sixteen-foot golden Buddha-body. Our job as practitioners is to keep coming back and make our best effort.

Dōgen writes in "Sesshin Sesshō" (Speaking of Mind, Speaking of Essence):

> We can never attain the Buddha-way by abandoning the Buddha-way. . . . Extremely stupid people think that when

we are learning the Buddha-way we have not arrived at the Buddha-way; they think that it is the Buddha-way only in the time beyond realization. . . . they do not know that the whole way is expounding of the way, they do not know that the whole way is the practice of the way, and they do not know that the whole way is experience of the way.[9]

How is it that in the midst of our unskillful actions, when we are suffering and causing suffering, we can still be practicing? Can we presence ourselves in a difficult situation and see our effort as well as the effort of the other person? Can we hold the nondual position that nothing is missing in the midst of the relative situation that something more is needed? This is entering the mud, entering the water. This is seeing in our all-too-red lump of flesh the true Dharma eye's presence. This is practice. We want to cultivate confidence in our ability to make this effort and have faith that our practice is an expression of realization. Mistake after mistake, making our best effort, we should never be discouraged.

The horses and sheep now arrayed throughout the world are each dharma stages dwelling in their suchness and moving endlessly up and down. Rats are time. So are tigers. Sentient beings are time, Buddhas as well. This time realizes the entire world by being a creature with three heads and eight arms, and realizes the entire world by being a sixteen-foot golden body.

HORSES, SHEEP, RATS, and tigers are all hourly divisions of a day in the Chinese and Japanese time systems.[1] But Dōgen's inclusion of these animals as particular times is not intended as an example of sequential time. Instead, it is an example of each being-time having its particularity or dharma position. When Dōgen juxtaposes the hours represented as animals arrayed throughout the world as dharma stages dwelling in suchness, he is stressing a particular moment as one unique, total expression of right-here-and-now.

This section of "Uji" draws directly from a line of the *Lotus Sūtra*: "The Dharma abides in its place in the Dharma, / And the form of the world is constantly abiding . . ."[2] Dōgen restates this line in a Dharma Hall Discourse given at Eiheiji Monastery as "All dharmas dwell in their Dharma positions; forms in the world are always present."[3]

Each existence is residing in the state of suchness or the state of one's true nature. These existences or forms constantly abide as particular things: rats, sheep, tigers, sentient beings, and buddhas. Continuing the quotation from Dōgen's Dharma Hall Discourse above, Dōgen gives other examples of beings dwelling in their dharma positions:

"Wild geese return to the [north] woods, and orioles appear [in early spring]. Not having attained suchness, already suchness is attained."[4]

These examples of dharma stages are not static. They move up and down endlessly; they are, for example, the wild geese flying. A dharma position is dynamic; its movement is the totality of all being(s)-time(s) interacting and being actualized within the context of a particular situation. Moving up and down is the activity of completely expressing this moment. Each now is a being-time: a vibrant and separate response. Although each dharma position has complete integrity separate from all other dharma positions, it also includes those dharma positions. If it did not have this inclusive quality, there could be no passage, which is enacted through interpenetrating being-times. Dōgen writes earlier in "Uji" that "each being-time is without exception entire time."[5] Each individual moment is unique and universal.

Steven Heine comments on what seems to be a contradiction: the dharma position of each moment including all being-time and, at the same time, has particularity unto itself. He writes:

> The first dimension of [a dharma position] refers to the aspect "possessed of before and after," encompassing the totality of simultaneous possibilities. The second dimension is the directness, immediacy, and spontaneity "cut off from before and after," without endurance or substance.[6]

A dharma position's inclusive and exclusive simultaneity expressed as a particular person, being, or situation is what Dōgen is calling the state of "dwelling in suchness and moving up and down." This movement must interpenetrate with other dharma positions in order for things to change. This state is also at the being-time of (as he wrote in the Dharma Hall Discourse above) both having attained suchness and not having attained suchness. The attainment or lack of attainment is the interplay between all of reality arising without obstruction and our relative experience.

A mundane example of how each dharma abides and moves might be the occasion of making a purchase. We have in the past learned how to use money, and we have the expectation that payment will be accepted. Yet simultaneously we have many ways to pay. We might use several different combinations of coinage and bills or we might be able to barter or swap for the item. We could use a credit card, a debit card, bitcoins, or online accounts. We might decide not to purchase the item after we discover the price. There are many possibilities for this or any other situation, and for that reason it is completely different from all other situations. Yet it also contains the history and expectation of previous encounters, and it may be the springboard for other events. There are many possibilities for a creative and skillful response.

Although each moment includes all other moments, we are going to narrow our focus to what is important at that moment. In the example given, what is foremost at the moment of buying something is how to pay for it. But just because we have made a choice, it does not negate all the other possibilities that are arising simultaneously.

How we narrow our focus is determined by our understanding of the totality of that moment. If we include self and other, our actions will be skillful. If we are only concerned with our own gain, we will probably act unwisely. Making a purchase is dynamic yet simple. It is one instance. It resonates, it moves, and it is even an enactment of suchness, perhaps expressed or not, but always abiding.

MOVING ENDLESSLY UP AND DOWN

Dynamic movement can also be understood as a moment abiding as impermanence. Tanahashi translates this section as "actualized by ascending and descending of the time-being at each moment,"[7] suggesting a quality of staying put yet dynamically moving.

If you are a dancer, you respond to sound and rhythm with your body. Yet each dance has its own demands or particularity. If you are a ballerina, you have a certain set of forms defining the style of how you will dance, yet within those parameters, your options of expression are innumerable. As you dance, that moment also holds the moment of the music's composer, the moment of composition, the history and culture of the music, the creativity of the choreographer, endlessly naming and including everything in the universe. There is also the nondual, total inclusivity of each moment, as the dance dances the dance—no subject and no object. At the same time, there is just the unique, independent, exclusive moment of the individual dancer dancing. Both are happening together, both depend upon the other for being-time's expression. This is the moment's constancy in the midst of dynamic expression.

Abiding in this moment is the right-here-and-now of our experience: it is enduring suchness. This suchness is the dynamic interpenetrating connection with all of reality. You may have a feeling that this moment is tranquil and quiescent, separate and complete. Yet, this moment is still interacting with all of reality. We're not usually aware of the universality of the moment, but that does not negate its expression.

This moving up and down can be understood as a kind of deep penetration of a particular occurrence of our being-time. At the same time, it is all being-time. The universal quality is the connective glue of all dharma positions as they simultaneously actualize being-time. Because each moment is interpenetrating being-time and also independent in and of itself, we get a sense of impermanence expressed.

A Glimpse of the Entire World

Continuing the paragraph, Dōgen writes, "This time realizes the entire world by being a creature with three heads and eight arms, and realizes the entire world by being a sixteen-foot golden body." Dōgen is reiterating that a particular dharma position's independent nature might be perceived as a creature with three heads and eight arms or a sixteen-foot golden body.

When we perceive a sixteen-foot golden body or a three-headed demon, we are only seeing a glimpse of what is actually present. This inclusive presencing is the moving up and down, the full range of expression of a dharma position of a being-time. We might only see one side or the other, but both are present at the same time. Dōgen is trying to describe being-time's true nature as unique moments, each dwelling in suchness.[8] In this case we have the dharma positions of horses, sheep, rats, tigers, sentient beings, and buddhas. We may label them as this or that, or as a sixteen-foot Buddha or a creature with three heads and eight arms, but it is just each dharma stage abiding in the nondual nature of reality as expressed in our everyday life.

Throughout "Uji," Dōgen returns to the problem of how we misunderstand spiritual practice as a sequential passage moving from delusion to realization and the problems that arise when we want to characterize our experience as good (sixteen-foot golden body) and/or bad (a creature with three heads and eight arms). We can't jettison one and get fixated upon the other. Neither position serves us well.

Katagiri once said, "Misunderstanding is also in the big ocean. Misunderstanding cannot exist separately from understanding, so understanding is there too, whether you believe it or not."[9] Fully expressing a dharma position includes everything and completely penetrates our life.

Entirely worlding the entire world with the whole world is thus called
penetrating exhaustively.

WHEN DŌGEN USES the same word as subject, object, and verb, he is
using this grammatical structure to indicate that each dharma is so
intimately penetrating its dharma position that it is freed from itself
in such a way that it becomes liberated to express itself completely in
and through existence's totality. His methodology is meant to indicate
being-time as *gūjin*, often translated as "total exertion,"[1] or *ippō gūjin*,
"the total exertion of a single thing." In Dōgen's example of the world
worlding the world, there is the world as a singular dharma position
making complete effort as itself 100 percent, resulting in the simultaneity of the whole world expressed with nothing left out. For us, this
would be a completely unselfconscious immersion in one's activity.

Steven Heine writes:

> The total penetration and realization of any single practice,
> explanation or experience at this very time fully discloses
> the entire Dharma-realm because all beings, all selves and
> all buddhas at each and every moment are harmoniously and
> simultaneously linked together.[2]

This nondual expression of a particular practice, explanation, or experience happens in everyday life. When a sailor goes out in a boat on
the ocean and has the experience of simultaneity with all aspects of

that dharma position—ocean, boat, self, and everything simultaneously presencing—he or she is having a direct experience of the world making the world.[3] Setting oneself out in array by responding without separation to the totality of a situation is penetrating exhaustively. Our sailor might not know that this is happening because she is not observing herself; she is just responding to what is. When this happens we might say sailing sails sailing. This is total exertion as complete interconnected intimate involvement with "what is" through a particular activity.

DEEP INVESTIGATION

In the United States, we often hear about mindfulness associated with Buddhism. A popular definition of mindfulness is a kind of complete attention on an activity and its object. For instance as we are washing dishes, we might be saying to ourselves, "I am washing a plate," and focusing our thoughts on the feeling of the activity itself. We might slow down, follow our breath, and put all our focus on the sensation of the task as an object of our attention.

This would not be how Dōgen would approach the practice of deep investigation or exhaustive penetration. He might describe the activity of washing dishes as washing washes washing, thereby removing the subject-object relationship. Mindfulness may be a dharma gate to intimacy, but it is not the Zen practice of exhaustively penetrating the totality of one's experience. In the true intimacy of complete engagement there is no labeling of self or other that comes from paying attention to something outside the self.

When engaging in work practice, a Sōtō Zen student is interacting with the totality of all the elements arising within the context of that activity. This means that one makes effort to fulfill the task in such a way that one is respectful of the tools used, the context of the work, the instructions of the work leader, the time allotted for the task, and working in unison with others. The purpose of our effort is to complete the job through our total exertion and practice with the task itself. It is not to be mindful of the activity as an object of our attention. When we are able to engage in work this way, we drop our own agenda and fully engage with the complete activity of cleaning and community.

Included in this intimate total immersion in the being-time of a particular moment is the simultaneous arising of all being-time. This nondualism is not separate from the relative or everyday. Washing dishes is not special. By entering the world of washing dishes, we enter the whole world, which is our world, by jumping in with wholehearted effort.

DHARMAS ARE REAL FORM

Nishijima and Cross translate Waddell and Abe's "penetrating exhaustively" as "perfectly realizing" and associate it with a phrase from the *Lotus Sūtra*: "buddhas alone, together with buddhas, can perfectly realize that all dharmas are real form."[4] Dōgen unpacks the meaning of real form in "Shohō Jissō" (All Dharmas Are Real Form):

> Real form is all dharmas. All dharmas are forms as they are, natures as they are, body as it is, the mind as it is, the world as it is, clouds and rain as they are, walking, standing, sitting, and lying down, as they are; sorrow and joy, movement and stillness, as they are; a staff and a whisk, as they are; a twirling flower and a smiling face, as they are; succession of the Dharma and affirmation, as they are; learning in practice and pursuing the truth, as they are; the constancy of pines and the integrity of bamboos, as they are.[5]

This perfect realization is all dharmas totally expressing their true nature. Identifying real forms as all dharmas is washing dishes, for example, and when it is fully expressed (*gūjin*), it is the realized activity of buddhas. When we can fully express or enact the total exertion of a single thing, we are expressing our true nature. We are "buddhas alone, together with buddhas." We remember the true state of ourselves and all being(s).

The integrated self is therefore not separate from all being-time. For this reason, Dōgen writes earlier in "Uji," "to set the self out in array is to make the world,"[6] which is the singular expression of "entirely worlding the entire world with the whole world."

A BUDDHA'S DIGNIFIED ACTIVITY

In his fascicle "Gyōbutsu Yuigi" (The Dignified Behavior of Acting Buddha), Dōgen discusses the activity of a buddha realized as worlding the world:

> Dignified behavior as the whole cosmos and dignified behavior as the whole Earth, we should learn in practice, as the whole world, the state of never having been hidden. What has never been hidden is not only the whole world, but also that which perfectly hits the target of acting buddha: dignified behavior.[7]

This dignified behavior is setting the self out in array, which is not different from the world worlding the world. Although we may not be aware of this practice, it is not a hidden activity. Rather it is being present for what is all around us. Unfortunately we are often so caught up in our own agenda that we are unaware. Arraying oneself is to drop the self-absorbed self and to be unified with all that is presencing.

We enter this paradigm through sincere practice. Our sincere practice is the dignified behavior of a buddha. Dōgen encourages us in "Gyōji" (Continuous Practice), when he writes that although we may not always hit the mark of being in accord, we must not abandon our effort in practice. "Sometimes these merits of continuous practice are not evident . . . but you should understand that even though these merits are not revealed, they are not concealed."[8] Earlier in the same text, Dōgen defines our effort and the effort of all beings as mutually supportive:

> The merit of this continuous practice upholds oneself and others, because due to one's own effort, all worlds in the universe all the way up to the heavenly abodes immediately share in its benefits. Even though you may not be aware of it yourself and others are not aware of it, that is the way it is.[9]

Further elaborating this point, Dōgen writes:

> Because of this continuous practice, there are sun, moon, and stars. Because of this continuous practice, there are earth, sky, and the heart within and body without, the four elements and the five skandhas.[10]

Our bodhisattva vow is to continuously make effort to alleviate suffering as best we can. We are motivated by our understanding that through a buddha's activity we express our interconnected nature. Our activity makes the world. The world makes the world. We do not know the consciousness of rocks, tiles, clouds, insects, or other animals, but we do understand our mutual identity. This becomes a motivation for concerted effort to enact the Buddha Way. This conscious activity is practice-realization.

Faith in Penetrating Exhaustively

My relationship to the world changes when I have faith that this teaching is true. One result is an optimistic view of the difficulties of our human society. If I have faith that my practice and effort to integrate myself with all being will bear some fruit beyond my intellectual comprehension, then I am heartened by my effort. My effort is not just about making something better for myself, it is about wholeheartedly engaging with the world. This may take many forms.

In the summer of 1987, I spent a month at Hōkyōji Monastery in Minnesota. Dainin Katagiri Roshi, the founder of Hōkyōji and the Minnesota Zen Center, was leading the practice period. One afternoon when we were having formal tea, a young man asked Katagiri Roshi a question. He said that his parents were political activists and they had questioned him as to why he felt going to a monastery would make the world a better place. They asked, "Wouldn't your time be best spent out in the world helping people?" Katagiri Roshi responded that sitting meditation, following the monastic rules, and leading a practice life were important. Even if we could not see the effect of this practice, it spread out from the monastery and positively affected all beings.

Manifesting the Tall Golden Buddha   18

To immediately manifest the bodying of the tall golden Buddha with the body of the tall golden Buddha as the arising of the religious mind, as practice, as enlightenment, as nirvāṇa—that is being, that is time.

WHEN WE ARE in accord with our situation, we are immediately manifesting the bodying of the tall golden buddha. This Buddha has the aspect of both a totality of expression—the first "tall golden buddha"— and the buddha deconstructed as "religious mind, as practice, as enlightenment, as nirvāṇa." These two buddhas are not different; both are being-time. One buddha appears to have transcended duality and the other to be embodying duality or stages of the path. Neither is caught, both are the simultaneous aspects of the dharma position of buddha. There is universality and independence in moments of aspiration, practice, enlightenment, and nirvāṇa.

At the beginning of "Uji," Dōgen writes: "The sixteen-foot golden Buddha-body is time; because it is time, it has time's golden radiance. You must learn to see this glorious radiance in the . . . hours of your day."[1] You might question the idea that you are also a buddha. Dōgen addresses this question in "Yuibutsu Yobutsu" (Only a Buddha and a Buddha):

How, then, are we to understand that this state of buddha is the same as us? To begin with, we should understand the action of buddha. The action of buddha takes place in unison with the whole earth and takes place together with all living beings. If it does not include all, it is never the action of buddha. Therefore, from the establishment of the mind until the attainment of realization, both realization and practice are inevitably done together with the whole earth and together with all living beings.[2]

Practice-realization is to immediately manifest as the tall golden Buddha as the arising of our religious mind, our practice, our realization, and nirvāṇa. To intimately engage the world, or exhaustively penetrate each moment through our wholehearted practice, is the expression of our buddha-nature fully realized. This is aspiration, action, realization, and attainment. It is being-time expressed.

In "Bendōwa" (Wholehearted Practice of the Way), Dōgen writes, "You must come to fully realize that birth-and-death is in and of itself nirvāṇa. Buddhism never speaks of nirvāṇa apart from birth-and-death."[3] Contrary to an often held view that nirvāṇa is a state that exempts us from our day-to-day existence, Dōgen clearly indicates that nirvāṇa and our life of birth-and-death are synonymous. Birth-and-death, often characterized as *saṃsāra*, is not to be shunned or escaped. We are not to chase after nirvāṇa. In "Shōji" (Birth-and-Death), Dōgen spells out for us the relationship between birth-and-death and nirvāṇa:

> If you search for a buddha outside of birth-and-death, it will be like trying to go to the southern country of Yue with your spear heading toward the north, or like trying to see the Big Dipper while you are facing south; you will cause yourself to remain all the more in birth-and-death, and miss the way of emancipation. Just understand that birth-and-death is itself nirvāṇa. There is nothing such as birth-and-death to be avoided; there is nothing such as nirvāṇa to be sought. Only when you realize this are you free from birth-and-death.[4]

Dōgen collapses the common conception of practice as beginning with aspiring to be buddha and ending with attaining buddhahood into nondual being-time. He is saying that all stages are present and manifest simultaneously. "Uji" is about taking our conceptualization of practice out of the realm of sequential steps-and-stages mapping to the realization that everything is present: nothing is missing. We don't have to wait for realization to arrive. It is already here if we can enact it. Equating nirvāṇa with birth-and-death removes the aspiration of transcending our human life, as is suggested in the early Buddhist path.

Nirvāṇa, birth-and-death, and saṃsāra are not different because both are empty of inherent existence. Yet, this is not a nihilistic state, because it is only through our buddha eyes that we can truly comprehend the meaning of this teaching. Immersing ourselves in the "mud and water" of our saṃsāric life, we realize it is just nirvāṇa.

Dōgen's understanding of nirvāṇa as this life of birth-and-death locates practice and attainment within the context of daily life. Since being-time holds both the aspects of nonduality and one's individuality, it follows that practice-realization, the tall golden buddha, aspiration, enlightenment, and nirvāṇa are never enacted in a rarefied arena alien to daily life. Dōgen writes in "Gyōji" (Continuous Practice), "Arousing the thought of enlightenment, practice, bodhi, and nirvāṇa have not the slightest break, but are continuous practice which goes on forever."[5] This reinforces the understanding that we do not practice to attain realization; rather our practice is an enactment of realization.

When I spent four years living at Tassajara Zen Mountain Monastery, it was clear to me that I had not left my daily life nor my difficulties behind. Besides all the mundane tasks of cooking, washing clothes, bathing, and cleaning, I was beset with all the problems I brought from the "outside." I might have thought the monastic life would free me from my daily concerns: it did not. Saṃsāra is a state of mind, not a state of objectified being.

To look at our person and our life as *uji* is the realization of a buddha. Whether we can understand or enact this principle, it is still our true state. Dōgen writes, "If we reflect upon and illuminate the moment before and the moment behind this body and mind, the human being behind this investigation is not I and not [another] person."[6] This is another way to talk about no-self. "Not I" is to see we are not separate. "Not another person" is recognizing our state as a particular independent moment of is-ness: the true person being present.

Yet to be buddha-nature does not mean that we always actualize buddha-nature. If we are acting in a selfish way, we are not actualizing what is already present—our interconnected nature with all being. As soon as we enact our true nature, then our buddha-nature presents itself. It has been there all along. This is difficult to describe, because clarification is reliant upon dualistic sequential language.

Dōgen expresses it in this way in "Busshō" (Buddha-Nature):

> The truth of the Buddha-nature is that the Buddha-nature is not endowed before actualizing a buddha, but endows itself after actualizing a buddha. The Buddha-nature and buddha-actualization always go simultaneously.[7]

The first sentence in this translation gives us a sense of sequential passage: Buddha-nature comes before buddha-actualization. But the second sentence pulls the rug out as it ties the two "stages" together into the simultaneity of being-time. On one hand, it is true that we don't always act in ways that reflect our actual state of connection with all being. When we act selfishly, our actions are not that of a buddha actualized, although it is still a moment of buddha-nature. Even if we are being selfish, it does not change the truth of our interbeing. As soon as we enact intimacy with all of reality, then both buddha-nature and buddha-actualization or enlightened action arise simultaneously and reveal themselves.

Simultaneity of buddha nature buddha actualized, practice realization, aspiring for realization, and attaining realization are all enacted within the context of being-time as this birth-and-death.

Everything is happening right now. Right now is a holistic nonsequential connecting event. We cannot perceive its totality with our limited physical senses. Yet, how else can we enact our realization except through the already presencing moment that is expressing itself as and through ourselves?

Why is understanding that practice-realization is completely interwoven with all of reality's arising so important to our practice? First it addresses the misconception that we are not good enough right now. Shunryū Suzuki Roshi is said to have remarked: "Each one of you is perfect the way you are . . . and you can use a little improvement."[8] He is expressing Dōgen's teaching that we are buddha-nature. We don't need to go somewhere else or find some other body-mind. Although we are completely one with the world's activity, our discordant activities indicate the need for improvement. This is how we understand the state of buddha as the same as us.

The question of relative and absolute practice is the riddle of practice-realization. Perfection is just our unobstructed true nature. Our practice is the enactment of our body-mind as buddha within the context of this imperfect or obstructed life. Realization is remembering our body-mind with all body-minds as buddha. Practice is the expression of a buddha; we do not practice to become buddhas. When we engage in the practice of the arising of the bodhi-mind, there is at that very moment the enlightened mind and nirvāṇa. Where else would it be? If it were not already present, we would not have the ability to aspire to practice. That intention is also practice-realization. We may experience our spiritual path as a linear progression, but it is much more inclusive and all-encompassing than we realize.

CONFIDENCE AND FAITH IN PRACTICE

To acknowledge that our effort is not in vain requires confidence in practice-realization. When we begin, belief in our ability to practice might be more difficult because we have a tendency to judge our effort in ways that are not helpful. If we question our effort and feel that we are mired in mistakes, we can become discouraged. Knowing that our effort is the effort of a buddha builds our confidence. Shunryū Suzuki Roshi was keen on a practitioner having confidence in the path and in herself. He taught: "We want strong confidence, or you may say faith, a kind of faith in our teaching that we have originally Buddha-nature. And our practice is based on this faith."[9] He also taught,

> If we make our best effort on each moment with confidence, that is enlightenment. When you ask whether your way is perfect or not, there is an insidious idea of self. . . . There is no special way to attain enlightenment. Enlightenment is not some certain stage. Enlightenment is everywhere. Wherever you are, enlightenment is there. [Whatever] you do with best effort enlightenment follows. This is very important for our Zen practice and our everyday life. We should make our effort in our everyday [life] as well as in [our formal] practice of Zen.[10]

Confidence and confirmation of our practice lie in knowing that we have given it our best effort. Like practice-realization, confidence and effort arise simultaneously. Interestingly, but not surprisingly, Shunryū Suzuki Roshi reminds us that when we get caught in questions of perfection, we are falling into the quagmire of engaging the small self. This "insidious idea of self" is embedded in asking if your way is perfect. Our faith is in the Buddha Way, but we often are caught in our interpretation of a buddha's path. This interpretation is not Buddha's Way; it is our way. Unfortunately, when we are caught, we don't know the difference. When this happens, our effort is obstructed by questions that are not productive.

Returning to the sentence under discussion in this chapter, we find several practice admonitions. First, Dōgen reminds us that practice-realization resides in this body-mind. This means it must be enacted in our daily life, as the person we are right now. Second, our body-mind is the embodiment of the tall golden Buddha, and it is this tall golden buddha that drives our effort and is the source of our confidence. Third, at this very moment is the simultaneous manifesting of deciding to practice, practicing, enlightenment, and attainment. Finally, Dōgen ends with "that is being, that is time," indicating it is "just this" right now.

Having faith that we are capable of this practice, that our sincere effort is realization, and that effort is enacted being-time right now is paramount. Each moment we cultivate faith that this is true for ourselves and for others, we will find that realization will arise in accord with our effort. Francis Cook, in *How to Raise an Ox,* presents a helpful definition of faith in Buddhism:

> Buddhist faith is a very deep certitude in the veracity of a certain doctrine, accepted and used as a touchstone for conduct in the faith that practice will verify its truth. The object of faith may be an idea, one's teacher, or the trustworthiness of the Buddha himself, but in any case, there is a complete certainty that one is confronting something on which one may totally rely. The object of faith may be trusted provisionally because Buddhism itself teaches that the faith will eventually be replaced by knowledge and that any teaching not verifiable in this way ought to be rejected.[11]

Dōgen has presented his understanding of the Buddha Way, in which he has total confidence. His teaching is dependent upon the teachings of the Buddhist masters who preceded him and his personal exploration of the Buddhist path. As a Sōtō Zen practitioner, I have placed my faith in Dōgen's presentation of Buddha's Way. I have faith in the parts I don't understand and confidence that what appears hidden to me will be revealed during the course of my effort in practice.

I have a vivid memory from my own experience of the kind of faith

Cook has defined as Buddhist. I was washing dishes in my apartment and thinking about the doctrine of emptiness. In the course of my musing I reached a point in thinking about practice that seemed to dead-end in nihilism. Since I knew the teachings are not nihilistic and I have faith in the teachings, I knew that my understanding was incorrect. My effort at that moment was to back up, let go of my distress, and have confidence that my understanding would clarify itself as I practiced with the material.

Another example is my faith in zazen. I sit because it is the practice-realization of a buddha. Do I sometimes have doubts about my zazen? Yes. Does it keep me from sitting? No. I have faith that this is the Way. My experience has been that what seems unclear to me now will become a kōan incorporated into my daily practice, almost without effort. If I keep paying attention to my life as it unfolds, have confidence in practice-realization, and keep coming back to the teachings for guidance, my confusion will fade over time.

Even if we cannot completely understand Dōgen's teaching, it will still impact our practice. His vision of life is vast, poetic, and concrete all at the same time. Sometimes it feels as if we are hanging on to a dragon's tail, like a prayer flag flapping in the wind. We don't know what or how, yet we just hang on, making our effort. This is just the nature of being a prayer flag waving from a dragon's tail. No problem.

One does nothing but penetrate exhaustively entire time as entire being. There is nothing remaining left over. Because any dharma left over is as such a leftover dharma, even the being-time of a partial exhaustive penetration is an exhaustive penetration of a partial being-time. Even a form [of understanding] that appears to be blundering is being. On a still broader plane, the time before and after one immediately manifests the blunder are both, along with it, dwelling positions of being-time. The sharp, vital quick of dharmas dwelling in their dharma-positions is itself being-time. You must not by your own maneuvering make it into nothingness; you must not force it into being.

REALITY, or just this moment, is the arising of all being-time (universal) and each being's time (particular) fully presencing in each moment. This arising is separate from your judgment or description of that moment. The moment is just this unobstructed moment, fully expressed. Any qualifier we attach to a moment's expression is an idea we have about that moment. For that reason "a leftover dharma" is still "a leftover dharma" fully expressed.

Even when we are not fully present for our life, our true nature is still presencing. Removing the personal pronoun from the opening sentence clarifies this idea. The sentence reads, "Being-time does nothing but penetrate exhaustively entire time as entire being." Expressing it in this way reveals the inclusiveness or no-self of reality. When we understand that our being-time includes all being-time expressed, our effort is not singular but part of the larger practice of all beings making the world.

We cannot make exertion without the support of all beings. If our effort reflects this deeper understanding, we see our endeavors are supported by everything. Our effort is the moment's effort. It is the expression of the exertion of all beings expressed, as we are the expression of all beings. That expression cannot be partial. A dharma can only be fully expressed, it cannot be expressed one-half or two-thirds. It is just this, complete in itself. This view of the expression of being-time is deeper than any ideas or definitions we have about our experience. In "Uji," Dōgen only seems to be interested in presenting how the world is, in and of itself. For this reason, a moment is always fully expressing what is arising at that time.

Even Blundering Is Being

Even our blunders or mistakes are a complete expression of the moment of their expression. We may wonder about our effort to avoid these mistakes. Is Dōgen saying that whatever we do is acceptable because it is fully expressing being-time? No. Dōgen teaches in "Gyōji" (Continuous Practice):

> You may sometimes try to conceal the deluded thought of trying to avoid continuous practice when you neglect it by saying that "even avoiding continuous practice is itself continuous practice," but this is a half-hearted continuous practice, and it cannot be considered to be seeking continuous practice. Truly, it is like a poor person throwing away his inheritance and wandering off to some other land.[1] . . . Therefore, continuous practice should never be neglected for even a second.[2]

Dōgen brings us back to our situation as real action, not an intellectual abstract discussion of being-time. We make mistakes. We make effort in practice. His point is that each mistake is still a fully expressed dharma. He is not saying that a fully expressed dharma blunder is an enactment of realized Buddha-activity. We cannot hide behind buddha-nature's encompassing scope.

AVOIDING TWO EXTREMES

At the end of this paragraph, Dōgen writes, "You must not by your own maneuvering make [practice] into nothingness" and "you must not force [practice] into being." Dōgen is delineating two mistakes we make in practice.[3] First, we should not understand this passage to mean that anything we do is an expression of penetrating exhaustively each moment. If you think he is saying anything you do is acceptable or that your actions don't matter, then your understanding of the passage is nihilistic. Nihilism refers to setting aside morals and ethics because you think your actions are of no consequence. A person caught in nihilistic thinking believes that since everything is empty of inherent existence or no-self, that life has no meaning. She might think it would be pointless to engage in ethical concerns, since nothing actually exists. Dōgen is saying exactly the opposite.

Because we are in a holistically connected system called reality, everything we do is important. Each thing, person, event has intrinsic value. And the connections we hold within the present moment cannot be other than a whole expressed. Each moment is what it is and that becomes its expression. In this way, our actions and the actions of all beings are of utmost importance.

As I wrote earlier, Dōgen seems to feel a certain freedom to fully explore our experience from the perspective of this web of connection. His audience is composed of practitioners who are already steeped in the truth of interbeing, mutual identity, and mutual penetration of all being-times. For this reason, morals and ethics are self-evident, and

Dōgen assumes we are acutely aware of the moral imperative of the Bodhisattva Path.

In addition, we are admonished to avoid forcing our practice into a shape that we think is enlightenment. We want to make realization a knowable entity, and thus we come to practice with a preconceived notion of enlightenment. We have a plan to transform ourselves, thereby meeting a list of attributes called enlightenment as embodied in our person. Inevitably, these ideas revolve around our idea of self. Stuck in these preconceived notions, we try to force it into being and propel ourselves further and further from the path.

Practice-realization is predicated on the actualization of our interconnection with all of life. Our practice is about realigning our behavior to reflect the truth of interconnection, not only from the perspective of the self, but also from the perspective of the totality of each thing arising simultaneously in this moment. Dōgen comments in "Gyōji" (Continuous Practice):

> When the continuous practice which manifests itself is truly continuous practice, you may be unaware of what circumstances are behind it, and the reason why you do not notice them is that to understand such a thing is not that special.[4]

When we don't force a moment of practice into a preconceived idea, we find that we may not recognize practice-realization when it arises. Dōgen writes in "Kajō" (Everyday Activity) that the Zen masters manifest their understanding while drinking tea and eating rice.[5] Understanding is manifest in the everyday activities in which we all engage. When we are trapped in the supposition that realization must have some special quality, we miss that fact. We tell ourselves that our current life is not special enough; therefore, it could not be a life realized.

If we follow this way of thinking, when we read that Zen masters express realization while drinking tea and eating rice, we believe that the being-time of their drinking and eating must be special and different from our time of eating and drinking. How could our eating and drinking be in the same league as that of a Zen master? Zen masters sit in grass huts, stillness radiating from the holy mountains that surround them, accompanied by the sound of a creek. Their tea is as green as the frog leaping into a nearby pool and their rice is infused with their enlightened nature. Surely they do not put their pants on one leg at a time!

From this erroneous view, we extrapolate that Zen masters are enlightened outside of the interactive arising of all dharmas, so-called daily life. Actually, Zen masters are Zen masters because they do not get caught in some idea about reality. Rather, they respond to the arising dharmas in such a way that they include the totality of each moment, thereby enacting realization. This is a fluid, continuous, impermanent response state.

When we respond with an idea about how we should be, we are forcing the moment. We get caught in thinking Zen is special and outside daily life. From this view, how could we understand our life as realized response? How can we possibly understand that when nothing special is happening, our life, just as it is, can resonate with realization? We don't recognize the skillful things we do as practice-actualization. Yet, each moment that we are able to fully participate in the totality of that moment is realized response. Enlightenment is not a fixed state residing within an individual. Rather we engage in enlightened behavior, at this time, responding in concord with the continuous practice of all beings worlding the world.

Do not underestimate your realization by negating it, and don't make it more than it is by concretizing it. Just pay attention to the business at hand. Zazen, going to the bathroom, chanting, going to work, or any other activity you can think of is an opportunity to fully inhabit our lives within the context of all of life. Most of the time we don't even notice when we are fully occupying a moment.

THE SHARP, VITAL QUICK OF DHARMAS

Whether we miss the mark or not, there is always "the sharp vital quick of dharmas dwelling in their dharma-positions." The word Dōgen uses for "sharp, vital quick" is *kappatsupatchi. Kappatsupatchi* is onomatopoeic in Japanese.[6] "Sharp, vital quick" is the sound of a fish leaping from the water, and the image is associated with complete integration.[7] This sound is Dōgen's concrete example of the immediacy and impermanence of intimate connection. Our true state is right now; no other place. Even if we think we are somewhere else, we cannot be anywhere but here and now. *Kappatsupatchi!* A fish leaps from the water and splashes down. We leap clear of fixed ideas and fully integrate with this moment's arising.

Imagine this sentence is like hands clapping together sharply or a ruler hitting a desk. Suddenly we perk up; we are fully present. "Wake up! Look! Look! Right now! A dharma position is dwelling here." Each moment gives us the opportunity to remember our interpenetrating state and act from that realization. Sometimes we do this without a thought—it just happens. Sometimes we do this despite our resistances. Sometimes we miss the mark. Yet, each time, we are freed to enter fully into the next moment and the next, endlessly renewing.

Do not give up, do not make up stories, get out of the way and just keep coming back to each moment as it is, responding as best you can. Like a fish we respond, leap, and land. It's just *kappatsupatchi!*

> The dragon's jewels are found in every wave.
> Looking for the moon, it is here, in this wave, in the next.[8]

You reckon time only as something that does nothing but pass by. You do not understand it as something not yet arrived. Although our various understandings are time, there is no chance for them to be drawn in by time. There has never yet been anyone who supposed time to be coming and going who has penetrated to see it as being-time dwelling in its dharma-position. What chance is there, then, for a time to arrive when you will break through the barrier [into total emancipation]? Even if someone did know that dwelling-position, who would be able truly to give an utterance that preserved what he had thus gained? And even were someone able to utter such an utterance at will, he could still not avoid groping to make his original face immediately present.[1]

FIRST, WE TEND TO SEPARATE TIME from our own being. We experience time as a dimension that we cannot see, which functions alongside our particular existence. We are caught by time, like a leaf spinning in a stream. Or, we are running to catch up to time, in order to have a sense of control over our life. Like the White Rabbit in Lewis Carroll's *Alice in Wonderland*, we run along with our watch held out in front of us fretting for time past or for time not yet arrived. We fear time will pass us by. We can never seem to catch up to the time of realization or control its appearance.

We may veer between the sense that we don't have enough time or we have all the time in the world. In the first occasion, we may practice with an intensity that is misguided and has the quality of impatience, fear, or anxiety. In the second instance we are lax, wandering and indulging our whims. When we practice with a teacher within the context of a well-established tradition, our effort is guided between these two extremes.

BEING DRAWN IN BY TIME

"Although our various understandings are time, there is no chance for them to be drawn in by time" refers to the difficulty of decoding the teaching of being-time when we are looking at the problem incorrectly. One of Dōgen's aims is to create a model of practice that clearly delineates how we should think about practice. Here he is saying, our insights about realization are time, yet we do not comprehend the true nature of this time because we are not "not drawn in by" time. For example, insights about practice may occur at a certain time for us, but somehow we don't connect it with our present circumstances. If we separate the time of insight from time-being, a gap is created and we are not "drawn in" by time's true nature. We are not looking for it, so we don't see it.

THE TIME NOT YET ARRIVED

Time not yet arrived is being-time right now. If we wait for some moment to arrive, we will never penetrate the truth of this moment's now. Dōgen writes in "Busshō" (Buddha-Nature) about the conditions of the time of practice-realization:

> "If it arrives" is like saying "it has arrived." If it were "if the time arrives," the buddha nature would not arrive; therefore, since the time has already arrived, this is the appearance of the buddha nature. Or [as Baizhang says,] "its principle

is self-evident." In some there has never been a time when the time does not arrive, nor a buddha nature that does not appear.[2]

The conventional idea of "not yet arrived" practice is waiting for a particular set of causes and conditions that will enable us to enact buddha-nature. The quotation above counters this idea by pointing out that since buddha-nature is the nature of reality itself, reality or being-time-right-now is nothing more than this time. Since this is the case, how could it be something that is not already present? For Dōgen, this presencing is a fundamental aspect of buddha-nature or being-time. Realization itself is always present and accessible.

Therefore the sentence "You do not understand it as something not yet arrived" means that you don't understand that "it" is here now.[3] This not only harkens back to the quotation from "Busshō," but also to Dōgen's comment at the beginning of "Uji," "There is an arising of the religious mind at the same time, and it is the arising of the time of the same mind. So it is with practice and attainment of the Way."[4] Practice-realization, attainment, aspiration, and our mind as it is right now are synonymous.

Yet, transformation is called for. We must change, but the change is not about being somewhere else or waiting for some future time. The change referred to is a state of mind, a turning of our understanding. What we turn toward or actualize is already here. The second aspect is that if we do wait, we will never experience realization. The idea that we must wait for something (or someone) outside ourselves to create the conditions for realization will only take us further away from freedom.

COMING AND GOING

When we experience coming and going as a constant sequential stream without pause, we will not settle into the present moment. Our experience becomes like a stone skipped across the top of a lake. When we fully engage right now, we lose the sense that time is getting away from us and we fully embody our current circumstances. This is the stone sinking all the way to the bottom.

Furthermore, this teaching is not about being pulled around by circumstances and neglecting to anticipate needs. Often we think that an admonition to live in the present moment means that we let go of planning for the future. This is not the point of being present. Fully engaging a moment is about paying attention to our life as it is. This is a different experience than that of being pulled around by circumstances.

Coarising with all being, we are able to fully engage this being-time. Without this total immersion, we cannot know what is the most skillful response. This is one reason we cannot attain realization through intellectual understanding. Our intellect is not enough; we must be present, body and mind, not separated by thinking about our experience. If we understand time only as coming and going, we cannot understand both the autonomous aspect of each moment and that moment's unobstructed cocreation with all being.

Dōgen does not deny that we have a past and future. Yet, the true freedom of realization is the ability to be simultaneously independent while responding to this moment's totality. In this way, no previous obstacles or future desires that might hinder our skillful response bind us. A skillful response is determined by our ability to be present with all of the various aspects of our situation that are germane to the interaction as it unfolds.

Unfortunately, we get tripped up by delusional thinking. Our fixed ideas about how things should be, separated from how they are, become a cage that traps us into acting in ways that create suffering. We become blind to all the possibilities that could be because our view is narrowed by preexisting emotions and preconceived ideas. This is the nature of being human. Our practice is to become aware of being caught, wake up, and free ourselves. We must consider that the map in our mind may be wrong. We need to look up, stand on the mountaintop, and see the totality of that moment. When we can do this, we are completely free from all the moments that preceded it and all the moments that follow. We have dropped the hindering small self and brought forth our true person by engaging the whole of being-time just as it is.

WHERE IS THE DHARMA GATE OF TOTAL EMANCIPATION?

Considering all these misunderstandings about the nature of our experience, how are we going to be able to understand being-time as the dharma gate of total emancipation? And even if we did have some insight into this state, how can we express it? Could you say something that would make it true for the other person, every time? Even if this were possible, we cannot escape that this truth must be enacted in each situation. The truth of being-time cannot be codified and transmitted outside of the presencing moment. It is only our common understanding of being-time as sequential that gives us the impression that we can approach our practice with such a limited view.

In the fascicle "Dōtoku" (Expressions) Dōgen gives an explanation of what he considers to be the process and enactment of "break[ing] through the barrier" or actualization of being-time.

He writes:

> There is an expression right now, an understanding right now . . . the practice right now is practiced by the expression and by the understanding. The grip of this practice accumulates in months and years and lets go of the practice from the months and years in the past. When it is about to drop away, the skin, flesh, bones, and marrow also affirm the dropping away; the nation, land, mountains, and river together affirm the dropping away. . . . So at this very moment, an expression is actualized without being waited for.[5]

In this passage, Dōgen places the enactment of realization in the present moment. This appearance is not solely the act of the individual, but is also enacted by practice, expression, and understanding. Here he acknowledges that actualization is the result of "months and years" of practice that are "let go of" as we enter each moment. This is the same idea found in an earlier section of "Uji" concerning swallowing up and spitting out each moment. We can't hold on to any particular way of expression, we cannot bottle and sell enlightenment. Enacting the present results in the small self dropping away. This breaking through or dropping away is affirmed by "the nation, land, mountains, and river[s]." The teaching of the time right now is "not being waited for" or as the time "not yet arrived." It is the time right now expressed.

ORIGINAL FACE IMMEDIATELY PRESENCING

Yet, we are still beset with our difficulties. Dōgen writes in "Genjōkōan" (Manifesting Suchness), "The dusty world and the Buddha Way beyond may assume many different aspects, but we can see and understand them only to the extent that our eye is cultivated through practice."[6] And, he continues, "the inexhaustible [treasure] store is present not only all around us, it is present right beneath our feet and within a single drop of water."[7] Despite our mistakes, it is all present. Yet, we can only access and actualize our understanding based upon where we are right now. These are the results of months and years of practice.

We are constantly being humbled by our present circumstances. We understand our limitations. As the Shin Buddhists say, we are "foolish human beings."[8] Yet in the midst of our ignorance there is "the time arrived." We must continue to investigate and try to understand our true situation. We can speak about this Dharma, but our true expression is what we do, how we respond. We do not need to grope for our original face; our original face is just this moment. Grounded in our present circumstances, educated by our past experience, guided by our aspiration to follow the bodhisattva vow, we enter this singular moment, holder of all being-time, and we respond. We make our best effort and then we make our next effort.

Do not get caught thinking intellectual understanding is enough. We have to put our bodies out there on the playing field, make our mistakes, pick ourselves up, and go forward. This is our true effort. Our original face is also the face of all of reality because we are not separate from reality. This is what guides our practice. We don't have to talk about it, we don't have to call it this or that, and it is not the product of our will. It is just a fish leaping clear of the water. It is our pure response; leaping clear of attachment, unobstructed by any ideas we might have about coming and going.

Left entirely to the being-time of the unenlightened, both enlightenment and nirvāṇa would be being-time that was nothing more than
an aspect of going-and-coming. [But] no nets or cages remain for
long—all is the immediate presencing here and now of being-time.
The deva kings and deva multitude actually presencing to the left
and right are even now being-time that puts forth my total exertion.
And everywhere else in the universe the hosts of being-times in water
and on earth are now immediately manifesting themselves in the full
power that I exert. Entities of every manner and kind being time in
the realms of darkness and light are the immediate manifestation
of my full exertion, all my full exertion makes a passage. One must
learn in practice that unless it is one's self exerting itself right now,
not a single dharma or thing can either immediately manifest itself
or make a passage.

DŌGEN PICKS UP the theme from the previous paragraph by stating that if we understand our realization to be dependent solely upon
sequential practice, that practice would be based upon only one aspect
of coming and going. This is what he is calling the "being-time of the
unenlightened." It is incorrect to understand enlightenment or nirvāṇa
as the fruits of sequential practice.[1] As Hee-Jin Kim writes:

> Realization . . . in Dōgen's thought rejected such a process of
> evolutionary becoming, or "coming and going" and "arising

and perishing" for that matter. Rather, it meant that reality in its realized state was always a self-sufficient, yet dynamic whole.[2]

From the perspective of nonduality, being-time must be one thing; nothing is missing. We can think of reality as an interpenetrating interactive process rather than a series of discrete things or occurrences. Reality as process is reality as one thing. Events may be viewed as going and coming, but their real nature is the totality of all going and coming. This totality is not sequential, because it is nondual and all-encompassing.

Nets and cages fall away because reality just is and cannot be tainted by our incorrect views about realization and delusion. Reality is whole, whether we see it or not. Realized response includes everything—going beyond delusion or realization. Selfish response includes just a narrow view predicated on clinging and desire, regardless of the needs of the larger situation.

Dōgen is not denying that we experience transformation as our practice matures. There is progression from this moment to the next, but that passage comes about from interpenetrating connections. This passage of no-passage from delusion to realization occurs because of an interpenetrating impermanent discrete moment's intimacy with all being. Thus, our focus is on the present moment's expression, not a model of sequential passage. We are embedded in what is arising in and with us, and not trying to conceptualize or compare our experience with the vermilion palace of our imagined realization.

My Total Exertion

Dōgen writes the "deva kings and deva multitude" that are presencing themselves "left and right" are still part of the "being-time that puts forth my total exertion." This is another place in "Uji" when the translation can emphasize one person's effort, as in "my full exertion," or the effort of the group, as in Kim's "their utmost efforts."[3]

Hee-Jin Kim translates this passage as:

> All in all, never caught in nets or cages, "existence-time" is realized. The deva kings and hosts of heaven—now manifested on the right now on the left—are the "existence-time" which, even now, they continue to exert through their utmost efforts. The "existence-time" of the hosts of other waters and lands is that which they themselves now realize through their utmost efforts. Various beings and various events existing as "existence-time" in the invisible and visible worlds all realize themselves through their utmost efforts; they pass through themselves by way of their utmost effort. Unless it is a passage of its own utmost efforts at this moment, not a dharma, not a thing, can ever realize itself or pass through itself. This we should study.[4]

Kim does not use the pronoun "my" or "one's self" in his translation. Without the personal reference, we are less confused about our role in making the world. The problem with a translation using a personal pronoun is that we, the practitioner, might think our effort is the only effort being expressed. On the other hand, when this passage is personal, we become aware of the importance of our effort. We are not given a free pass. Our practice is as important as that of the deva kings, deva multitudes, water and land hosts. Reality itself is neither someone else's effort nor self-effort. All beings' time, a being's time, and all being-time are simultaneously engaged in total exertion. Again we return to the idea of reality as a totally impermanent, interpenetrating process without beginning or end.

Our individual separate effort, our self-identified realization, makes possible the practice or manifestation of others but only in accord with all the various beings that make possible the activity of reality. Steven Heine, in a note to his translation of this paragraph, writes:

> Dependence upon *jinriki* [sustained effort], however, does not suggest a subjectivistic[5] causal principle. One's own efforts are equally dependent upon the exertions of all other beings. In Shōbōgenzō "Gyōji," Dōgen writes that the unrelenting activity of sustained exertion (*gyōji*) right-now is the basis of all selves and all buddhas, all moments and all phenomena . . .[6]

When our activity, in concert with all beings—in this case deva kings, deva multitudes, earth hosts and water hosts—actualizes interconnected interpenetrating response and is not hindered by attachment to self, it can then be characterized as "my total exertion." Total exertion, by definition, must include everything, seen and unseen, simultaneously presencing itself. From the position of absolute reality, this means nothing is left out. Kim's translation makes this idea clearer.

Because nothing is ever left out, "no nets or cages remain for long." As Dōgen expresses earlier, "a partial exhaustive penetration is an exhaustive penetration of a partial being-time."[7] These phrases are difficult sentence structures, but they are simply stating that reality itself cannot be expressed partially or be caught up in our misunderstanding about its true nature. Since we are also reality, our essential nature is not caught either.

Nevertheless, we do get caught. But if we continue our effort in practice, eventually we will become freed from nets and cages or erroneous ideas about coming and going. And as we make our sincere effort, we are fully engaged in practice. This full engagement cannot really be called partial, because it is the best effort we can make at this time. And the kind of effort we make is key. If our effort is sincere and continuous, we will "break through the barrier into total emancipation."[8] This breakthrough is dependent upon our ability to firmly set ourselves in the midst of our lives, with our dharma eye open.

But this looking has to go beyond the notion that we stand in the center of a circle conducting our experience. Gratitude is a strong source of equanimity because it joins us with all beings and takes us out of our self-absorption. In gratitude we are acknowledging the simultaneity and connection we have with all of life. In gratitude we feel joy as we see the continuous practice of all beings. We begin to feel some ease from our own desires and our awakened eye senses the deva kings and earth hosts. We are open to understanding the effort of trees and rain. We feel comradeship with our environment and with all the foolishness of our fellow human beings. These are the hosts of water and earth beings whose effort is in concert with our own. There is no separation. Life is intimacy.

We will not experience this gratitude unless we are able to get out of our limited view. A member of our saṅgha had surgery that rendered her housebound for several weeks. Before the surgery she had many ideas about who would help her and exactly what kind of help she would receive. In short, she had a plan based upon some preconceived idea about how she would best like her situation to evolve.

The person who was going to help her was not able to come and stay with her. Suddenly all the ideas about how things were going to happen fell apart. This moment included her past experiences and planned future—immediately present, and they were not working out the way she thought they would. Stopping and allowing this moment to be as it is right now let her take stock of the situation, alleviate some of her suffering, and acknowledge what was now possible.

The moment of realizing that things are not going to work out as planned cannot be skipped. Because my friend accepted what was happening, along with her disappointment, she was able to transform her view. This transformation came when she accepted the help that was coming forward from an unexpected quarter. Discussing the situation with her teacher guided her process. Often we do not see and accept help when it is offered because it is not the help we have imagined. We resist and complain about our situation because it does not meet our expectations. When she opened up to the totality of the situation, she discovered that her neighbors wanted to be of assistance. Two women in her saṅgha who live nearby became primary helpers and later friends.

Perhaps most important, after her initial shock of having to let go of her plans, she began to feel deep gratitude. She realized that by letting herself participate in the being-time that was present, not the being-time she imagined, she began to transform and feel a deeper connection with all the people around her. This transformation has continued.

Because the independent aspect of being-time experienced is not really separate, it can become the pivotal point of transformation. It is this moment that is the realization of suchness, of fully exhausting our immediate experience without obstruction. This moment is the now in which we are able to turn and be turned by including everything as it is. If our understanding is grounded in practice-realization, then we have a better chance for transformation to occur. My friend's full exertion, her openness, even in the midst of her resistance, was what allowed passage to happen and transformation to occur. It is also what allowed other solutions to arise. These problems/solutions are the continuous practice of all beings.

DARK AND LIGHT

The light and darkness Dōgen mentions is not a metaphor for good and evil. Light refers to what we see or where our attention is focused. Dark refers to what we can't see. Hee-Jin Kim translates dark and light as invisible and visible.[9] Fazang, one of the shapers of the Chinese Huayan School, writes that light (disclosure) and dark (concealment) are illustrated by imagining a lion made of gold. When we see the lion, we just see a lion, not gold. When we are focused on the golden aspect, the lion aspect recedes. If we look at both simultaneously, both sides are alternately disclosed (light) and hidden (dark).[10] When something is light, or easily seen, we say it is apparent to us. If something is dark and therefore we are unable to see it, we call it hidden. Yet, things are neither light nor dark; it is just our perception or focus that varies.

Dōgen's teaching in "Uji" is that we must hold more than one view. Our tendency is to see things as this or that. When we see time, being is hidden. When we see being, time is hidden. When we focus on the past, the present is hidden. When we focus on the future, the past is hidden. We see an experience as past, but no longer present. We understand the future is not yesterday. We become attached to our views, reify our thinking, and do not recognize other aspects. Thus our effort is hindered and obstructed. We don't question the veracity of our own view.

Dōgen observes in *Sansuikyō* (Mountains and Rivers Sūtra):

> You should question this matter right now. Are there many ways to see one thing, or is it a mistake to see many forms as one thing? You should pursue this beyond the limit of pursuit. Accordingly, endeavors in practice-realization of the way are not limited to one or two kinds. The ultimate realm has one thousand kinds and ten thousand ways.[11]

These ten thousand ways are the continuous practice of all beings. We can't necessarily see them, but we should know that they are there. We are not the only ones engaged in practice-realization. We are not the only ones living as this being-time.

Sometimes we see the fruits of our practice and at other times we do not. In "Gyōji" (Continuous Practice), Dōgen says:

> The merits of this continuous practice are sometimes not hidden, and so beings arouse the thought of enlightenment and begin to practice. Sometimes these merits of continuous practice are not evident, and so beings do not see and hear

them and do not come to understand them. But you should
understand that even though these merits are not revealed,
they are not concealed.[12]

We may not be aware of the merits of our own practice. Yet Dōgen
extols us to enact continuous practice and to understand that our practice is essential as is the practice of all beings whether we see it or not.
Dōgen continues in "Gyōji" (Continuous Practice):

> The time when continuous practice is manifested is what we
> call "now." Consequently, one day of continuous practice by
> us becomes the seed of all the Buddhas; it is the continuous
> practice of all the Buddhas. On the basis of this continuous
> practice, all the Buddhas are manifested.[13]

For Dōgen, it is vital that we engage in the activity of continuous practice. Like buddha-nature and practice-realization, continuous practice is the time right now. Immediately upon our effort to follow the
Buddha Way, we become one with the Buddha's Way. Becoming one
with the Buddha Way is to enact the Buddha Way. Enactment must
include both dark and light: that which seems to be hidden and that
which is revealed. This seeing goes beyond intellectual understanding.
Full exertion is going beyond the distinctions of one side or the other.

In his book *Realizing Genjokoan*, Shohaku Okumura makes an
important observation about practice: "Dōgen, however, said that to
see one reality from two sides is not enough; he said we should *express*
these two sides in one action."[14] How do we express this understanding?
Okumura says that we might create a false dichotomy when we think
that practicing for the community hinders our own spiritual growth.
An individual's practice would be "light" to them and community
practice would be hidden or "dark." He writes:

> We have to find out how we can best serve the whole commu-

nity, yet we must do this through our own personal action and responsibility. We are completely independent while at the same time we are fully part of the community. So, how can we actualize both sides of our lives within one action? This is really the basic point of our lives.[15]

When I was living in a practice community, sometimes students would say, "I can't take a job supporting the community because it will interfere with my practice." They believed that the added responsibility of taking care of the community would make their life so busy that their spiritual practice would suffer. In their mind, spiritual practice did not include taking care of the larger community. "Practice" was only the activities that seemed special, such as chanting, ōryōki, or sitting in meditation. When we realize that continuous practice includes all beings, our kōan becomes, "How can I be of service to the community and also find my way in practice?" As we take on this question and express our practice-realization through our activity, we see that one does not hinder the other. Both sides are illuminated. We understand that the community and self are not different.

Furthermore, knowing that one is practicing with all beings can be encouraging. I find it heartening to know that I am not alone. I am embedded in a vast interconnecting mutual activity called life. My life is not diminished or obstructed by the life of others. My life becomes the life of the whole world and as such is the whole world. My practice matters, yet my mistakes are workable. My life and death become no beginning and no end. The "I" is independent and simultaneously all being. Each makes the other. Together "no nets or cages remain for long," and I am freed to see my intimate life with all beings.

You must not construe this passing to be like a squall of wind and rain moving from place to place. The entire world is not changeless and immoveable, nor unprogressing and unregressing—the whole world is passing seriatim. Passing seriatim is like spring, for example, with all of its many and varied signs. That is passing seriatim. You should learn in practice that passing takes place without anything extraneous. For example, springtime's passage invariably passes through spring. The passage is not spring, but as it is the springtime's passage, passing attains the Way now in the time of spring. All of this you must give careful and repeated examination.[1]

IN THIS PARAGRAPH, Dōgen explains how transformation or passage[2] happens within the context of being-time. His discussion of passage is not just how one thing becomes another or how many things are simultaneously one thing. His investigation of passage is also about how we are to understand the progress of our spiritual transformation.

From a universal perspective, there is nothing in the world that is not passage. This passage is more than sequential movement from east to west, from past to future, from delusion to realization. It is the movement of interpenetrating interconnected events all arising simultaneously at the intersection of a particular being-time. Passage happens as each independent moment is expressed. A moment's interactivity with all of reality makes passage. It is not to be characterized as delineated moments in sequential causal relationships. Dōgen is asking us to understand these innumerable multiplicities of interpenetrating events as simultaneously arising, interacting, and thereby making passage.

PASSAGE IS THIS MOMENT'S PASSAGELESS-PASSAGE

A moment does not become another moment by progressing from one finite delineated time element to another. It is our mind that defines a being-time's boundaries and seeks out sequential passage. A moment's passage cannot be strictly sequential because a moment is impermanence and thus interpenetrating. It has no duration, no real demarcations, as it is just this mind's moment. That is why a moment's passage is actually no-passage. This passage is predicated upon something deeper than the causes and conditions we perceive as a moment and then cognize as leading into the next.

Furthermore, we might observe that the stages of so-called sequential time are not actually available to us. Time's past and future are only a concept we have of the past or future in this moment. What is available to us is our direct experience of now. This "now" includes remembrance of the past and projections into the future. This now being-time is all being-time (universal) and all beings' time (particular) arising and changing simultaneously at the intersection of this moment. For the most part, this too is not accessible as it is not apparent to us—it is hidden, and because it is hidden it is not conceptualized. As soon as we conceptualize our experience, that idea is just another moment. To go beyond the hidden and the revealed is to respond to passage as passage. This is penetrating the totality of each moment with our effort in response to that moment as it is, not as we would like it to be.

Our actual experience of passage is nonconceptual, since to fix it as a concrete moment is to think about what has happened and give it a name. Immediate experience is to be simply immersed in what is. Even the act of naming something is still the act of just this moment, and just this moment is enacted before the naming of it. Yet this does not deny that each moment has an aspect of individuality, nor does it deny that naming our experience can be useful.

The whole world makes passage. Yet, the world does not move in lockstep. The passage of being-time is not a continuous series like dominoes carefully lined up to create a cascading progress as they fall. Instead it is many, many particular impermanent, independent, interconnected, and interpenetrating moments that make passage at this time. This passage is the continuous practice of all beings making the world. Passage is the interpenetrating connected moment of all beings simultaneously responding-acting that moves a moment along. Dōgen offers the example of spring to demonstrate how this operates.

Spring is not a date on the calendar, spring is not just seeing a robin on your lawn, spring is not only about the daffodils blooming—there is so much more going on. It is infinite and interconnected, not sequential. It is the befores and afters manifesting as the moment we call spring. Spring is a concept or name we give to a simultaneous passage of being-times that we winnow out of the totality of all of reality. Spring could not be spring without the universal activity of all being-time. The effort of each thing and all things makes up the seasons. Dōgen acknowledges the independent dharma position of spring when he writes "springtime's passage invariable passes through spring." Spring is the effort of the arising of one (or all) dharma(s) or being(s) right now.

A WIND-BELL IN SPACE

Dōgen offers an example of the multiplicity of passage as the transmission of Buddhist ancestors in his fascicle "Maka Hannya Haramitsu" (The Perfection of Wisdom):

> My late Master, the eternal Buddha says:
> Whole body like a mouth, hanging in space;
> Not asking if the wind is east, west, south or north,
> For all others equally, it chatters prajñā:[3]

Chin Ten Ton Ryan Chin Ten Ton.

This is the chattering of prajñā [transmitted] by Buddhist
  patriarchs from rightful successor to rightful successor.
  It is prajñā as the whole body, it is prajñā as the whole of
  others, it is prajñā as the whole self, and it is prajñā as the
  whole east, west, south and north.[4]

The wind-bell exemplifies passing in and through this moment's
moment. The particular moment of the wind-bell's sounding is the
culmination of the passage of wind, metal, sound, the bell, and the
effort of all being-time throughout time and space. It is not just
the direct cause and effect of wind moving the clapper.

A wind-bell hangs in space. This bell exists as an independent
moment of being-time. It does not try to control the direction of the
wind. The wind-bell does not perceive the wind as sequential. The wind
itself is just the is-ness of the being-time of passage, it has no particular
agenda called "moving the wind-bell's clapper." This wind's arising and
this bell's being-time are mutually penetrating and mutually engaged
in their activity. There is the passage of the bell and the passage of the
wind. The bell is pure response. The wind is pure response. The east is
response. The west is response, south and north are response. Nothing
is left out. The wind-bell's song is the mutual penetration of everything
seen and unseen. All passage is just this, and yet there is the moment of
the wind-bell's sounding. This can be said of each element mentioned
in the poem.

All together, affirming, rings out the voice of "Chin Ten Ton Ryan
Chin Ten Ton." Because the wind-bell's voice is also the voice of all
being-time, Dōgen writes this is the affirmation of wisdom transmitting passage from "rightful successor to rightful successor."[5] It is the
wisdom of the whole body of universal being-time. This is also true for
spring's passage. It is the wisdom of the particularity of a dharma that
is both the independent self and the self of no-self of that dharma. It is
the wisdom of everyday life called spring's-passage-being-time.

PASSAGE COMPLETES THE WAY

Steven Heine translates the end of this paragraph of "Uji" as, "Passage is not just spring; however, since it is the passage of spring, passage now completes the Way at the very time spring appears."[6] A paraphrase of this sentence might be: The activity of passage—the world worlding the world—is not just the moment called spring. However it is, in this example, spring's passage. Inasmuch as spring is all being-time actualized, spring accords itself with all being-time and is realization. Thus it "completes the Way." This realization is the time right now actualizing the time right now, called spring. Like buddha-nature, spring is already present, yet is not manifest until it is spring.

This procession of moments is also the how of our spiritual journey. Our progress is made up of many, many moments each in their turn the passage of the various being-times interpenetrating that moment. The spiritual journey in Zen Buddhism is epitomized by the phrase transmissionless transmission. This is the passageless-passage of the Dharma. How is it that we pass from ignorance to wisdom? What elements are necessary for transformation?

Dōgen tells the story of a student's progress in Zuimonki (Record of Things Heard) prefaced with this simile:

> An ancient has said, "Associating with a good person is like walking through the mist and dew; though you will not become drenched, gradually your robes will become damp. This means that if you become familiar with a good person, you will become good yourself without being aware of it."[7]

In the main story, a young man was a student of Master Gutei. This student didn't seem to realize what he was learning or practicing. Dōgen comments, "a boy who attended Master Gutei (Jūdi), without noticing when he was learning or when he was practicing, realized the

Way because he served as a personal attendant to the master who had been practicing for a long time."[8] In the course of attending to Master Gutei, he attained realization.

By focusing on the activity of helping Master Gutei every day, the student was not aware he was being trained. He probably spent his time making the master's bed and fetching tea. Yet those activities, in accord with Master Gutei's instruction, created his passage from student to master. This transformation was due to the confluence of all the activities: all the befores and afters and the independent moments of the student's life with the master. His interactions with Master Gutei resulted in his total immersion in practice-realization. Transformation was always present, yet there was a particular moment of its recognition when Master Gutei acknowledged his passage into spiritual maturity.

Another example is found in "Udonge" (The Udumbara Flower). Dōgen explains the awakening of Buddha's disciple Mahākāśyapa. Buddha holds up a flower. Mahākāśyapa, seeing the flower, smiles. The moment of Buddha-flower-smile is passageless-passage. Dōgen describes it this way:

> All instances, however many, of the twirling of flowers, are individual instances of [the transmission from] rightful successor to rightful successor; they are the actual *existence* of the *transmission*. Indeed, forget the World-Honored One's twirling of a flower! . . . Because the time of twirling of flowers is the whole of Time itself, it is the experience of the same state as the World-Honored One, and it is the same twirling of flowers. The meaning of *"twirling flowers"* is flowers displaying flowers [phenomena manifesting themselves as they are]: it is plum flowers, spring flowers, snow flowers, and lotus flowers.[9]

Furthermore,

> Twirling flowers are twirled by eyes, twirled by mind-
> consciousness, twirled by nostrils, and twirled by flowers
> twirling. In general, the mountains, rivers, and the Earth;
> the sun and moon, the wind and rain; people, animals, grass,
> and trees—the miscellaneous things of the present display-
> ing themselves here and there—are just the twirling of the
> udumbara flower.[10]

Just one flower being held up for display is passage through all time
and being, awakening each and every thing. This is what Mahākāśyapa
realized. Essentially his realization was already present as his own
being, yet it was the passage of all buddha-nature in and through him
that revealed his true nature. This is our passage too.

CAREFULLY EXAMINE THE MATTER

Dōgen ends this paragraph with the admonition "All of this you must
give careful and repeated examination." At each critical juncture of the
text, Dōgen reminds us to pay attention. We want to grapple with this
teaching in such a way that it brings us back to our present situation.
In particular, understanding passage is critical to conceptualizing how
practice-realization is enacted. In this case, the story of Gutei's student
is instructive. His awakening is the result of his complete immersion
in the activity of his life, through the guidance of his teacher. His realization did not come about because of his preconceived idea about
enlightenment.

Realization is not intellectual understanding. Dōgen warns us in
"Bendōwa" (Wholehearted Practice of the Way):

> We should remember that from the beginning we have never
> lacked the supreme state of bodhi, and we will receive it and

use it forever. At the same time, because we cannot perceive it directly, we are prone to beget random intellectual ideas, and because we chase after these as if they were real things, we vainly pass by the great state of truth.[11]

Of course, this book, Dōgen's "Uji," and all of Buddhist writings and teachings are a product of the mind and heart. We must use them as pointers along the path of practice. Deep understanding of Buddhism is always grounded in dharma teachings, dharma teachers, and dharma community. Guidance in practice happens within the context of connection with these three elements. Teachings, teachers, and community give us the forum to explore, actualize, and be confirmed in our understanding. In this way we are able to "carefully explore the matter" of being-time's actualization in daily life, not in our heads.

Before I began to write this book, I did not realize the immense scope of Dōgen's vision of being-time. But no matter what I think I know about being-time, it is stopping and being in my being-time just as it is, enacting the no-self of my exertion with all being that is actualizing being-time. This is enacted in the context of my Buddhist practice community. It is actualized at the supermarket, while driving my car, or when walking the dog. Nothing other than living one's life completely in the Way is actualizing being-time's passage.

How Long Does Enlightenment Take?

If, in speaking of a "passage," you imagine that the place of passage lies somewhere outside, and the dharma of the one doing the passage moves toward the east [like the spring] through 100,000 worlds over 100,000 kalpas of time, that is a result of not giving total devotion to the single-minded practice of the Buddha Way.

THIS PARAGRAPH is a reinterpretation of the Buddhist doctrine that innumerable lifetimes are necessary for awakening.[1] Dōgen writes that if we hold to this sequential view of spiritual progress, we have not wholeheartedly dedicated ourselves to practice-realization.

A traditional teaching of both the Theravāda and Mahāyāna Schools of Buddhism is that we acquire realization over the course of many, many lifetimes.[2] Various schools, at various times, have versions of this teaching. After many eons of practice through innumerable lifetimes, we arrive at the point where we are able to put it all together and attain realization. For Dōgen this is dualistic thinking and does not mesh with his understanding of authentic Buddhist practice.

To believe that innumerable rebirths are the primary means to attain the Way would negate Dōgen's understanding of nonsequential passage, buddha-nature, practice-realization, being-time, and other key teachings. Dōgen's practice model, based upon the immediacy of one's buddha-nature, is in direct line with the schools of Buddhism that were developed in China and transmitted to Japan. The critical point for us as practitioners is that practice-realization is possible in each moment.

Dōgen understands our essential nature to be buddha-nature. This essential nature is not something we acquire over many lifetimes; it is reality itself. As reality itself, buddha-nature is not only a human attribute but the essential being-ness of everything. It is the world made up of the particularity of form and activity. Buddha-nature is not a substrata from which things come; it is things manifest in all their myriad forms. Because reality itself is buddha-nature, it is inherent to all beings regardless of their understanding. For this reason Dōgen writes that buddha-nature is not dependent upon karma or causes and conditions.[3] In other words, buddha-nature is not about a process of acquisition over many lifetimes of Buddhist practice. Buddha-nature is fundamental nature as it manifests in each dharma's particularity. Furthermore, reality's expression is not obstructed by anything. Since buddha-nature is the totality of being as each being, anything we perceive as obstructive is still just reality expressing reality in its nondualistic whole.

Buddha-nature, because of its fundamental character, is not dependent upon a particular time of arrival for its appearance. Buddha-nature is not potential; it is always fully presencing right now. This fully present buddha-nature is being-time. Buddha-nature is actualization in the immediate now, within temporal conditions. Our realization is not dependent upon eons of lifetimes; it is dependent upon waking up to the true nature of our experience right now. Realization is buddha-nature's emancipated suchness.

Hee-Jin Kim comments: "What matters most in religion, as Dōgen saw it, is not . . . an eternal recurrence of rebirths, but the realization of enlightenment here and now."[4] Kim also writes, "Dōgen . . . was not interested in any theoretical involvement with the problem of rebirth, but simply accepted the doctrine and used it practically as a mytho-poeic framework for our moral freedom and responsibility in determining our own destiny."[5]

Throughout this book we have been examining Dōgen's rejection of sequential time as a primary view of being-time's true nature. To discuss the Buddhist path as a specific and sequential series of cause and effect resulting in a good or bad rebirth would not be Dōgen's characterization of the spiritual path.[6] For Dōgen, cause and effect are directly enacted and understood from the dharma position of now. Each being-time, as it is right now, becomes the locus of our effort to enact the Dharma. In this way, a dharma position of being-time is not caught by previous deeds in a former lifetime or even in this one. We are free to turn toward and enact the moment's pure unobstructed passage at any time.

Are we absolved from all responsibility or repercussions for our actions? No. Does this mean that anything we do is buddha-nature? On one level it does. Are we as embedded buddha-nature expressing buddhahood no matter what we do? No.[7]

Actualizing Right Now

Steven Heine writes:

> There is no being-time that is not Buddha-nature; on the other hand, Buddha-nature is not manifested unless and until—or, more positively, only upon—one's realization of *uji* [being-time] as the insubstantiality of all phenomena.[8]

Again as Dōgen succinctly says in "Busshō" (Buddha-Nature):

> A fundamental principle of Buddha-nature is that it is not invested prior to attaining Buddhahood but incorporated upon attainment of Buddhahood. Buddha-nature and attainment of Buddhahood are always simultaneous.[9]

While buddha-nature is always present, its actualization is called buddhahood. When we express the truth of buddha-nature (interconnected, interpenetrating nature expressed), then we are manifesting our true nature, unobstructed and presencing now. Buddha-nature is already fully present, but it does depend upon our expression of it to call that expression buddhahood. Dōgen writes in "Bendōwa" (Wholehearted Practice of the Way); "The Dharma is amply present in every person, but without practice, it is not manifested; without realization, it is not attained."[10] For this reason Dōgen is adamant that practice itself is not separate from realization. He writes in "Bendōwa" (Wholehearted Practice of the Way):

> To think practice and realization are not one is a non-Buddhist view. In the Buddha Dharma, practice and realization are one and the same. As your present practice is practice within realization, your initial negotiation of the Way is in itself the whole of original realization. That is why from the time you are instructed in the way of practice, you are told not to anticipate realization apart from practice. It is because practice points directly to original realization.[11]

We do not engage in practice in order to attain anything. Our practice is an expression of a buddha's activity. For this reason, practice, as much as it is an expression of buddha-nature, cannot be separated from realization. Our aspiration to practice arises because our essential nature is realization. Our practice may miss the mark, but it is still generated from our true nature. Nevertheless, make no mistake: Dōgen is adamant that practice is necessary and our responsibility. In "Gyōji" (Continuous Practice) he admonishes the practitioner:

> Continuous practice that actualizes itself is no other than your continuous practice right now . . . not sustaining your continuous practice . . . is like leaving behind the treasure at the home of your true parent and wandering poor in another land. Wandering through wind and water at the risk of your life, you should not discard the treasure of your own parent. While you were searching in this way, the dharma treasure

would be missed. This being so, continuous practice should not slacken for a minute.[12]

Practice-realization is only expressed in the now. Practice-realization is not something acquired and then never revisited. A fully realized being can constantly express buddha-nature in a continuous series moment after moment. As Dōgen says (again in "Gyōji"):

> On the great road of buddha ancestors there is always unsurpassable practice, continuous and sustained. It forms the circle of the way and is never cut off. Between aspiration, practice, enlightenment, and nirvāṇa, there is not a moment's gap; continuous practice is the circle of the way.[13]

REALIZATION IS MANIFEST IN EACH MOMENT

As I wrote at the beginning of this section, the critical point for us as practitioners is that enacted practice-realization is possible in each moment. I find this very encouraging in several ways. First, there is the very good news that our actualization of the Buddha Way is attainable in this very moment, as it cannot be expressed at any other time. My lifetime is not in preparation for realization; rather, it is an expression of Buddhadharma—if I practice.

Furthermore, no matter how often I miss the mark, I am free to turn and be turned by the Dharma, thereby rectifying my mistakes. I am not caught in a cage of karmic repercussions that must be systematically eradicated before I can actualize my understanding. The immediacy of actualization is that this very moment liberates us from a purgatory of atonement.

And concurrent with this immediacy of expression is my practice with all beings. I make the world and the world makes me. There is no separation. Together my life and the lives of all beings make passage. Expressing this passage is actualizing the Way. It is my responsibility, as a being of this world, to make this world by realizing my place in it. Responsibility in practice should not be viewed as a burden. Taking up the mantle of our aspiration to enact a buddha's life does not require that I wait for anyone or anything. It is all right here in front of me. As soon as I take up practice, each being comes forth to confirm and meet my effort.

Yaoshan Bites the Iron Bull 24

DŌGEN PRESENTS this kōan:[1]

Once Yaoshan Hongdao,[2] at the direction of Wuji Dashi,[3] went to Zen master Mazu[4] with a question. "I believe I have a fair grasp of the three vehicles[5] and the teaching of the twelve divisions,[6] but what about the meaning of the First Patriarch's [Bodhidharma][7] coming from the west?"

Mazu said:

> For the time being, I let him raise his eyebrows and
>   blink his eyes.
> For the time being, I don't let him raise his eyebrows and
>   blink his eyes.
> For the time being, my letting him raise his eyebrows
>   and blink his eyes is correct.
> For the time being, my letting him raise his eyebrows
>   and blink his eyes is not correct.

When Yaoshan heard this, he achieved great enlightenment. He told Mazu, "When I was at Shitou's, it was like a mosquito on an iron bull."

Yaoshan asked his first teacher Wuji Dashi (more commonly known as Shitou) almost the identical question. There is a translation of this dialogue between Yaoshan and Shitou in Andy Ferguson's book *Zen's Chinese Heritage*. Yaoshan says:

"Now I want to find out about the southern[8] teachings of pointing directly at the mind, seeing self-nature, and becoming a buddha. Truly, I'm not clear about this teaching and I ask for the master's compassionate instructions." Shitou says, "You can't attain it this way. You can't attain it not this way. Trying to attain it this way or not this way, it can't be attained. So what will you do?" Yaoshan was confused.[9]

Since Yaoshan was having problems understanding Shitou, Shitou suggested Yaoshan go study with Mazu. Shitou must have felt that Yaoshan would benefit from Mazu's style of teaching.

Yaoshan presents his understanding to Mazu, just as he had to Shitou using similar language. Yaoshan tells Mazu that he has studied the major doctrines of Buddhist studies and attained a solid foundation of the doctrinal teachings of Buddhism. Nevertheless, he doesn't understand the essence of Buddhist practice. He expresses this by saying, "I don't understand the meaning of Bodhidharma coming from the west."[10]

Yaoshan can't answer this kōan with his doctrinal knowledge, so he asks Mazu how he should proceed. The remainder of "Uji" revolves around variations of Mazu's answer to Yaoshan.

The phrase "For the time being, I let him raise his eyebrows and blink his eyes" can also be translated as "Being-time makes him raise his eyebrows and blink his eyes."[11] Now there is the connotation that one's actions are being guided by the totality of a particular situation or being-time. The expression "raising the eyebrows and blinking the eyes" means bringing forth one's understanding through everyday actions.[12] It refers to a particular response to a particular situation. Yaoshan is being encouraged to let go of his intellectual knowledge and respond to what is.

The kōan ends with Yaoshan's enlightenment and his comment "When I was at Shitou's, it was like a mosquito on an iron bull."[13] The image of a mosquito biting an iron bull is a vivid example of how frustrating it can be to try to penetrate a seemingly impenetrable situation.

These two dialogues are concrete examples of a student inquiring about how to fully express each moment and the student's confusion about how to proceed. What is right? What is wrong? How can we know? Just like Yaoshan we bite an iron bull and are unable to let go.

What Mazu utters is not the same as other men. Here eyebrows and eyes must be mountains and seas, because mountains and seas are eyebrows and eyes. Within this "letting him raise," you should see mountains. Within this "letting him blink," you should essentiate the sea. "Correct" enters into intimate terms with "him." "Him" is ushered in by "letting." "Not correct" is not "not letting him," and "not letting him" is not "not correct." All of them are equally being-time.

DŌGEN WRITES of Mazu that he "is not the same as other men" and therefore, we are to pay attention. Mazu stands atop the highest peak and walks the floor of the deepest ocean; his dharma eye is open. He understands and enacts the true Dharma.

Lifting eyebrows and blinking eyes, mountains, and seas together are our life and all beings immediate presencing. Our practice, our individual being (here characterized as lifting an eyebrow and blinking), is in concert with the mountains and seas as they represent the dynamic presencing of all of life.

Dōgen writes in "Yuibutsu Yobutsu" (Only a Buddha and a Buddha), "A buddha's practice is to practice in the same manner as the entire earth and all beings. If it is not practice with all beings, it is not buddha's practice."[1] Like practice-realization, the time of raising one's eyebrows and blinking is the same time as realizing mountains and seas. Mazu understood this and was trying to convey it to Yaoshan.

WHO IS RAISING AN EYEBROW OR BLINKING?

We should also ask about the phrases "letting him raise" and "letting him blink." Who is "him"? Waddell and Abe explain that "him" in Japanese can be either a personal pronoun or a demonstrative pronoun.[2] In this case, "him" could refer to Bodhidharma or an unnamed person, such as one's original nature. Nishijima and Cross say that it is Mazu referring to himself.[3] From a practice point of view, I think this must be taken as an ambiguous reference to Bodhidharma, Mazu, Yaoshan, ourselves, or any practitioner. It could be a reference to Buddha transmitting the dharma seal to Mahākāśyapa. Perhaps the Buddha blinked, and Bodhidharma raised his eyebrows. Doesn't each being-time of Mazu, Bodhidharma, Yaoshan, Mahākāśyapa, Śākyamuni, you, and me include every being-time?

As Dōgen writes earlier in "Uji," "Past time and present time do not overlap or pile up in a row—and yet Qingyuan is time, Huangbo is time. Mazu and Shitou are times too. Since self and other are both times, practice and realization are times."[4] The being-times of the various teachers do not obstruct each other, yet they still inform and interpenetrate each other. What is understood is the same in all cases, although how it is expressed or actualized by the individual is predicated upon the particular circumstances. This is true of any or all of the possibilities above. The important point is that the response is in accord with the myriad aspects of the situation. We are interested in what is most skillful and most in harmony with the actualized moment. There is no abstract right answer.

LETTING AND MAKING

Most of the English translations of this passage read "if you let him," but some are translated as "if you make him."[5] In English "letting" and "making" have different connotations. Letting something happen has the quality of allowing circumstances to drive the direction of an outcome; making something happen is more directed and controlled. From a practice point of view, realized response must include both letting and making.

I grew up in San Antonio, Texas, where it rains heavily in the spring and fall. Often this means that freeway underpasses are flooded. Every year, people drive into these flooded areas, stalling their cars, and have to be rescued. At other times of the year the road is dry and safe. Obviously my decision to go under a freeway overpass will be determined in part by whether it is raining or not. I "make" a decision about the route I am going to take. I "let" the weather determine, in some part, what that route will be. The unwise action is to drive into a flooded underpass. On the other hand, there might be a time when I need to make the choice to chance it. Clearly present circumstances, past experience, and my intended route must all be taken into consideration. There is no one path to my destination that will always be the right way. The totality of my particular being-time will both figuratively and literally make passage from this moment to the next. How that passage happens is determined by the moment itself and my response to that moment.

DŌGEN'S TETRALEMMA

To say "'not correct' is not 'not letting him,' and 'not letting him' is not 'not correct'" is Dōgen's way of keeping us engaged in the intimacy of the situation. Dōgen will not land anywhere, nor should we. This is Dōgen's version of the logic device called a tetralemma. A tetralemma is a philosophical presentation developed in India that is formulated as *a* is, *a* is not, *a* is and is not, *a* is neither *a* nor not *a*.[6] Joan Stambaugh writes of Dōgen's use of this logic in her book *Impermanence Is Buddha-Nature*:

> One might say Dōgen does his own "*uji*-version" of Nāgārjuna's tetralemma. Whereas Nāgārjuna had exhausted the possibilities of assertion and denial by showing that all four

were false (*a*, not *a*, both *a* and not *a*, neither *a* nor not *a*), Dōgen gives us two versions of the tetralemma and then modifies them.[7]

Stambaugh continues:

Nāgārjuna had stated that you cannot say anything; Dōgen goes beyond this to make different statements, none of which is true to the exclusion of others. They are all true (sometimes), which is another way of saying that everything is being-time.[8]

In the opening verses of "Uji" the phrase "for the time being" conventionally has the aspect of something happening within time, possibly giving us the illusion of fixed positions. But Dōgen's examples of "correct," "letting," etc., are without handles; things appear very slippery. We no longer have the option of conceptualizing this situation as rules for behavior. Like Nāgārjuna's tetralemma, this "*uji*-lemma" keeps us from reifying being-time. Dōgen shifts the descriptive aspects of the opening verses to the active response of lifting the eyebrows and blinking one's eyes. The being-time of lifting and blinking, being correct or not, never stops morphing from one view to another. This is the actualized response of someone who is firmly rooted in the needs of the situation, unobstructed by ideas about the situation. There is not one thing we can hold on to.

We want to know which way is correct. It would be so nice to have a formula that would tell us what to do. In Buddhism we do have admonitions, such as the precepts, that give us guidance. We need to thoroughly study their meaning. Once we are firmly grounded in the basics we have to use our own discernment within the context of this being-time. At some point we let go of our ideas about what is right and wrong and trust our response. Do I raise an eyebrow? Do I blink? There cannot be any hard and fast rule; it is our best, most sincere response, at that moment, to the myriad things coming forth to greet us. After offering various permutations of this phrase, Dōgen writes: "All of them are equally being-time." Therefore, each version is meeting our life. Each response has its position, passage, interpenetration, and individuation.

> Mountains are time, and seas are time. If they were not time, there
> would be no mountains and seas. So you must not say there is no time
> in the immediate now of mountains and seas. If time is destroyed,
> mountains and seas are destroyed. If time is indestructible, moun-
> tains and seas are indestructible. Within this true dharma, the
> morning star appears, the Tathāgata appears, eye-pupils appear, the
> holding up of the flower appears. This is time. If it were not time,
> things would be not-so.

In Dōgen's earlier commentary on Mazu's teaching to Yaoshan,
Dōgen makes explicit that a unique realized response (raising the eyebrows and blinking) is all being-time (mountains and seas). He writes,
"Eyebrows and eyes must be mountains and seas, because mountains
and seas are eyebrows and eyes."[1] I understand this to mean that eyebrows and eyes are the particular occasion of a person's response and
mountains and seas represent the larger universal world of realized
activity. When a person's dharma eye is open, that person perceives
not just his or her own view, but that of mountains and seas. They are
born together. This is the activity of unhindered enlightened response.

Dōgen completes his train of thought in the paragraph above. He
connects the dots, if you will. Mountains and seas, representing being,
are also time. Since being and time are not different, they are mutually
dependent within each particular manifestation. They are identical
and do not exist without the other. Still, it is the fact of the mountains'

(and seas') particularity that also allows for the unique moment of raising the eyebrow and blinking the eyes. This independent aspect of reality is the circumstance of realized response.

Dōgen continues by interjecting that if time is finite ("mountains and seas are destroyed"), then beings (mountains and seas) are finite. Conversely if time is infinite, then beings are infinite. Inferred in the juxtaposition of finite and infinite is their nondual nature. Like "is correct" and "is not correct," they are both true, not true, both true and not true, and neither true nor not true.

The totality of being-time's presencing is the circumstance of each thing's appearance. Being-time (like buddha-nature) is not separate from a thing's being-time or buddha-nature. Hence, when one responds and sees with the Buddha eye, one experiences both the impermanence or temporality of a particular situation and the totality of all situations arising simultaneously within the context of that one thing.

Because there is the particular presencing of being-time, such as mountains and seas, there is also the occasion of realizing the Buddha Way. In *Sansuikyō* (Mountains and Rivers Sūtra), Dōgen writes that mountains and waters are integral to realization's expression: "If [mountains] walking had ever rested, the buddhas and ancestors would never have appeared; if walking were limited, the buddha dharma would never have reached us today."[2] Mountains and rivers can be both the universal and particular aspect of being-time, in this case representing buddha-nature's full enactment. This universal particularity of being-time embodies the action (walking, blinking, or raising eyebrows) of realized response.

Since a being-time holds both universal and particular, its appearance (buddhas and ancestors) as realization is dependent upon the activity of all beings (mountains walking). This is the connection between the beginning of Dōgen's thought above and the conclusion that, for this reason, the "morning star appears," along with the other instances of awakening he cites.

EVERYTHING IS BORN TOGETHER

Imbedded in the logic of this paragraph is Dōgen's teaching that each thing's appearance rebirths the whole world. In other words, the appearance of eyebrows and eyes and mountains and seas are born together. He alludes to this earlier in the text when he writes "we set the self out in array and make that the whole world,"[3] "each of the forms exists as the entire world,"[4] and "each being-time is without exception entire time."[5] Later he tells us that the being-time of those we can see and those we cannot "are all the immediate manifestation of my full exertion"[6] The implications of being-time's finite infinity is that within each particular arising of a dharma position the world is born. Within the context of the morning star's appearance and the other examples given, the world is born or uniquely presencing within the context of each dharma position.

In the fascicle "Yuibutsu Yobutsu" (Only a Buddha and a Buddha) he writes: "An ancient buddha said, 'Mountains, rivers, and the earth are born at the same moment with each person. All buddhas of the past, present, and future are practicing together with each person.'"[7] He explains this as:

> If we look at mountains, rivers, and earth when a person is born, this person's birth does not seem to be bringing forth additional mountains, rivers, and earth on top of the existing ones. Yet, the ancient buddha's words should not be a mistake. How should we understand this? . . . Understand that the ancient buddha teaches that your birth is not separate from mountains, rivers, and earth.[8]

At the moment of the arising of a particular time-being, the world accords itself and makes passage to include this "new" element. Yet, there is nothing "new" happening. The particular unique finite nondual moment reflects its particularity and in a sense changes the whole world. In this way the mountains, rivers, and earth are born with us. In this way, the very personal singular moment of the arising of the mind to practice is also the completed path of attainment with all beings. This finite moment of effort includes the infinity of all buddhas and ancestors. This is the intersection of all being-time as this being-time. It is mountains and seas arising within one blink of an eye, it is a flower being held up, it is a buddha awakening.

Each moment is born with us and includes all activity occurring everywhere, even if we cannot see it. Within this finite infinity, when we die, we are not dead. When we are born, we are not born. From this view, the self is not the self. The self is all being(s), and all being(s) are the self. The self is the form of the mountains. The self is blinking and raising the eyebrows. When we allow the totality of being to presence itself to us and we to it, something special happens. This special moment is just the everyday occurrence of unobstructed response, yet it is a revelation to us. This is the Tathāgata's appearance.

REALIZATION AS EYE-PUPILS APPEARING

Responding skillfully to the world's total functioning is represented by the metaphor of the eye-pupil. Awakened activity is like a pupil's constant adjustment to light and dark. In "Ganzei" (Eye-Pupil) Dōgen teaches:

> Taking up the practice of boundless eons and perfecting it comprises myriads of eye-pupils. . . . This manifesting [of the eye-pupil] and functioning are called "eye-pupil." "Mountains, rivers, and the great earth," just as they are, are the subtle and mysterious nondivisibility of the disclosure of the eye-pupil.[9]

Manifesting and functioning is the continuous practice of all beings and an individual being. The eye-pupil is a specific example of a person's response. The affirmation of our particular abilities unfolds as our daily experience within the structure of formal practice and with our teacher. Dōgen writes, "the essential functioning [of the eye-pupil] is that of testing with blows and shouts."[10] In Dōgen's example cited in "Ganzei" (Eye-Pupil), his teacher, Rujing, delivers "the blows and shouts." In "Uji," Zen master Mazu expresses his understanding as seemingly contradictory statements that function as a test and an answer for Yaoshan. These tests are the direct activity of learning the truth of being-time through the student-teacher dynamic. Dōgen also writes,

> "Testing" is the disclosure of the eye-pupil. It is the manifest-
> ing of the Buddha eye, the living eye-pupil. "Seeing anew" is
> union. This seeing and uniting is like a thunderclap resound-
> ing throughout heaven and earth.[11]

This thunderclap may be as soft as the smile of Mahākāśyapa[12] or as resounding as the ping of a pebble hitting bamboo; each moment is fully realized by the one awakened and the one awakening. Each moment is this moment's birth and expression. It is the passageless-passage of the eye-pupil's expansion and contraction. The transmission between student and teacher is a living eye-pupil, and it is testing.

Mind-to-mind transmission of passageless-passage is dependent upon our practice-verification with a teacher. Dōgen writes in "Gakudō Yōjin-shū" (Guidelines for Studying the Way), "To understand dharma and attain the way can only be the result of studying with a teacher."[13]

Mazu and Yaoshan are verifying the way together. At the time of face-to-face transmission, it is Master Śākyamuni holding up a flower and disciple Mahākāśyapa's smile. This is testing and verification of being-time. Our life tests us continuously. Can we respond by drop-ping our agenda and our need to defend our self-image? When we can, wisdom and compassion come forth and realization is born. Can we include everything? Every moment that we see anew is rejoining the myriad things. It is remembering our humanity, and it is setting the self out in array. We respond by raising an eyebrow or blinking. We respond by not raising an eyebrow and not blinking. Who can say what is correct or not correct? Only the affirmation of the thunderclap of the moment expressed will show us the correct path. This is confirmed by our teacher's testing.

THE TRANSMISSION OF BEING-TIME

Śākyamuni's realization occurred when he understood that the morning star was none other than being-time. Mahākāśyapa awakened with all beings when he acknowledged the flower held aloft by Śākyamuni as an expression of being-time. Their being-time is still present as our being-time.

Furthermore, within the moment of Śākyamuni's awakening is the appearance of a buddha, the appearance of awakening itself, and the appearance of its transmission passage to Mahākāśyapa. Within the moment of an awakened person's raised eyebrow or blink of an eye, mountains and rivers are born, Śākyamuni appears and the transmission of affirmation is possible between master and pupil.

Dōgen references the awakening experiences of our ancestors throughout the Shōbōgenzō as examples of practitioners who embodied being-time. The transmission of being-time, for us, is to be face-to-face with the Buddhist ancestors as being-time's passageless-passage. In that moment all other ancestors come forth and are no longer hidden. Dōgen stresses that, for us, this transmission is not bestowed upon the self but, rather, acknowledged by a living teacher. This is why, as we near the end of "Uji," we are given examples of teachers and students. Dōgen observes in "Menju" (Face-to-Face Transmission):

> Without the face-to-face transmission from the Buddha's face, we are not buddhas. Śākyamuni Buddha's direct meeting with the Venerable [Mahā]kāśyapa is the immediate

transmission. . . . The World-Honored One saw sharing his
seat and sharing his robe with Mahākāśyapa as his lifetime
of Buddha-behavior. The Venerable Mahākāśyapa through
face transmission, mind transmission, body transmission,
and eye transmission, has intimately received the face-to-
face transmission of the World-Honored One; he has served
offerings to, venerated, made prostrations to, and served
homage to Buddha Śākyamuni.[14]

And when that moment of face-to-face transmission occurs:

At the time of bowing formally to Śākyamuni Buddha's face,
the fifty-one buddha ancestors and the Seven Buddhas are
not present side by side or in one line. But it is face-to-face
transmission among all the buddha ancestors at the same
time. If you do not see in just one generation all the masters,
you are not a disciple. If you do not see in just one generation
all the disciples, you are not a master. Masters and disciples
always see one another when transmitting and inheriting
dharma. This is the realization of the way, face-to-face transmission of the ancestral source. Thus, masters and disciples
bring forth the luminous face of the Tathāgata.[15]

A being-time has various aspects: the right-here-and-now, the
interconnected-interpenetrating being-time of all beings-times, its
unobstructed nature and passage. All these aspects exist as the true
dharma eye of being-time and are transmitted through our unfolding
intimacy with all being. Our understanding is verified by both life itself
and within the context of Zen's student-teacher relationship. Realization happens at a particular being-time: a flower held up, the morning
star rising. This moment is also all being's-time's birth. It is the activity
of all buddhas expressed through the present moment. Nothing is left
out, nothing is obstructed or hidden. This is the aspect of being-time as

nonduality, as both finite and infinite. This is a moment's passageless-passage. The verification of our understanding of this dynamic is acknowledged by one who has previously been recognized by his or her teacher as having opened the eye of practice-realization.

The Mind Is a Donkey, the Word Is a Horse

Zen master Guixing of Shexian, a Dharma descendant of Linji and direct Dharma heir of Shoushan, once instructed the assembly of monks:

> For the time being, the mind reaches but the word does not.
>
> For the time being, the word reaches but the mind does not.
>
> For the time being, the mind and word both reach.
>
> For the time being, neither mind nor word reach.

Uji CONTINUES:

Mind and the word are equally being-time. Their reaching and not-reaching alike are being-time. Even when the time of their reaching is not yet over, the time of their not-reaching has arrived. The mind is a donkey, the word a horse, making the horse a word and the donkey mind. "Reaching" is not coming; "not-reaching" is not yet. This is how being-time is.

GUIXING'S TEACHING

As in the earlier text, the lines begin with the phrase "for the time being," indicating this time-being, all time-being, and/or a time-being. Guixing's main instruction is close to a classic tetralemma,[1] which can be understood from a relative as well as an absolute point of view.[2]

From the relative perspective, Guixing may be discussing the modes or stages of attainment and expression. This interpretation can be pretty straightforward. In this moment, our intention or mind[3] is in a state of attainment, but we can't express it. Or we make enlightened response, but we are not aware of it. Or our awareness and our expression both hit the mark. Or finally, we don't get it at all.

Dōgen's commentary on Guixing's teaching points toward an absolute understanding of mind, word, reaching, and not-reaching as all expressions of a moment's nondual totality. In "Shinjin Gakudō" (Body-and-Mind Study of the Way), he combines both aspects (relative and absolute):

> Everyday mind opens the gate of the inner chamber. Because thousands of gates and myriads of doors open and close all at once, it is everyday mind. Now, this boundless sky and entire earth are like unrecognized words, a voice from the deep. Words are all-inclusive, mind is all-inclusive, things are all-inclusive. . . . If you arouse the aspiration for enlightenment, you will move forward on the way of enlightenment. The moment is already here. Do not doubt it in the least.[4]

The state of intention or mind, words, reaching, and not reaching are all part of our everyday mind. Fully investigating our everyday life encompasses dharma gates without end. Since, as Dōgen mentions earlier in "Uji," "each of the forms exist as the entire earth,"[5] we know that thoroughly investigating one thing will illuminate everything.

Language or words are themselves a living entity. As Dōgen instructs, they are all-inclusive and are the sky and the entire earth. Hee-Jin Kim writes that for Dōgen,

Language is as dynamically alive as any living being in the
world. . . . In essence, the interior dynamics of words and
letters amount to neither more nor less than the temporal
dynamicity of existence-time.[6]

Words are dharmas also, and as such, they are being-time. Intention
is being-time; reaching is being-time. Mind is intention both conscious and beyond consciousness. This intention includes our heart's
expression, effort, and the continuous practice of all beings. It is the
moment already here. The word may be understood as how we express
ourselves, and it is also the sūtra of myriad things coming forth. It is
"a voice from the deep." Reaching is the state of actualization and not
reaching may also be understood as being-time expressed. As we open
to the various connotations of each state expressed as mind, word,
reaching, and not reaching, we realize that our experience goes beyond
fixed states of this or that.

Sincere Expression Is in Each Moment

Conventionally, a discussion of how we approach realizing our true
nature will involve separating various aspects of practice such as effort,
expression, or examining goals. Zen master Guixing's four possibilities present the components of a being-time's dharma position and
buddha-nature's actualization. As Dōgen writes in the previous section, "This is time. If it were not time, things would not be so."[7]

The independent aspects of intention, expression, reaching, and
not-reaching cannot be ignored. When we are reaching, there is just
reaching. When we are not-reaching, there is just not-reaching. Each
aspect is a fully expressed being-time. Each moment of mind, speech,
and expression is an actualization of our understanding. Each aspect
is being-time's expression, thus cannot be other than a fully expressed
dharma. The moment of our transformation resides within the time

of the independent aspect of a dharma position. It is in the particular moment of aspiration, expression, reaching, or not-reaching that practice-realization is enacted. We cannot skip over the effort and attention required to attend to each particular moment's requirement.

ONE IS NOT BETTER THAN THE OTHER

Dōgen writes in "Gabyō" (Painted Rice Cakes):

> All buddhas are realization; thus all things are realization.
> Yet, no buddhas or things have the same characteristics. . . .
> Although there are no identical characteristics . . . at the
> moment of your actualization, numerous actualizations
> manifest without hindrance. This is the straightforward
> teaching of the ancestors. Do not use the measure of oneness
> or difference as the criterion of your study. Thus, it is said,
> "To reach one thing is to reach myriad things."[8]

If we deeply investigate the nature of reaching, not-reaching, intention, or words, we will find that as we intimately practice with one situation countless doors and gates will open. The distinct qualities of reaching, not-reaching, mind, and word are all incorporated in a buddha's realization. Each state has different characteristics, yet they do not hinder one another. The various aspects of our effort—intention, exertion, and expression—are all the activity of practice-realization.

We might think as we read Guixing's instructions to the assembly that one or two of the lines are better outcomes than one or two of the others. But Dōgen clearly writes that mind, word, reaching, and not-reaching are all being-time. Each aspect deserves our study. Do not reject one above the other. Within the moment of reaching is the moment of not-reaching, and within not-reaching is the moment of reaching.

A Complete Expression Includes Total Functioning

Dōgen introduces an aspect of passage in this section when he writes, "Even when the time of their reaching is not yet over, the time of their not-reaching has arrived." In "Busshō" (Buddha-Nature), Dōgen writes, "You should know that throughout the twenty-four hours of your day no time passes without its already being come."[9] All possibilities, both reaching and not-reaching, are interpenetrating. Reaching is "not yet over" because it is now; not-reaching "has arrived" as it has already come.

The simultaneity of intention, expression, reaching, or not-reaching is what causes passage. Passage is the nonsequential transformation of each aspect's interpenetrating movement. The being-time of intention fulfilled (reaching) or unfulfilled (not-reaching) is a moment of practice-realization (sincere expression). This expression results from the totality of each moment. If our effort were just expression without intention, then we would be caught without direction. If our effort contains just intention without expression, we would never actualize practice.

The question of incorporating and expressing passage is also addressed in "Busshō" (Buddha-Nature): "A fundamental principle of the Buddha-nature is that it is not invested prior to attaining Buddhahood but incorporated upon attainment of Buddhahood."[10] From this perspective although things are fully present, their appearance only happens at the time of expression. Reaching is reaching upon the actualization of reaching, and not-reaching can only appear within the context of its particular expression. We must make the effort to actualize what is present. Practice and realization are the moment of incorporation and expression of each being-time as it moves from one moment to the next.

THE MIND IS A DONKEY, THE WORD IS A HORSE

Dōgen's use of the donkey and the horse analogy may refer to the kōan "Changqing's Clarification of Understanding."[11]

> Huileng of Changqing studied with Lingyun and asked him, "What is the essential meaning of Buddhadharma?"
>
> Lingyun said, "When the donkey matter has not yet left, the horse matter arrives."[12]

Dōgen uses the image of unfinished donkey business while horse business is arriving several times in the Shōbōgenzō.[13] In almost all cases he is describing how an event's passage has particularity, expressed as donkey or horse, yet is enacted as the moment's totality, expressed as one arriving before the other has left, demonstrating the simultaneity, interpenetration, and immediacy of passage, rather than conceptualizing a moment as sequential transformation.

Gudo Nishijima comments that "Before the donkey business has finished, horse business has arrived" means "one thing happening after another in day-to-day life."[14] As each moment is intimate engagement, there is the simultaneity of other being-times engaging. The non-sequential simultaneity of mutual penetration and continuous practice connects each being-time and all being-time, thereby making passage. The impermanence of each moment flows each moment into the next while still retaining the independent immediacy of this moment's particularity.

The donkey might seem inferior to the horse, but despite their independent characteristics they just follow one after another. The donkey has its function, the horse has its function, and neither obstructs the other.

DRINKING TEA WITH ZHAOZHOU

In a footnote to this section, Waddell and Abe cite the kōan "Zhaozhou's Cup of Tea"[15] to illustrate how we might understand the relationship between reaching and not-reaching. The story goes like this:

> Two monks visited Zhaozhou. He asked one of them: "Have you come [reached] here before?" "I've never come before," the first monk replied. Zhaozhou said: "Have a cup of tea." Then he asked the second monk the same question. "I've come before," he answered. Zhaozhou said: "Have a cup of tea." A senior monk said: "Why did you give them the same response?" Zhaozhou said: "Have a cup of tea."

Dōgen is interested in how we respond, at this time, to the moment. It doesn't matter if you have "reached" this place before. It is just this place now. In "Kajō" (Everyday Activity), Dōgen comments on this kōan:

> "*Here*" is beyond the brain, is beyond the nostrils. . . . Because it springs free from "here," *it has already arrived here* and *it has never been here before. This place is the place where the ineffable exists,* but they discuss it only as *having already arrived* and *never having been before.*[16]

For this reason, arriving here or not arriving here has nothing to do with being offered a cup of tea. We might get distracted by the idea of attainment, as did the senior monk. He thought Zhaozhou should have treated each monk differently based upon their seniority. But Zhaozhou just met each monk at that moment, fully incorporating the moment.

Zhaozhou greets everyone with tea. Each monk has his own before and after, as does Zhaozhou, and at the same time there is just the independent being-time of drinking tea with the master. To equate attainment and tea means clinging to some idea about the meeting that is extra. In this case, to act from this idea is an obstruction of the actualized moment. Having come or not having come is the donkey leaving and the horse arriving at the time of "here."

Reaching is impeded by reaching and not impeded by not-reaching. Not-reaching is impeded by not-reaching and not impeded by reaching. The mind impedes the mind and sees the mind, word impedes word and sees word, impeding impedes itself and sees itself. Impeding impedes impeding—that is time. Although impeding is employed by other dharmas, there has never yet been impeding that impedes another dharma. The entire world, exhaustively, with no thing or time left out, is impeding. I encounter a man. A man encounters a man. I encounter myself. Going forth encounters going forth. If they do not obtain the time, it cannot be thus.

IN THE PREVIOUS SECTION, Dōgen discusses the state of reaching and not-reaching as flowing states of passage illustrated by the metaphor of the donkey leaving and the horse arriving. Here he is concentrating on the independent aspects of reaching, not-reaching, mind, and word. Each state is seen from the point of view of its particularity and how that particularity is defined.

Dōgen's use of the word *impeding* does not have the conventional meaning of "getting in the way of or obstructing something." Counter-intuitively, Dōgen's understanding of impediment is liberation.[1] The logic of this liberation is that through limiting or impeding itself a dharma position is liberated to fully express itself within its independent being-time. Essentially it is limiting itself to itself. If this were not true, a thing, person, event, etc., would be completely nondual and cease to exist as a recognizable particular being-time.[2] If a thing were not impeded it would have no particular characteristics. By saying "reaching is impeded by reaching," "not-reaching is impeded by not-reaching," "mind impedes mind," and "word impedes word," Dōgen is distinguishing and acknowledging that there are the states of reaching, not-reaching, mind, and word. They are different, but do not obstruct each other. Furthermore, these states are each an entrance to realization. What is impeded (an independent state) is the subject of impediment or investigation.

For example, reaching impedes (reveals) reaching. Its revelation is predicated upon its own limiting of itself; otherwise there would be nothing to be considered. This in turn allows the thing itself to "see" itself, thereby seeing into its own true nature resulting in liberation. Reaching revealed is just the thorough investigation of reaching itself by reaching. This deep penetration is the liberation and freedom of the being-time of reaching (or mind, word, not-reaching). In this way, reaching (subject) reaches (verb) reaching (object) becomes the no-self of just this moment expressed as reaching.[3]

IMPEDING IS EXHAUSTIVE PENETRATION

When limited or particularized, a dharma can completely, exhaustively penetrate the nature of that being-time. This is the simultaneity of a moment's independent manifestation as it is also interpenetrating-interconnecting with all being and making passage. In this way, we go deeply into our experience; we do not skip over the top or relegate it as outside of our own sphere. It is through this complete investigation and expression that we are liberated from the delusional self. This inquiry can only happen in the context of a unique being-time, or in our case a particular self-time.

If we completely immerse ourselves in the particularity of a moment, we are fully realizing and including the totality of that moment. If we are always rejecting a moment's arising, in and of itself, by saying, "This thing does not exist; this moment has no substance," we will not realize how things really are. For example, we might constantly want to negate the self as empty of inherent existence. Yet, it is through allowing ourselves to meet ourselves that we liberate ourselves. Dōgen writes in "Genjōkōan" (Manifesting Suchness), "Enlightenment does not destroy man any more than the moon makes a hole on the surface of the water."[4] We do not cease to be recognizable as a particular person at the moment of realization.

From another perspective, the fully expressed independent moment is a moment that allows us to respond unfettered by previous ideas, prejudices, or experiences. It is this independent aspect that frees us to skillfully respond to the present moment regardless of our previous mistakes. When each moment is freely expressed, in and of itself, then buddha-nature is always accessible. Otherwise expressing our true state would be dependent upon and the result of lifetimes "piling up," rather than integrating with what is right now.

Furthermore, if we understand our practice as attaining the absolute, we may encounter the problem of thinking our everyday life is of no consequence. We might believe that our effort is to transcend daily life and enter a rarefied and imagined spiritual state. It is imperative that we understand our everyday life as being-time's complete expression. A bodhisattva's liberation is enacted as the activity of entering the water, entering the mud. This is the impeded or limited state of just this.

IMPEDING SEES ITSELF

Impeding (as an independent dharma position) realizes itself (impedes) and thereby "sees" its true nature. "Impeding impedes itself and sees itself. Impeding impedes impeding—that is time." As mentioned earlier, the noun verbing itself is Dōgen's well-known grammatical technique for expressing the dynamic activity of a dharma position's passage within the context of its own activity, such as "the world worlding the world."

Structuring a sentence in this way creates a situation in which words go beyond pointing to liberation and become an agent of liberation. This happens when we are jarred free from our usual way of understanding subject and object relationships. This phrasing allows us to understand an activity's expression without the self as the center of the activity. The small self's effort is removed, and we are left hanging in the multiplicity of all of reality's passage, not just our individual passage.

Dōgen expresses this methodology of fully investigating the impeded self in his well-known formula for forgetting the self in "Genjōkōan" (Manifesting Suchness):

> To learn the Buddha Way is to learn one's self.
> To learn one's self is to forget one's self.
> To forget one's self is to be confirmed by all dharmas.
> To be confirmed by all dharmas is to cast off one's body and
>   mind and the bodies and minds of others as well.[5]

First the self of no-self is affirmed or recognized as an independent dharma position (impeded), thereby learning the Buddha Way through the self. Then the self of no-self is viewed from the position of mutual identity and interpenetration with all being-time. Having learned the self, one "forgets" the self. At this juncture the self of no-self is both particular (an independent actualized dharma position) and universal (a mutual identity interpenetrating dharma position) and now can be confirmed or actualized as an expressed being-time. This impeded self is both manifesting and responding as independent and interpenetrating simultaneously, which Dōgen calls dropping off body-mind (*shinjin-datsuraku*). This whole process of awakening is predicated upon the impediment or particularity of the self that is no-self. In "Genjōkōan" (Manifesting Suchness), Dōgen finishes this thought with "All traces of enlightenment disappear, and this traceless enlightenment continues without end."[6] This is being-time actualized.

IMPEDING DOES NOT IMPEDE OTHER DHARMAS

Separation and harmony occur when "impeding is employed by other dharmas, [and] there has never yet been impeding that impedes another dharma." This is a rather convoluted way of saying that a dharma's particular aspects, such as being a human being, do not get in the way of any other dharma. These unique causes and conditions arise because of the impeded independent state. Simultaneously there is the state of each thing's interpenetration. Unique characteristics are passed on uniquely through the impeded state, yet at the same time do not obstruct the universal. This being so, the particular aspects of reality don't get in each other's way. Dogs exist, chairs exist, cockroaches exist, clouds exist, and so on, yet all coexist without hindrance.

From the standpoint of no-self, it is when the self-centered aspect of our personality comes forward that we find ourselves caught by duality. Duality or our relative nature is not the problem. Problems arise when we get attached to any one thing. Existence itself is not hindered by all dharmas presencing.

IMPEDING AS MISTAKES

Let us look at the nature of a mistake from the perspective of impeding. Conventionally, when we think about our mistakes, we think they prevent or block access to realization. Therefore, the way to deal with a mistake is to cut it off.

Yet a mistake is also part of a not-mistake. This nonreification of mistakes means that we can, in this moment and the next, do something different. We don't have to run away from unskillful actions; rather we place ourselves in the middle of our life, warts and all, and learn about transformation through our mistakes. Mistakes see mistakes, thereby transforming mistakes, and make passage.

If I have a problem with anger, I cannot ignore my anger. If I try to cut off or push away what I find difficult, that difficulty will continue to plague me. In this case, I must accept, define, or impede anger as anger. I must acknowledge that right now there is anger, my anger. The first step of working with a problem is knowing and accepting that there is a problem.

Atonement or transformation of a problem can only happen through the problem. Dōgen writes in "Kattō" (Twining Vines), "In general, although sacred beings all aim to learn that cutting of roots of the complicated, they do not learn that cutting means cutting the complicated with the complicated. . . ."[7] By acknowledging and thoroughly investigating the problem or complication, we will find the means of transformation.

MEETING SOMEONE

"I encounter a man. A man encounters a man. I encounter myself. Going forth encounters going forth" is just the intimacy of everyday experience. The "I" is an instance of impeding. The "man" is an instance of impeding. The "self" is an instance of impeding. "Encountering" is impeded "going forth."

I meet someone. I am a dharma meeting another dharma. In meeting a person/dharma I meet myself. I meet myself because essentially we are one and the same, although, at the same time, separate. Dōgen writes in "Gabyō" (Painted Rice Cakes), "To reach one thing does not take away its inherit characteristics. . . . To try to make it different is a hindrance. . . . Reaching one thing is reaching myriad things."[8]

Dōgen's "I encounter a man" may refer to a dialogue[9] between San-sheng (Master Enen of Sanshō temple) and Cunjiang (Master Koke) found in his collection of three hundred kōans:

Master Enen of Sanshō temple in the Jin district said: "When I have a chance to meet people, I meet them, but even if I meet them I do not always teach them." Master Koke said: "When I have the chance to meet people, I do not always meet them, but when I meet them I teach them."[10]

This kōan is an example of variations of realized action. Sansheng and Cunjiang say there is meeting and not meeting; there is coming forth and not coming forth. True meeting is meeting the person and not meeting the person. It is no-person meeting no-person.

In meeting a person, Sansheng meets that person without "meeting" them or guiding them. He "goes away." Then there is Cunjiang. His style is different. He gets right down in the student's face. He takes them by the arm, leading them. Is one better than the other? Daido Loori's comment about these styles is "though born the same way, one rolls it in, the other rolls it out."[11] It is "a silver bowl filled with snow."[12] It is "raising the eyebrow, blinking the eye; not raising the eyebrow and not blinking the eye."[13] The Buddha's tongue is one vast teaching rolling it in and rolling it out. Either way, the Dharma is revealed.

Moreover, the mind is the time of the immediately present ultimate Dharma. The word is the time of the key to higher attainment. Reaching is the time of the body of total emancipation. Not-reaching is the time "you are one with this and apart from this." You should attest and affirm thus. You should being-time thus.

DŌGEN, after exploring the importance of how an independent dharma position is defined, now addresses the realized aspect of each state.[1]

We commonly think that bringing forth the mind[2] that has the intention to practice is the beginning of enacting the Buddha Way. Conventionally we refer to this beginning as "awakening our intention." Yet the whole path is present at the time of the arising of the thought of Buddha. Dōgen writes in "Bendōwa" (Wholehearted Practice of the Way), "[Practice] now is also practice in the state of experience; therefore, a beginner's pursuit of the truth is just the whole body of the original state of experience."[3] And in "Gyōji" (Continuous Practice) he says:

> The great Way of the Buddhas and ancestors always consists in these supreme activities: the desire for enlightenment, practice, enlightenment, and nirvāṇa. These four activities are never interrupted in their continuation and never allowed even a single interval between them. This is the perpetuation of the Way through activity between them.[4]

Who or what mind makes the intention to awaken? It is the awakened mind itself. This awakened mind includes the totality of this moment and all beings. Our intention is an expression of the whole world awakening with us. We vow to practice, and this practice is an expression of realized action. Our wisdom comes forth; our compassion is evident.

IMMEDIATE PRESENT, ULTIMATE DHARMA

Since our activity is not a progression from delusion to enlightenment made solely by the independent self, Dōgen defines the first thought of practice as "immediate present ultimate Dharma" or *genjōkōan*: "the presence and perfection of all dharmas as they are in the here-and-now."[5] Hee-Jin Kim further explains the meaning of *genjōkōan*:

> It does not suggest an evolutionary ascent from hidden-ness to manifestation, or from imperfection to perfection, or conversely, an emanational descent from one to many, or from reality to appearance. Rather, things, events, beings are already unmistakably what they truly are; what is more, they are vibrant, transparent, and bright in their as-they-are-ness.[6]

This "mind" of or intention for "immediate present ultimate Dharma" is things-as-they-are-ness, or being-time. When we find ourselves wishing that we could experience our life with equanimity, compassion, and wisdom, we are listening and connecting to what is already present within ourselves and all of life. This inmost request[7] is an expression of each being's continuous practice-realization. Even when we feel most alone, we are still embedded in community. Even when we think our delusion cannot go deeper, we are accompanied by enlightenment. In each moment that we glean a small part of the totality of life, the whole is never missing. As Dōgen Zenji says, "But do not ask me where I'm going / As I travel in this limitless world / Where every step I take is my home."[8]

KEY TO HIGHER ATTAINMENT

For Dōgen, words are not merely signifiers; they are much more. A word or words are "the time of the key to higher attainment" (*kōjō kanrei*).[9] Such a key to higher attainment can also mean a pivot or a vital element necessary for turning. It may be that Dōgen is referring to the pivot of the turning word of the kōans he has cited. It may be that this is a description of the importance of a teacher's guidance. He may be referring to the sūtras taught as an expression of the whole universe.[10]

Higher attainment can be embedded in speech. Dōgen writes in "Bukkōjō-ji" (Beyond Buddha), "If there is no speech, there is no experience of that which is beyond Buddha."[11] Here speech becomes the enactment of the ascendant state of a buddha, only spoken by one who knows.[12] Despite Bodhidharma's apocryphal dictum stating that Zen is "a special transmission outside the scriptures,"[13] Dōgen believes in the power of words. In his fascicle "Mitsugo" (Intimate Language), he tells the story of those who say that the Buddha's true teachings are transmitted only through action rather than words, because words are inadequate. Dōgen comments, "What a pity! The degeneration of the buddha way has resulted from this."[14] He debunks the example of the Buddha holding up a flower and Mahākāśyapa's smile as the only expression of Buddhist truth. He writes:

Upon seeing Mahākāśyapa smile, the World-Honored One said, *I have the treasury of the true dharma eye, the wondrous heart of nirvāṇa. I entrust this to Mahākāśyapa.* Is this statement words or no words? If the World-Honored One avoided words and preferred holding up a flower, he would have held up a flower again and again.[15]

"Uji" itself and all of Dōgen's writings are predicated upon the belief that we can gain understanding through intimate words. These are the words that become a key, a pivot point resulting in higher attainment. Words can open dharma gates resulting in casting off body-mind (*shinjin-datsuraku*). These words do not just represent ideas; words themselves have an important function in our learning and expressing the Dharma. A word, a shout, a series of words, the word of the Buddha, the word as just this—each is a dharma position and, as such, the place of practice-realization. They, too, are being-time. Dōgen's use of language is his own attempt to directly express *genjōkōan*, immediate present ultimate dharma.

REACHING IS TOTAL EMANCIPATION

"Reaching" (*dattai*)[16] refers to total emancipation or dropping off body-mind. Dōgen explains "casting off body-mind" in "Genjōkōan" (Manifesting Suchness) as "To be confirmed by all dharmas is to cast off one's body and mind and the bodies and minds of others as well. All trace of enlightenment disappears, and this traceless enlightenment continues on without end."[17]

Steven Heine describes casting off body-mind as a "genuine self-forgetfulness . . . to 'cast off' all delusory or inauthentic bifurcations between mind/body, self/other, self/non-self as well as between enlightenment/delusion and impermanence/permanence."[18] This state of casting off body-mind is the state of *uji* or total immersion, engagement, and expression of being-time.

ONE WITH THIS AND APART FROM THAT

"Not-reaching" as "one with this and apart from this" is a bodhisattva's willingness to stand in the middle of this messy life. "Being one with this and apart from that"[19] is the same as "being splattered with mud and getting wet with water."[20] This is the bodhisattva's realized activity happening in the midst of daily life. The bodhisattva sits in the middle of all emotions: sorrow, pain, joy, jealousy, anger, and elation—one with this life, yet not caught by its suffering. When we manifest the immediate present of our life, we are that bodhisattva. We are simultaneously one with and apart from.

BAIZHANG'S SECOND VISIT TO MAZU

Being "one with this and apart from that" is associated with a kōan called "Baizhang's Second Visit to Mazu." Here is the kōan as Dōgen presents it in the Eihei Kōroku (Dōgen's Extensive Record):

> Baizhang met again with Mazu. Mazu held up his whisk. Baizhang said, "Do you identify with this function or separate from this function?" Mazu hung the whisk in its place. [Baizhang] stood waiting for a little while. Mazu said, "Later when you are flapping your lips, how will you be of help to people?" Baizhang took the whisk and held it up. Mazu said, "Do you identify with this function or separate from this function?" Baizhang hung the whisk back in its place. Mazu immediately shouted. Later on, Baizhang said to Huangbo, "At that time, when Mazu shouted at me, I was deaf for three days."[21]

Here's another story about a student's awakening experience as he explores what it means to teach the Dharma. Dōgen says of this kind of encounter that they are examples of not being "caught up in the stages from living beings to Buddha . . . transcending the boundaries of delusion and enlightenment."[22] These encounters should not be compared with students "who wait for enlightenment . . . verification . . . and who recognize shadows rather than their true self; or those who abide in intellectual views about their essence, and chase after lumps of dirt, never acting for the sake of others."[23] These encounters are "the direct understanding beyond words."[24]

Practice-realization is not predicated upon stages. Teaching or being helpful is not about holding up the whisk (an indication of a teacher's authority) or hanging up the whisk. Continuous practice is beyond delusion and enlightenment and enacted in "mud and water." The time right now is the time arrived. Nothing is actualized through intellectual interpretation, although intellectual understanding may be important in practice. These last paragraphs of "Uji" return to this theme over and over.

YOU SHOULD BEING-TIME THUS

Our realization is expressed through practice. Practice-realization is the actualization and enactment of being-time. Practice-realization is not the intellectual deconstruction of the concept of being-time. Dōgen makes being-time a verb to emphasize this point. This practice is *genjōkōan*—present ultimate Dharma. The actualized *nikon*, the right now of our life, is our expression of practice-realization. It cannot happen in any other being-time than this being-time. It is the freedom from our past and future: it is right now, unhindered, uncaught. Having reached this place of totally being the self and dropping the self, of entering the mud and water, we respond to all being-time as it arises in this moment both as self and other. We set ourselves out in array, we respond, unhindered, and we are free to play in the field of just this.

We need to investigate the how of this. The investigation itself is practice-realization, intention, present Dharma, reaching and not-reaching, being one with this and apart from this. We engage our investigation with a teacher, embedded in saṅgha as the Buddha Way guides us. Let being-time be the verb of your life. Dōgen writes, "You should being-time thus." We should be guided by being-time and moved by being-time. This has been his whole point. If we ask the right questions, we will crack open the great mystery of our existence.

We have seen above how the respected elders have both spoken. Yet is there not something even further to utter?

We should say:

> Half reaching of mind and word is also being-time.
> Half not-reaching of mind and word is also being-time.

Your investigation must go on like this.

> Letting him raise his eyebrows and blink his eyes
>   is a half being-time.
> Letting him raise his eyebrows and blink his eyes
>   is a "Wrong!" being-time.
> Not letting him raise his eyebrows and blink his eyes
>   is a half being-time.
> Not letting him raise his eyebrows and blink his eyes
>   is a "Wrong!" "Wrong!" being-time.

Such investigations continuing is thoroughgoing practice—reaching here and not reaching there—that is being-time.

DŌGEN ASKS THE QUESTION, "Is there anything more to be said?" Then he reworks Mazu and Guixing's verses. It might be helpful to add Dōgen's response to the verses of Mazu and Guixing.

Mazu said:

> For the time being, the mind reaches but the word does not.
> For the time being, the word reaches but the mind does not.

For the time being, the mind and word both reach.
For the time being, neither mind nor word reach.

Dōgen responds:

Half reaching of mind and word is also being-time.
Half not-reaching of mind and word is also being-time.

Guixing said:

For the time being, I let him raise his eyebrows and blink his eyes.
For the time being, I don't let him raise his eyebrows and blink his eyes.
For the time being, my letting him raise his eyebrows and blink his eyes is correct.
For the time being, my letting him raise his eyebrows and blink his eyes is not correct.

Dōgen responds:

Letting him raise his eyebrows and blink his eyes is a half being-time.
Letting him raise his eyebrows and blink his eyes is a "Wrong!" being-time.
Not letting him raise his eyebrows and blink his eyes is a half being-time.
Not letting him raise his eyebrows and blink his eyes is a "Wrong!" "Wrong!" being-time.[1]

Immediately, two things stand out about how Dōgen restructures the verse. First, Dōgen moves and retranslates the phrase "for the time being" to the end of each sentence as "being-time." By shortening "for the time being" as "being-time" and moving it to the end of the sentence, he emphasizes the central role of *uji* or being-time. There is no ambiguity that "being-time" is the activity of each response. This activity is expressed as the particular need of a hypothetical situation.

Second, Dōgen introduces the variable of half being-time and wrong being-time. He links the two sets of verses with "your investigation must go on like this." The second set of verses is Dōgen's example of how we might continue our investigation.

HALF BEING-TIME

The "half" of reaching or not-reaching is being used to convey the same idea as "partial exhaustive penetration" about which Dōgen writes earlier in "Uji."[2] These examples are real, concrete, individual moments of being-time.[3] Reaching, not-reaching, or half reaching indicate moments of practice.[4] In the time of our sincere effort we will hit the mark and miss the mark; this is things-as-they-are. Dōgen writes in the fascicle "Sanjūshichi Bon Bodai Bunpō" (Thirty-Seven Elements of Bodhi): "Total happening means half-happening. Half-happening means what is happening here and now."[5] Half reaching or not-reaching is about the issues and problems that arise in our daily lives. It is about how we respond to real situations.

When Dōgen writes about half reaching and half not-reaching, he acknowledges that our response may not be completely in accord with the situation (partial or half realization), it is just partial realization. "Just" does not mean things do not matter. It means at this time. After all, "at this time" is the only time we can enact practice. Furthermore, we are always in the state of half reaching and half not-reaching: this is the donkey leaving and the horse arriving. It is the state of being human. What we think or say about reality and how we respond sometimes function and sometimes do not. The confirmation of this function as expressed being-time can only come from each moment's actualization. But even that is too abstract. It always comes back to grounded practice-response based upon our understanding and enactment of connection with others. We don't always know what to do, but we can rely upon remembering our relationship with all beings as a guide.

"WRONG! WRONG! WRONG!"[6]

Dōgen's repeated exclamatory use of "Wrong!" is probably a reference to the kōan "Tianping's Three Wrongs."[7]

> Congyi of Tianping, during his traveling, visited Siming Monastery. He often said, "Don't say that in the present time you can encounter the Buddhadharma. When we look for someone who can, it is impossible to find one." One day Tianping came out of the dharma hall. Abbot Xiyuan Siming called out to him, "Tianping!" Tianping looked up. Xiyuan said, "Wrong." Tianping took a few steps. Again Xiyuan said, "Wrong." Tianping went close to him. Xiyuan said, "Are these two wrongs my wrongs or your wrongs?" Tianping said, "My wrongs, Master." Xiyuan said, "Wrong." Tianping gave up. Xiyuan said, "Senior monastic, stay here for a while, and let us examine these wrongs." Tianping walked away.

Most commentaries[8] criticize Tianping for his pride and attachment to intellectual understanding. All of the wrong-ing was about getting Tianping to drop his intellectual stance and pride. Xiyuan's efforts were to no avail. Don't get caught in trying to figure out who is wrong. If you do that you are just falling into the trap of intellectual investigation. Yuanwu Keqin[9] comments about this case:

> Some say that Tianping didn't understand, and thus was wrong; and some say his not speaking was wrong. But what connection is there? They hardly realize that these two "wrongs" are like stone struck sparks, like flashing light-

ning. . . . If you can travel on the sword's edge, then you will be free in all ways.[10]

Daido Loori adds, "If you can't say a word, then it's time to just shut up and sit. We should finally understand that these three wrongs notwithstanding, from the beginning, nothing whatsoever is lacking."[11] Saying a word or not saying a word; sit zazen. Even if there are three wrongs, there is still "just this being-time."

Knowing something with our mind is not the same as enacting our understanding. Yet knowing with our mind can be helpful. We should not discard intellectual understanding altogether, nor should we be led around by it. Our practice is on the edge of Mañjuśrī's wisdom sword. If we know how to travel that fine edge, we are free from this or that. The two wrongs become sparks from a stone, intimacy's immediate fire, and lightning's flash in the dark night. It is only through engaging our life that we will find our path along the edge.

LEAPING BEYOND HALVES AND WHOLES

Dōgen writes earlier in "Uji" about the "sharp, vital quick," the *kappatsupatchi* of dharmas.[12] Our life is ideally an expression of a keen discernment and a dynamic vitality that respond to each situation we encounter. This is only achieved when we go deeply into each moment. Going into a moment is not mindfulness practice; rather, it is zazen. It is the activity of embodying a moment's passage. We are not caught by our situation, and we are not outside our situation. Our situation swallows up all that has come before and spits out a response. What has come before is not a Western psychological reenactment of our mistakes or neurotic tendencies; it is the totality of our being-time incorporated into the present moment.

Spitting out is a fish leaping clear of the water; it is being one with all being-time and individuating as being-time. The synthesis of being-time, or arraying oneself, includes both and goes beyond both. Our response has to incorporate the whole and then just leap responding to what is. This is to leap out of or to leap into oneself or itself. This act of leaping or going beyond is letting go of the dichotomies of this or that. Understanding leaping clear involves asking "leaping clear of what?"

"Uji" helps us answer this question by guiding us up to the point of leaping. Yet, we cannot just leap off any old cliff. We must leap off the cliff of intellectual grasping for our original face and into the vast ocean of the Buddha Way. We incorporate our investigation of the particular and the universal as they exist in accord and mutual penetration. If we think our particular life is delusion and the universal is realization, then we have a problem. Yet even if we know that the particular as the whole is "it," we might still have a problem. Do we raise an eyebrow or wink? Is this a half understanding or a whole? We don't have to worry about halves and wholes as long as we do our best to fully engage in our life as both an individual and as one among the many beings practicing the continuous activity of worlding the world.

When we go to the zendo to sit zazen and we have the experience of complete integration with our surroundings, where does our individual self go? When we hear the bell, we stop sitting, and stand by our seat. Where has the absolute gone? When we leave the zendo and clean the temple, which is better? Cleaning or sitting? Each activity is just the appropriate response to the situation. We hear the signal to go to the zendo, and we go to the zendo. We hear the bell, and we stand by our seat. We are given cleaning jobs, and we clean the temple.

When we follow the schedule, it helps us to understand the activity of "things just as they are." When we resist the schedule, we get to investigate the nature of our aversion. We don't deny our problems, and we still show up. We listen to life with every pore of our body. We listen and hear the voice of the other as well as the self. To leap clear is to avoid getting caught. To leap clear is to recognize that we have likes and dislikes and they do not obstruct setting the self out in array.

Dōgen writes in "Kembutsu" (Seeing the Buddha) that when we hear that each form is Buddha, we think that in order to be Buddha each form should be understood as no-form. We want to negate the form aspect of our lives and immediately experience nonduality. But it is through the form realm or, as Dōgen says, our half being-time that we enter practice. Dōgen quotes Fayan, who says, "If you see that all forms are beyond forms, you don't see the Tathāgata."[13] Dōgen comments on this:

> These words by Fayan are the utmost statement. . . . Accept his words with trust and practice. See thoroughly that all forms are Tathāgata forms and not beyond forms. See the Buddha in this way, make up your mind, realize trust, and maintain these words. . . . Thus, keep seeing and hearing these words with your ears and eyes. Have the words drop away in your body, mind, bones and marrow. . . . Do not think your own words and actions cannot awaken your own eye. . . . In this way, there is a single path to study. No forms are beyond forms, beyond forms are all forms.[14]

Clearly we should not dismiss the activities of our everyday life as something to be transcended. Our everyday life is the dharma gate of practice-realization. Where else will our practice be enacted?

Your Investigation Must Go On like This

We must keep trying to place our understanding in the realm of a buddha's activity as our everyday life. A buddha's field is formal practice with a teacher, and it is going to work and shopping for groceries. We cannot understand practice unless we practice, and then we don't need to worry about realization. Practice is intimately interacting with life. From a traditional Buddhist view, we cannot practice without a teacher, a sangha, and the Dharma. Our practice is embedded in community and communion with all beings. This is actualized being-time.

First, our practice must be established within this context. Once we have found a teacher and a saṅgha, we stay put and settle into our investigation of self. We must have a feedback system. We cannot discern on our own if our understanding is correct.

Dōgen writes in "Bendōwa" (Wholehearted Practice of the Way):

> Clearly, the Buddha-Dharma is never known with the intellectual understanding that we ourselves are just buddha. . . . Solely and directly, from our first meeting with a good counselor, we should ask the standards of good practice, and we should single-mindedly pursue the truth by sitting in Zazen, without allowing a single recognition or half an understanding to remain in our minds. Then the subtle method of the Buddha-Dharma will not be [practiced] in vain.[15]

In this quotation, we are given five necessary components for practice: (1) going beyond our intellectual understanding, (2) finding a good teacher, (3) following the practice standards, (4) sitting zazen, and (5) not judging our effort.

In searching for authentic practice Dōgen left his home in Japan and made the dangerous journey to China. Through his unwavering effort, discerning mind, and openness, he found what he was missing. It is in China that he encountered his root teacher, Rujing. It is here he discovered the importance of practice integrated into daily life, through his interactions with the *tenzo* monk Lu.[16]

As Dōgen ends "Uji," he encourages us by using the example of other Zen masters and their students as an illustration of understanding. The last line of the text states that it is through the investigation of "reaching here and not reaching there" that we will enact practice. This is the dharma gate of being-time. Ultimately it is being-time itself that verifies Dōgen's actualization and ours.

On the same day Dōgen completed writing "Uji," he lectured on the meaning of Buddha's robe (in *Kesa Kudoku*, Power of the Robe).[17] How fitting that on that day, he sat in front of his students and spoke of his deep faith and commitment to following the Buddha Way. At heart, "Uji" is not an intellectual thesis on the nature of being and time; it is an impassioned exploration of the deepest aspects of the spiritual path.

At the end of *Kesa Kudoku* (Power of the Robe)—a long text on the history, meaning, construction, and care of the ordination robe— Dōgen offers a personal anecdote. He writes,

> When I was in Song China . . . at the beginning of zazen in the morning, . . . [the monks] would hold up their kaṣāyas,[18] place them on their heads, and chant the robe verse quietly with palms together. This was the first time I had seen the putting on of the kashaya in this way and I rejoiced, tears wetting the collar of my robe.[19]
>
> > How great, the robe of liberation,
> > A formless field of merit.
> > Wrapping ourselves in Buddha's teaching,
> > We free all living beings.[20]

Dōgen continues,

> At that time, there arose in me a feeling I had never before experienced. [My] body was overwhelmed with joy. The tears of gratitude secretly fell and soaked my lapels. . . . Then I secretly vowed: "One way or another, unworthy though I am, I will become a rightful successor to the Buddha-Dharma. I will receive the authentic transmission of the right Dharma and, out of compassion for living beings in my homeland I will cause them to see and to hear . . . the Dharma. . . ."[21]

In the midst of his emotions, his feelings of inadequacy, in his joy and gratitude, he vows to make a sincere effort to enact the Buddhadharma.

"Uji" is one of Dōgen's most revered and difficult texts. In it, he attempts to clearly elucidate the meaning of practice within the context of the totality of the world's expression. Reaching or not-reaching, blinking an eye, reciting the robe verse, driving to work, caring for a parent, or weeding the garden—in every activity, we transmit and receive the Buddhadharma. Everything recites the sūtra of *uji*, in the midst of joy and gratitude, grief and pain. Heeding the words of Old Buddha Dōgen, we have faith that nothing is missing; practice-realization is not apart from us.

Notes

---◆

EPIGRAPH

1. Stephen Heine, *The Zen Poetry of Dōgen: Verses from the Mountain of Eternal Peace* (Boston: Charles Tuttle, 1997), 97.

PREFACE

1. Dainin Katagiri, *Each Moment Is the Universe: Zen and the Way of Being Time* (Boston: Shambhala Publications, 2007).
2. Norman Waddell and Masao Abe, trans., "Uji," *The Heart of Dōgen's Shōbōgenzō* (New York: State University of New York Press, 2002), 53.
3. Waddell and Abe, "Uji," *The Heart of Dōgen's Shōbōgenzō*, 53.
4. Gudo Nishijima and Chodo Cross, trans., "Uji, Existence-Time," *Master Dōgen's Shōbōgenzō* (Woods Hole, MA: Windbell, 1994), bk. 1, 113.
5. Kazuaki Tanahashi, ed., "The Time-Being, Uji," *Moon in a Dewdrop: Writings of Zen Master Dōgen* (San Francisco: North Point Press, 1985), 79.
6. Waddell and Abe, "Uji," *The Heart of Dōgen's Shōbōgenzō*, 49.

INTRODUCTION

1. There are many short biographies of Dōgen available. Two sources are: Kazuaki Tanahashi, ed., *Moon in a Dewdrop: Writings of Zen Master Dōgen*, 3–25; and Hee-Jin Kim, *Eihei Dōgen: Mystical Realist* (Somerville, MA: Wisdom Publications, 2004), 14-49. Kim's essay is also reprinted in Shohaku Okumura, *Realizing Genjokoan: The Key to Dōgen's Shōbōgenzō* (Somerville, MA: Wisdom Publications, 2010), 211–61.
2. This has been particularly true of the Critical Buddhism movement. This movement as it pertains to Dōgen is explored in Steve Heine's chapter "Critical Buddhism and Dōgen's *Shōbōgenzō*: The Debate over the 75-Fascicle and 12-Fascicle Texts," in *Pruning the Bodhi Tree: The Storm over Critical Buddhism,* ed. Jamie Hubbard and Paul Swanson (Honolulu: University of Hawaii Press, 1997), 251–85.
3. I am indebted to Taigen Leighton, who pointed this out to me after he had read an early version of one of the chapters of my book. For this reason, I return to this topic throughout the book.

4. Nishijima and Cross, trans., "Shoaku-makusa, Not Doing Wrongs," *Master Dōgen's Shōbōgenzō*, bk. 1, 99.
5. William Bodiford, trans., "Treasury of the Eye of the True Dharma, Book 31 Not Doing Evils (*Shoaku* makusa)," *Sōtō Zen Journal Dharma Eye: News of Sōtō Zen Buddhism Teachings and Practice*, no. 11 (December 2002), 22.
6. Nishijima and Cross, "Shoaku-makusa, Not Doing Wrongs," *Master Dōgen's Shōbōgenzō*, bk. 1, 102.
7. Waddell and Abe, "Uji," *The Heart of Dōgen's Shōbōgenzō*, 48.
8. Waddell and Abe, "Uji," *The Heart of Dōgen's Shōbōgenzō*, 48.
9. Waddell and Abe, "Uji," *The Heart of Dōgen's Shōbōgenzō*, 55.
10. Tanahashi, "Guidelines for Studying the Way, Gakudō Yōjin-shū," *Moon in a Dewdrop: Writings of Zen Master Dōgen*, 38.
11. Heine, *The Zen Poetry of Dōgen: Verses from the Mountain of Eternal Peace*, 103.
12. Taigen Leighton writes about zazen as ritual: "The point is to enact the meaning of the teachings in actualized practice, and the whole praxis, including meditation, may thus be viewed as ritual, ceremonial expression of the teaching, rather than as a means to discover and attain some understanding of it. Therefore, the strong emphasis in much of this approach to Zen training is the mindful and dedicated expression of meditative awareness in everyday activity." "Zazen as Enactment Ritual," *Zen Questions: Zazen, Dōgen and the Spirit of Creative Inquiry* (Boston: Wisdom Publications, 2011), 37.
13. Shohaku Okumura and Taigen Leighton, *The Wholehearted Way: A Translation of Eihei Dōgen's Bendōwa* (North Clarendon, VT: Tuttle Publishing, 1997), 24.
14. Nishijima and Cross, "Jinzū," *Master Dōgen's Shōbōgenzō*, bk. 1, 75.
15. Waddell and Abe, "Fukanzazengi," *The Heart of Dōgen's Shōbōgenzō*, 3–4.
16. Tanahashi, "Guidelines for Studying the Way, Gakudō Yōjin-shū," *Moon in a Dewdrop: Writings of Zen Master Dōgen*, 38.
17. Nishijima and Cross, "Menju: Face-to-Face Transmission," *Master Dōgen's Shōbōgenzō*, bk. 3, 164.
18. Nishijima and Cross, "Menju: Face-to-Face Transmission," *Master Dōgen's Shōbōgenzō*, bk. 3, 164.
19. Hee-Jin Kim, *Dōgen on Meditation and Thinking: A Reflection on His View of Zen* (Albany: State University of New York Press, 2007), 123.
20. A phrase like "fences, walls, tiles, and pebbles" is shorthand for any concrete thing.

CHAPTER 1: *UJI* IS BEING-TIME

1. For a discussion of the pros and cons of existence v. being, see Rein Raud's "The Existential Moment: Rereading Dōgen's Theory of Time," in *Philosophy East & West* 62, no. 2 (April 2012): 158–59.
2. Hee-Jin Kim, *Dōgen on Meditation and Thinking: A Reflection on his View of Zen*, 70.

3. Other translations for "old" are "eternal," "ancient," or "the old buddhas say."
4. Waddell and Abe, "Uji," *The Heart of Dōgen's Shōbōgenzō*, 48. An alternate translation appears in Nishijima and Cross, *Master Dōgen's Shōbōgenzō*, bk. 1, 109–10.
5. Kaz Tanahashi in his translation of "The Time-Being, Uji" in *Moon in a Dewdrop: Writings of Zen Master Dōgen*, 246, n2, translates the source of these opening two lines, "Yaoshan Weiyan said: 'If you want to know human endeavors, then purify this noble form, hold a jar, and carry a monk's bowl. If you try to escape from falling into the lower realms, first of all you should not give up these practices. It is not easy. You should stand on the highest peak and go to the bottom of the deepest ocean. This is not easy practice, but you will have some realization.'" Yaoshan Hongdao (Yaoshan's posthumous name) appears later in "Uji" when his meeting with Mazu is recounted.
6. I owe this insight to Norman Fisher.
7. Waddell and Abe, "Uji," *The Heart of Dōgen's Shōbōgenzō*, 48, n2.
8. Nishijima and Cross, "Hotsu-bodaishin, Establishment of the Bodhi-mind," *Master Dōgen's Shōbōgenzō*, bk. 3, 268.
9. Nishijima and Cross, "Genjō-kōan, The Realized Universe," *Master Dōgen's Shōbōgenzō*, bk. 1, 34.
10. Huayan (also called Hua-yen) is a school of Buddhism established in Tang-dynasty China based upon teachings in the *Avataṃsaka Sūtra*. Its influence spread to all East Asian schools of Buddhism.
11. Nishijima and Cross, "Zenki, All Functions," *Master Dōgen's Shōbōgenzō*, bk. 2, 286.
12. Tanahashi, "The Time-Being, Uji," *Moon in the Dewdrop: Writings of Zen Master Dōgen*, 77.
13. Hee-Jin Kim, trans., "Gyōji, Activity-unremitting," *Flowers of Emptiness: Selections from Dōgen's Shōbōgenzō*, Studies in Asian Thought and Religion, vol. 2 (Lewiston/Queenston: The Edwin Mellen Press 1985), 192. In Kim's footnote addressing the meaning of the title, he writes *gyōji* denotes "not only spiritual discipline in the ordinary sense but the universal dynamics inherent in all reality," 197, n1.
14. Francis Dojun Cook, "Gyōji Continuous Practice," *How to Raise an Ox: Zen Practice as Taught in Master Dōgen's Shōbōgenzō* (Los Angeles, CA: Center Publications, 1978), 176.
15. Masao Abe, *A Study of Dōgen: His Philosophy and Religion* (Albany: State University of New York Press, 1992), 84. Abe translates *kyōryaku* as "passageless-passage" instead of the more typical "passage."
16. Kazuaki Tanahashi, trans., "Kai'in Zemmai, Ocean Mudra Samadhi," *Treasury of the True Dharma Eye: Zen Master Dōgen's Shōbō Genzō* (Boston: Shambhala, 2010), vol. 1, 385.
17. Waddell and Abe, "Uji," *The Heart of Dōgen's Shōbōgenzō*, 51, n18.
18. Hee-Jin Kim, *Dōgen on Meditation and Thinking: A Reflection on His View of Zen*, 3.

19. Nishijima and Cross, "Sesshin-sesshō, Expounding the Mind & Expounding the Nature," *Master Dōgen's Shōbōgenzō*, bk. 3, 55.
20. See Nishijima and Cross, "Juppō, The Ten Directions," *Master Dōgen's Shōbō-genzō*, bk. 3, 189. Also in "Bukkyō, The Buddha's Teaching" Dōgen writes, "The sands of the Ganges as the Buddha's teachings are a staff and a fist." Nishijima and Cross, "Bukkyō, The Buddha's Teaching," *Master Dōgen's Shōbōgenzō*, bk. 2, 66.

    Examples of Dōgen's comments on the staff, whisk, pillars, and lanterns are: "As regards the concrete situation of succession . . . and a certification of succes-sion . . . some receive . . . a staff . . . some a whisk," Nishijima and Cross, "Shisho, The Certificate of Succession," *Master Dōgen's Shōbōgenzō*, bk. 1, 191; "There are outdoor pillars and stone lanterns in great realization," Nishijima and Cross, "Daigo, Great Realization," *Master Dōgen's Shōbōgenzō*, bk. 2, 86; and "Because they are the ten directions, one direction, this direction, [my] own direction, and the present direction, they are the direction of the eyes, the direction of the fist, the direction of an outdoor pillar, and the direction of a stone lantern," Nishijima and Cross, "Juppō, The Ten Directions," *Master Dōgen's Shōbōgenzō*, bk. 3, 189.
21. Tanahashi, "On the Endeavor of the Way, Bendō-wa," *Moon in a Dewdrop: Writings of Zen Master Dōgen*, 152.

CHAPTER 2: THINGS JUST AS THEY ARE

1. *"Arutoki* for 'there is a time' (or 'sometimes,' 'once,' 'at a certain time,' etc.) . . . are now rendered by Dōgen as *u-ji* or *yū-ji*: *u* ('to be,' 'to have') and *ji* ('time')," Kim, "Uji, Existence-time," *Flowers of Emptiness: Selections from Dōgen's Shōbōgenzō*, 230, n5.

CHAPTER 3: TIME'S GLORIOUS GOLDEN RADIANCE

1. In Japan the monastic day is divided into twelve hours: 10 p.m.–2 a.m. is consid-ered midnight, 2 a.m.–6 a.m. is late night, 6 a.m.–10 a.m. is morning, 10 a.m.–2 p.m. is midday, 2 p.m.–6 p.m. is afternoon, and 6 p.m.–10 p.m. is evening. From Narasaki Tsugen, *Practices at a Zen Monastery* (Nīhama, Japan: Zuiōji Senmon Sōdō, 2011), 150. This system of time (*jūni ji*) is East Asian. The actual duration of each period of time varies depending upon the time of sunrise or sunset. The twelve hours is also a reference to the mundane or secular aspects of life. From Tanahashi, "Glossary: twelve hours," *Moon in a Dewdrop: Writings of Zen Mas-ter Dōgen,* 346.
2. Nishijima and Cross, "Kōmyō, Brightness," *Master Dōgen's Shōbōgenzō*, bk. 2, 241. The hundred weeds refers to myriad "concrete things," 241, n33.
3. Tanahashi, "Radiant Light." *Treasury of the True Eye*, vol. 1, 416.
4. Tanahashi, "Refrain from Unwholesome Action," *Treasury of the True Dharma Eye: Zen Master Dōgen's Shōbō Genzō*, vol. 1, 96.

5. Tanahashi, "On the Endeavor of the Way," *Treasury of the True Dharma Eye: Zen Master Dōgen's Shōbō Genzō*, vol. 1, 6.

CHAPTER 4: PRESENT DOUBT

1. Stepping off the hundred-foot pole refers to letting go of our attachments and presencing oneself with all being-time. In *Zuimonki* Dōgen writes, "An ancient master said, 'At the top of a hundred foot pole, advance one step further.' This means you should have the attitude of someone who, at the top of a hundred foot pole, lets go of both hands and feet . . ." Okumura, trans., *Shōbōgenzō-zuimonki: Sayings of Eihei Dōgen Zenji recorded by Koun Ejō* (Tokyo, Japan: Sōtō-shu Shumucho, 2004), 191.
2. Philip Yampolsky, trans., *The Zen Master Hakuin: Selected Writings* (New York: Columbia University Press, 1971), 144.
3. Shunryū Suzuki Roshi unpublished lecture transcripts, "Shōsan Ceremony Tassajara Lecture B" (San Francisco: San Francisco Zen Center), April 23, 1968, SR-68-04-23-BV, p. 12.

CHAPTER 5: EMBODYING THE WORLD

1. Tanahashi, "Only a Buddha and a Buddha," *Treasury of the True Dharma Eye: Zen Master Dōgen's Shōbō Genzō*, vol. 2, 880.
2. Kim, "Uji, Existence-time," *Flowers of Emptiness: Selections from Dōgen's Shōbō-genzō*, 224. Kim has a completely different translation of this line in *Eihei Dōgen: Mystical Realist*: "You should examine the fact that myself unfolds itself and makes the entire universe of it *(ware o hairetsu shi-okite jinkai to seri)*, and that all things and events of this entire universe are temporal particularities." Hee-Jin Kim, *Eihei Dōgen Mystical Realist* (Boston: Wisdom Publications, 2004), 151. Kim goes on to point out that Dōgen is not talking about an abstract self or selfish self. He writes, "Quite obviously, my self was not merely the psychophysical ego but that self which was one with the world—both the self and the world were the self expressions of Buddha-nature." Kim, *Eihei Dōgen Mystical Realist*, 151.
3. Kim, *Flowers of Emptiness: Selections from Dōgen's Shōbōgenzō*, 230, n8: "The original *ware*, translated here as 'self,' has two different interpretations; one takes it to mean 'time' . . . , the other to mean 'self'. . . ."
4. The question of effort in practice is an important one. Scholar Joan Stambaugh points out that while Dōgen does not specifically address the question of effort in "Uji," "The self set out in array in sustained exertion is a synonym for *uji*, and is, so to speak, a meeting-place or confluence for the presencing of all things in a total situation." Joan Stambaugh, *Impermanence Is Buddha-Nature: Dōgen's Understanding of Temporality* (Honolulu: University of Hawaii Press, 1990), 28. We often talk of our own effort, but our effort is only a portion of the sustained effort of all being. Our effort is supported by and aided by the effort *(gyōji/*

continuous practice) of each and every thing in this world. Removing the pronoun from the sentence "we set the self out in array and make the world" and
making it read "the self sets the self out in array and makes the world" is closer
to this actualized continuous effort of the world making the world. The self
becomes synonymous with the whole world.

5. Waddell and Abe, "Genjōkōan (Manifesting Suchness)," *The Heart of Dōgen's
Shōbōgenzō*, 40.

6. You may ask: How do we know the self is confirmed? I think this is a tricky
thing. If we want some sign of affirmation, isn't that just the self carrying itself
forward? Who is it that wants to know? On the other hand, it is not unreasonable
to want to know if you are on the right track. That is why the student-teacher
relationship is so important.

7. There are the three pure precepts: refraining from unskillful actions, practicing
all that is skillful, and sustaining all beings. There are the ten prohibitory precepts: to resolve not to kill, but to cherish all life; to resolve not to steal, but to
only take what is freely given; to resolve not to misuse sexuality, but to remain
faithful in relationships; to resolve not to lie, but to communicate the truth; to
resolve not to sell or use intoxicants that cause delusion, but to polish clarity; to
resolve not to dwell on the mistakes of others, but to create wisdom from ignorance; to resolve not to praise oneself at the expense of others, but to maintain
modesty; to resolve not to withhold material aid, but to share understanding; to
resolve not to harbor ill will, but to live in equanimity; and to resolve to uphold
the Three Treasures: Buddha, Dharma, and Saṅgha (community). There are
various wordings of the precepts, but they all list the ten basic prohibitions: not
killing, stealing, lying, misusing sexuality, engaging in intoxication, dwelling
on others' mistakes, praising self over others, harboring ill will, withholding the
teachings, abusing Buddha, Dharma, or Saṅgha.

8. Kim writes in reference to this sentence, "Here Dōgen uses four Chinese
ideograms, dō ('same'), hotsu ('to awaken'), ji ('time'), and shin ('mind'), and
arranges them as dō-ji hos-shin and dō-shin hotsu-ji. Time, mind, awakening,
and sameness are thus intertwined with one another to suggest the simultaneous
awakening of the self and the world." Kim, "Uji, Existence-time," *Flowers of
Emptiness*, 230, n10.

9. Kim, "Busshō: The Buddha-nature," *Flowers of Emptiness: Selections from
Dōgen's Shōbōgenzō*, 71. Brackets in original text.

10. Tanahashi, "On the Endeavor of the Way, Bendō-wa," *Moon in a Dewdrop: Writings of Zen Master Dōgen*, 146.

11. Leighton and Okumura, trans., *Dōgen's Extensive Record: A Translation of the
Eihei Kōroku* (Boston: Wisdom Publications), 521. Brackets in the original text.

CHAPTER 6: THE ONE HUNDRED GRASSES EXIST

1. Nishijima and Cross, "Genjō-kōan," *Master Dōgen's Shōbōgenzō*, bk. 1, 34.
2. Dainin Katagiri, *Each Moment Is the Universe: Zen and the Way of Being Time*
(Boston: Shambhala, 2007), 100.

3. Waddell and Abe, "Genjōkōan (Manifesting Suchness)," *The Heart of Dōgen's Shōbōgenzō*, 44.

4. The Huayan School's vision is vast and complicated in the way it describes the nature of reality. Of that vast vision two concepts are most germane to our investigation: mutual identity and mutual interpenetration. Hee-Jin Kim discusses this topic in *Eihei Dōgen Mystical Realist*, 145–47, as does Garman Chang in *The Buddhist Teachings of Totality: The Philosophy of Hwa Yen Buddhism* (University Park: Pennsylvania State University Press, 1977), 136–39. Other good sources for reading about Huayan philosophy are: Francis H. Cook, *Hua-Yen Buddhism: The Jewel Net of Indra* (University Park: Pennsylvania State University Press, 1977) and "Entry into the Inconceivable: An Introduction to Hua-Yen Buddhism," *Classics of Buddhism and Zen: The Collected Translations of Thomas Cleary*, vol. 1 (Boston: Shambhala Publications, 2002). Variations on spelling of this school are Hwa Yen, Huayan, Hua-yen, and Hua-yan, and in Japan it is called the Kegon School.

5. The definition of these terms and to what they apply are not uniform over all Buddhist schools. But, for the Huayan School, Zen, and Dōgen, the understanding that everything is impermanence applies.

6. Fazang (643–712) is the third patriarch of the Huayan School in China.

7. Francis H. Cook, *Hua-Yen Buddhism: The Jewel Net of Indra* (University Park: Pennsylvania State University Press, 1977), 77. Brackets in original text.

8. Tanahashi, "Dharma Blossoms Turn Dharma Blossoms," *Treasury of the True Dharma Eye: Zen Master Dōgen's Shōbō Genzō*, vol. 1, 186.

9. Waddell and Abe, "Uji," *The Heart of Dōgen's Shōbōgenzō*, 49.

10. "The 'mind here and now is Buddha' is living and dying, coming and going." Nishijima and Cross, "Soku-shin-ze-butsu, Mind Here and Now Is Buddha," *Master Dōgen's Shōbōgenzō*, bk. 1, 54.

11. "Living and dying, coming and going, are the real human body . . . to clarify the real body . . . may truly be the one great matter." Nishijima and Cross, "Shoaku-makusa, Not Doing Wrongs," *Master Dōgen's Shōbōgenzō*, bk. 1, 107–8.

12. "Remember, the instruction of the buddhas . . . [and] of Dharma preaching are each limitlessly establishing the teaching and limitlessly abiding in place. Do not look for the limits of their coming and going. . . . Thus, the planting of arrowroot and wisteria, and the entanglement of arrowroot and wisteria, are the nature and form of the supreme truth of bodhi." Nishijima and Cross, "Muchū-setsumu, Preaching a Dream in a Dream," *Master Dōgen's Shōbōgenzō*, bk. 2, 261. Arrowroot and wisteria mean the complications of the current situation.

13. "*Buddhas together* receive the Dharma for the benefit of *buddhas together*. On this basis living-and-dying and coming-and-going exist." Nishijima and Cross, "Shohō-jissō, All Dharmas Are Real Form," *Master Dōgen's Shōbōgenzō*, bk. 3, 82. Italics in original text.

14. Carl Bielefeldt, trans., "Treasury of the Eye of the True Buddha, Book 42, Talking of the Mind, Talking of the Nature, Sesshin Sesshō," *Sōtō Zen Journal Dharma Eye: News of Sōtō Zen Buddhism: Teaching and Practice*. no. 16 (September 2005), 16.

15. Nishijima and Cross, "Shoaku-makusa, Not Doing Wrongs," *Master Dōgen's Shōbōgenzō*, bk. 1, 107.
16. Katagiri, *Each Moment Is the Universe: Zen and the Way of Being Time*, 99.
17. Cook, *Hua-Yen Buddhism: The Jewel Net of Indra*, 77.
18. In Nishijima and Cross's translation of "Uji," their footnote states the phrase translated here as "field of suchness" is *inmo no denchi*. In English *denchi* means a specific place and *inmo* refers to reality itself. Nishijima and Cross, "Uji, Existence-Time," *Master Dōgen's Shōbōgenzō*, bk. 1, 110, n11. See also Nishijima and Cross, "Inmo, It," *Master Dōgen's Shōbōgenzō*, bk. 2, 119, opening comments.
19. Nishijima and Cross, "Shin-fukatoku, Mind Cannot Be Grasped," *Master Dōgen's Shōbōgenzō*, bk. 1, 230.
20. Katagiri, *Each Moment Is the Universe: Zen and the Way of Being Time*, 101.
21. Katagiri, *Each Moment Is the Universe: Zen and the Way of Being Time*, 102

CHAPTER 7: THE ONE HUNDRED GRASSES ARE TIME

1. Chang, *The Buddhist Teaching of Totality: The Philosophy of Hwa Yen Buddhism*, 160. Brackets in original text.
2. Okumura, *Realizing Genjokoan: The Key to Dōgen's Shōbōgenzō* (Somerville, MA: Wisdom Publications, 2010), 120.
3. Nishijima and Cross, "Genjō-kōan, The Realized Universe," *Master Dōgen's Shōbōgenzō*, bk. 1, 33.

CHAPTER 8: AM I A BUDDHA OR A DEMON?

1. This kind of thinking can be extremely harmful if we consider that enlightenment is a state achieved. An enlightened response must include the time of being. This means enlightenment is a response to what is arising in the moment, not a static state achieved by an individual. To think an individual achieves realization divorced from the totality of all being may result in immoral and unethical behavior. The person who "is enlightened" may think they are somehow above or beyond temporal or causal conditions.
2. Steven Heine has an interesting take on this journey. He writes that the delusional practitioner erroneously thinks attainment of the vermilion palace will be a place that shields one from the difficulties of life. This highlights one of the ways that we, as practitioners, avoid addressing the difficulties of taking responsibility for our unskillful actions. We hide in practice instead of being transformed by practice. It is, Heine writes, "a remote pinnacle from which he could idly oversee the landscape, feeling secure and triumphant, without having to labor through the task of making his way in the 'mud and water,' symbolic of the bodhisattva's compassionate vow to save all sentient beings. The palace symbolizes all the idle hopes and expectations which existentially fear or reject and ontologically deny through self-fixation here-and-now activity. Obsessed

with the fabricated and romanticized future represented by the grandiose palace, which may or may not exist or ever be reached, the past is considered to have vanished, and the present is overlooked or discounted so that the separation between self and mountain-river is as great as between heaven and earth." Steven Heine, *Existential and Ontological Dimensions of Time in Heidegger and Dōgen* (Albany: State University of New York Press, 1985), 53.

3. Heine, *Existential and Ontological Dimensions of Time in Heidegger and Dōgen*, 53.

4. "In general, although sacred beings all aim to learn the cutting of the roots of the complicated, they do not learn that cutting means cutting the complicated with the complicated, and they do not know that the complicated is entwined with the complicated." Nishijima and Cross, "Kattō, The Complicated," *Master Dōgen's Shōbōgenzō*, bk. 3, 35–36.

CHAPTER 10: WHOSE TIME IS IT ANYWAY?

1. Waddell and Abe, "Uji," *The Heart of Dōgen's Shōbōgenzō*, 50.

2. Tanahashi, "The Moon," *Treasury of the True Dharma Eye: Zen Master Dōgen's Shōbō Genzō*, vol. 1, 457.

3. Waddell and Abe, "Uji," *The Heart of Dōgen's Shōbōgenzō*, 50.

4. Waddell and Abe, "Uji," *The Heart of Dōgen's Shōbōgenzō*, 50.

5. Nishijima and Cross, "*Sangai Yuishin*, The Triple World Is Only the Mind," *Master Dōgen's Shōbōgenzō*, bk. 3, 45.

6. "The four, five, or six great elements, all elements, and immeasurable elements, are also great miracles that appear and disappear, are spit out and swallowed. The great earth and empty space are miracles that are swallowed and spit out." And "Thus, the buddha dharma is always actualized through miracles. When actualized, a drop of water swallows the great ocean and a speck of dust hurls out a high mountain." Tanahashi, "Miracles," *Treasury of the True Dharma Eye: Zen Master Dōgen's Shōbō Genzō*, vol. 1, 292 and 295, respectively.

7. Nishijima and Cross, "Jinzū, Mystical Power," *Master Dōgen's Shōbōgenzō*, bk. 2, 75.

8. Heine and Waddell and Abe essentially describe the same event from two viewpoints. Heine writes, "[Right-here-and-now] at once encompasses and underlines ('chew up') and over comes and refutes ('spit out') the conventional or derivative fixations and attachments." Heine, *Existential and Ontological Dimensions of Time in Heidegger and Dōgen*, 54. Waddell and Abe write, "Any time (being) always contains a principle of self-affirmation (in which all other times are negated) and a principle of self-negation (in which other times are affirmed). The time on the mountain swallows (negates) the time of the fine palace and spits it out (affirms, manifests it). The self-identity of this contradiction is always present in the being-time of the present now." Waddell and Abe, "Uji," *The Heart of Dōgen's Shōbōgenzō*, 50–51, n17.

9. There are differing views about the meaning of the vermilion palace. Heine (whose lead I have followed) writes, "The palace represents man's deficient attempts to escape from the responsibilities for authentic exertion in terms of an idealized and anticipated futural attainment." Heine, *Existential and Ontological Dimensions of Time in Heidegger and Dōgen*, 179–80, n13. Tanahashi defines the "vermilion tower" as a symbol for enlightenment in Tanahashi, "Glossary: vermilion tower," *Moon in a Dewdrop: Writings of Zen Master Dōgen*, 347.

10. "When you realize buddha dharma, you do not think, 'This is realization just as I expected.' Even if you think so, realization inevitably differs from your expectation." Tanahashi, "Only a Buddha and a Buddha," *The Treasury of the True Dharma Eye: Zen Master Dōgen's Shōbō Genzō*, vol. 2, 876.

CHAPTER 11: WHAT IS TODAY'S TIME?

1. Hee-Jin Kim describes the relationship of presencing delusion and enlightenment: "Delusion and enlightenment differ from one another perspectively, are never metaphysical opposites (such as good and evil, or the one and the many, as ordinarily understood), and are both temporal, coextensive, and coeternal as ongoing salvific processes. . . . They are orientational and perspectival foci within the structure and dynamics of realization and are never erased. Yet they are 'permeable,' so to speak, instead of 'incommensurable.' In light of such an intimate, dynamic relationship, enlightenment consists not so much in replacing as in dealing with or 'negotiating' delusion in the manner consistent with its principles. By the same token, delusion is not ordinary by any means; it is constantly illuminated and clarified by enlightenment in the ongoing salvific process ad infinitum." Kim, *Dōgen on Meditation and Thinking: A Reflection on His View of Zen*, 4.

2. John McRae, trans., *Vimalakīrti Sutra* (Berkeley, CA: Numata Center for Buddhist Translations and Research, 2004), ch. X, verse 15, 172.

3. John McRae, *Vimalakīrti Sutra*, 173.

CHAPTER 12: LEARNING INTIMACY

1. Nishijima and Cross, "Shohō-jissō, All Dharmas Are Real Form," *Master Dōgen's Shōbōgenzō*, bk. 3, 79.

2. Dōgen relates Chikan's awakening in two fascicles of the Shōbōgenzō. See Nishijima and Cross, "Keisei-sanshiki, The Voices of the River-Valley and Form of the Mountains," *Master Dōgen's Shōbōgenzō*, bk. 1, 87, and Nishijima and Cross, "Gyōji, [Pure] Conduct and Observance [of Precepts] – Part 1," *Master Dōgen's Shōbōgenzō*, bk. 2, 147.

3. Nishijima and Cross, "Gyōji, [Pure] Conduct and Observance [of Precepts] – Part 1," *Master Dōgen's Shōbōgenzō*, bk. 2, 147.

4. Nishijima and Cross, "Keisei-sanshiki, The Voices of the River-Valley and Form of the Mountains," *Master Dōgen's Shōbōgenzō*, bk. 1, 88.
5. Nishijima and Cross, "Keisei-sanshiki, The Voices of the River-Valley and Form of the Mountains," *Master Dōgen's Shōbōgenzō*, bk. 1, 88.
6. Nishijima and Cross, "Gyōji, [Pure] Conduct and Observance [of Precepts] – Part 1," *Master Dōgen's Shōbōgenzō*, bk. 2, 148.
7. Nishijima and Cross, "Keisei-sanshiki, The Voices of the River-Valley and Form of the Mountains," *Master Dōgen's Shōbōgenzō*, bk. 1, 88.
8. Okumura, *Shōbōgenzō-zuimonki: Sayings of Eihei Dōgen Zenji recorded by Koun Ejō*, 139–40. This book is not part of the larger work called Shōbōgenzō, but a separate volume.

Chapter 13: The Essential Point

1. "The world worlding the world" is in reference to the paragraph discussed in chapter 17 of this book: "Entirely worlding the entire world with the whole world is thus called *penetrating exhaustively*." Waddell and Abe, "Uji," *The Heart of Dōgen's Shōbōgenzō*, 53.
2. Francis Cook, "Gyōji, Continuous Practice," *How to Raise an Ox*, 176.
3. Waddell and Abe, "Uji," *The Heart of Dōgen's Shōbōgenzō*, 54.
4. Francis Cook, "Gyōji, Continuous Practice," *How to Raise an Ox*, 176.

Chapter 14: Time Passing

1. Waddell and Abe's translation of *kyōryaku* as "seriatim passage" is unfortunate. *Seriatim* implies an orderly sequence, thus making it easier to become confused about Dōgen's meaning. Waddell and Abe may want to point to the aspect of "coming and going" or sequential time that is not problematic. Or they may be acknowledging that our perception of being-time's passage has a linear aspect and is predicated upon causal relationships.

   However, "passage" is the most common translation for the Japanese word *kyōryaku*. Masao Abe translates *kyōryaku* as "passageless-passage," which may be the closest to Dōgen's meaning. Abe, *A Study of Dōgen: His Philosophy and Religion*, 84. Kim notes that while this word has the conventional meaning of to pass through or experience, Dōgen subtly shifts the meaning to "signify . . . 'the passage of time,' by which Dōgen denotes 'temporal dynamicity' or 'temporal movement'—the dynamics of the realized present, in and through which all time and all existence are salvifically actualized." Kim, *Dōgen on Meditation and Thinking: A Reflection on his View of Zen*, 70. In other words, understanding the how of passage in "Uji" is a dharma gate to realization and of actualized presencing. This passage is in conjunction with being-time as the realized now or *nikon*. Heine writes, "*Nikon* and *kyōryaku* are two inseparable, interpenetrating and ultimately selfsame, although provisionally distinguishable standpoints for understanding *Uji*. Neither has priority; the difference between them is a matter of viewing either the surface (*nikon*) or the cross-section (*kyōryaku*) of a total temporal phenomenon. . . . *Nikon* designates the particular and immediate activity . . . *kyōryaku* suggests the entire context and background of events of man and universe." Heine, *Existential and Ontological Dimensions of Time in Heidegger and Dōgen*, 130.

2. Stambaugh, *Impermanence Is Buddha-Nature: Dōgen's Understanding of Temporality*, 44.

3. Okumura, *Realizing Genjokoan: The Key to Dōgen's Shōbōgenzō*, 120.

4. Okumura, *Realizing Genjokoan: The Key to Dōgen's Shōbōgenzō*, 120. Italics in original quotation.

5. This kōan appears in the collections of *Mumonkan* (Gateless Gate) and *Shōyō Roku* (Book of Serenity). Dōgen discusses this kōan several places, in particular "Dai Shugyō" (Great Practice) and "Shinjin Inga" (Deep Belief in Cause and Effect). There is some controversy about how these two fascicles reflect Dōgen's understanding of karma. For a discussion of this question see Heine's "Critical Buddhism and Dōgen's *Shōbōgenzō*: The Debates over the 75-Fascicle and the 12 Fascicle Texts," *Pruning the Bodhi Tree, The Storm over Critical Buddhism*, 251–85.

6. Nishijima and Cross, "Dai-shugyō, Great Practice," *Master Dōgen's Shōbōgenzō*, bk. 4, 44.

7. Nishijima and Cross, "Dai-shugyō, Great Practice," *Master Dōgen's Shōbōgenzō*, bk. 4, 48.

8. "We should recognize that, just as it is inescapable for spring to be simply the spirit of spring itself, and for autumn likewise to be the beauty and ugliness of autumn itself, even if we try to be other than ourselves, we are ourselves. We should reflect also that even if we want to make these sounds of spring and autumn into ourselves, they are beyond us. Neither have they piled up upon us, nor are they thoughts just now existing in us. This means that we cannot see the four elements and five aggregates of the present as ourselves and we cannot trace them as someone else. Thus, the colors of the mind excited by a flower or the moon should not be seen as self at all, but we think of them as our self." Nishijima and Cross, "Yui-butsu-yo-butsu, Buddhas Alone, Together with Buddhas," *Master Dōgen's Shōbōgenzō*, bk. 4, 214.

9. The four elements are earth, water, fire, and air. The five aggregates (form, feelings, perception, volition, and consciousness) are another way to refer to a person.

10. Nishijima and Cross, "Yui-butsu-yo-butsu, Buddhas Alone, Together with Buddhas," *Master Dōgen's Shōbōgenzō*, bk. 4, 214.

11. Okumura, *Shōbōgenzō-zuimonki: Sayings of Eihei Dōgen Zenji recorded by Koun Ejō*, 174.

12. Heine, *Existential and Ontological Dimensions of Time in Heidegger and Dōgen*, 55. Brackets added to original quotation.

13. Waddell and Abe, "Busshō (Buddha-nature)," *The Heart of Dōgen's Shōbōgenzō*, 74. Brackets in original quotation.

14. *Mu busshō*'s literal translation is "no buddha-nature," meaning that reality is beyond saying there is buddha-nature or there is not buddha-nature. Expression of *mu* is essentially realization.

15. A *kaṣāya* (Skt.) or *okesa* (Jap.) is a large rectangular outer stole worn by Buddhist monks, nuns, and priests.

16. Tanahashi, "Transmitting the Robe," *Treasury of the True Dharma Eye: Zen Master Dōgen's Shōbō Genzō*, vol. 1, 144. Brackets added to original quotation.

17. Hee-Jin Kim expresses it this way: "Temporal passage . . . was not so much a succession . . . of inter-epochal wholes, as it was a dynamic experience of an intra-epochal whole of the realized now, in which selective memory of the past and the projected anticipation of the future were subjectively appropriated in a unique manner. In brief, continuity in Dōgen's context meant dynamism." Kim, *Eihei Dōgen: Mystical Realist*, 161–62.

CHAPTER 15: "LOOK! LOOK!"

1. Heine translates this section as "The views now held by the average man as well as the conditioned origination (*innen*, Skt. *pratītya-samutpāda*) of the views by which he tries to accord for his existence are by no means the *Dharma* of the average man; the *Dharma* for now sets the stage for the origination of his [*karmic*] conditions." Heine, *Existential and Ontological Dimensions of Time in Heidegger and Dōgen*, 157. Heine's note to this passage reads in part, "In the second part of the sentence, dependent origination is used as a verb *innen shite*." Heine, *Existential and Ontological Dimensions of Time in Heidegger and Dōgen*, 181, n21. Based upon Heine's understanding, I think we can interpret Dōgen's enigmatic sentence to mean that the Dharma from the absolute perspective is reality itself, and therefore supersedes the Dharma viewed from the relative, the karmic repercussion of causes and conditions that trap us.

2. The Japanese word used here is *hō*, which is a translation of the Sanskrit word *Dharma*. Dharma (with a capitalized *D*) can refer to the fundamental law of the universe and all of the Buddha's teaching. Small *d* dharma refers to individual things or persons. Dharma, a key concept in Indian religions, is also used in Jainism, Hinduism, and Sikhism, as well as Buddhism. In Japanese *hō* can mean the teachings of the Buddha, Buddhist scriptures, the Buddhist path, or reality/truth, things-as-they-are or phenomenal existence. This is the same character found in the Three Refuges. In this case Dōgen's definition is to speak of Dharma as all of reality.

3. Tanahashi, "Dharma Nature," *Treasury of the True Dharma Eye: Zen Master Dōgen's Shōbō Genzō*, vol. 2, 559. "Not form, perception, feeling, inclination, and discernment" are the five skandhas. Therefore Dōgen is saying it is beyond the duality of person, too.

4. Waddell and Abe, "Busshō (Buddha-nature)," *The Heart of Dōgen's Shōbōgenzō*, 66.

5. Okumura, *Shōbōgenzō-zuimonki: Sayings of Eihei Dōgen Zenji recorded by Koun Ejō*, 209.

6. Waddell and Abe, "Uji," *The Heart of Dōgen's Shōbōgenzō*, 53.
7. Ruth Fuller Sasaki, trans., *The Record of Linji* (Honolulu: University of Hawai'i Press, 2009), 4–5. The full kōan is: "The master, taking the high seat in the hall, said, 'On your lump of red flesh is a true man without rank who is always going in and out of the face of every one of you. Those who have not yet confirmed this, look, look!' Then a monk came forward and asked, 'What about the true man without rank?' The master got down from his seat, seized the monk, and cried, 'Speak, speak!' The monk faltered. Shoving him away, the master said, 'The true man without rank—what kind of dried piece of shit is he!' Then he returned to his quarters."
8. A rephrasing of the kōan cited. Sasaki, *The Record of Linji*, 4.
9. Nishijima and Cross, "Sesshin-sesshō, Expounding the Mind & Expounding the Nature," *Master Dōgen's Shōbōgenzō*, bk. 3, 55.

CHAPTER 16: HORSES, SHEEP, RATS, AND TIGERS

1. Rat: 11 p.m.–1 a.m.; tiger: 3 a.m.–5 a.m.; horse: 11 a.m.–1 p.m.; and sheep: 1 p.m.–3 p.m.
2. Nishijima and Cross, *Master Dōgen's Shōbōgenzō*, "Lotus Sutra References," LS 1. 120, bk. 1, 299. These lines can be found in chapter 2 of the sūtra. See Leon Hurvitz, trans., *Scripture of the Lotus Blossom of the Fine Dharma (The Lotus Sūtra)* (New York: Columbia University Press, 1976), 41.
3. Leighton and Okumura, trans., "An Everlasting Blossom Dharma Hall Discourse 91," *Dōgen's Extensive Record: A Translation of the Eihei Kōroku*, 133–34.
4. Leighton and Okumura, trans., "An Everlasting Blossom Dharma Hall Discourse 91," *Dōgen's Extensive Record: A Translation of the Eihei Kōroku*, 134.
5. Waddell and Abe, "Uji," *The Heart of Dōgen's Shōbōgenzō*, 50.
6. Heine, *Existential and Ontological Dimensions of Time in Heidegger and Dōgen*, 94.
7. Tanahashi, *Moon in a Dewdrop: Writings of Zen Master Dōgen*, 79.
8. The word "suchness" is *tathatā* in Sanskrit. Tathatā denotes the true state of things; it is the essential nature and beyond conceptual thought. Other synonyms for "suchness" include *emptiness, thusness, the limit of reality*, and *true suchness*. Damien Keown, ed., "tathatā," *The Oxford Dictionary of Buddhism* (New York: Oxford University Press, 2003), 296.
9. Katagiri, *Each Moment Is the Universe: Zen and the Way of Being Time*, 121.

CHAPTER 17: PENETRATING EXHAUSTIVELY

1. Nishijima and Cross's footnote concerning this sentence indicates that its translation may hold several possibilities for the translator. I have omitted the characters. "The original sentence is constructed with combinations of only three Chinese characters, JIN, KAI, GU. 'The whole Universe' is JINKAI; JIN, 'whole,' works as an adjective, and KAI, 'world,' works as a noun. 'Universally realize' is

KAI-JIN *su*; KAI, 'universally,' works as an adverb and JIN *su*, 'realize,' works as a verb. 'Perfectly realize' is GUJIN *su*; GU, 'perfectly,' works as an adverb, and JIN, 'realize,' works as a verb." Hence their translation becomes "To universally realize the whole Universe by using the whole Universe is called 'to perfectly realize.'" Nishijima and Cross, "Uji, Existence-time," *Master Dōgen's Shōbōgenzō*, bk. 1, 113, n27.

2. Heine, *Existential and Ontological Dimensions of Time in Heidegger and Dōgen*, 68.

3. Dōgen writes about this in "Zenki" (Undivided Activity/All Functions) from a sightly differerent point of view. "Birth is just like riding in a boat. You raise the sails and row with the oar. Althought you row, the boat gives you a ride and without the boat no one could ride. . . . When you ride in a boat, your body and mind and the environs together are the undivided activity of the boat." Tanahashi, "Undivided Activity, Zenki," *Moon in a Dewdrop: Writing of Zen Master Dōgen*, 85.

4. Nishijima and Cross, "Uji, Existence-time," *Master Dōgen's Shōbōgenzō*, bk. 1 113, n27.

5. Nishijima and Cross, "Shohō-jissō, All Dharmas Are Real Form," *Master Dōgen's Shōbōgenzō*, bk. 3, 79.

6. Waddell and Abe, "Uji," *The Heart of Dōgen's Shōbōgenzō*, 49.

7. Nishijima and Cross "Gyōbutsu-yuigi: The Dignified Behavior of Acting Buddha," *Master Dōgen's Shōbōgenzō*, bk. 2, 39.

8. Cook, "Gyōji, Continuous Practice," *How to Raise an Ox: Zen Practice as Taught in Master Dōgen's Shōbōgenzō*, 176.

9. Cook, "Gyōji, Continuous Practice," *How to Raise an Ox: Zen Practice as Taught in Master Dōgen's Shōbōgenzō*, 175.

10. Cook, "Gyōji, Continuous Practice," *How to Raise an Ox: Zen Practice as Taught in Master Dōgen's Shōbōgenzō*, 176.

CHAPTER 18: MANIFESTING THE TALL GOLDEN BUDDHA

1. Waddell and Abe, "Uji," *The Heart of Dōgen's Shōbōgenzō*, 48.

2. Nishijima and Cross, "Yui-butsu-yo-butsu, Buddhas Alone, Together with Buddhas," *Master Dōgen's Shōbōgenzō*, bk. 4, 217.

3. Waddell and Abe, "Bendōwa (Negotiating the Way)," *The Heart of Dōgen's Shōbōgenzō*, 22.

4. Tanahashi, "Birth and Death," *Treasury of the True Dharma Eye: Zen Master Dōgen's Shōbō Genzō*, vol. 2, 884.

5. Cook, "Gyōji, Continuous Practice," *How to Raise an Ox: Zen Practice as Taught in Master Dōgen's Shōbōgenzō*, 175.

6. Nishijima and Cross, "Yui-butsu-yo-butsu, Buddhas Alone, Together with Buddha," *Master Dōgen's Shōbōgenzō*, bk. 4, 218. Brakets in orginal quotation.

7. Kim, *Flowers of Emptiness: Selections from Dōgen's Shōbōgenzō*, 75. Kim's footnote clarifies Dōgen's use of the word "after." "Even so, the 'after' is crucially

important, because by this word it is made absolutely unequivocal that the Buddha-nature defines itself only through buddha-actualization; the Buddha-nature is to buddha-actualization, as ground is to a figure." Kim, *Flowers of Emptiness: Selections from Dōgen's Shōbōgenzō*, 91, n55.

8. David Chadwick, *To Shine One Corner of the World: Moments with Shunryu Shunryu Suzuki* (New York: Broadway Books, 2001), 3.

9. Shunryu Suzuki, "Traditional Zen Spirit," Cuke.com Shunryu Suzuki Transcript (January 5, 1967): http://www.shunryusuzuki.com/suzuki/ft.php?ID=141.

10. Shunryu Suzuki, "Most of You Are Beginners," Cuke.com Shunryu Suzuki Transcript (December 11, 1965, Lecture A), http://www.shunryusuzuki.com/suzuki /ft.php?ID=83.

11. Cook, *How to Raise an Ox: Zen Practice as Taught in Master Dōgen's Shōbōgenzō*, 21.

CHAPTER 19: NOTHING REMAINS

1. This is a reference to the *Lotus Sūtra's* chapter 4, "Belief and Understanding." See Bunnō Katō, Yoshirō Tamura, and Kōjirō Miyasaka, trans., "Chapter IV: Faith Discernment," *The Threefold Lotus Sūtra, Innumerable Meanings, The Lotus Flower of the Wonderful Law, and Meditation on the Bodhisattva Universal Virtue* (Tokyo: Kosei Publishing, 1989), 110–25.

2. Cook, "Gyōji, Continuous Practice," *How to Raise an Ox: Zen Practice as Taught in Master Dōgen's Shōbōgenzō*, 177.

3. The two extremes in Buddhist doctrine are "it is" and "it is not." In my interpretation of Dōgen's meaning, "it is" is the fixed notion of enlightenment as enacted outside the immediacy of all being arising. "It is not" is a nihilistic view that believes nothing exists; therefore, our actions have no repercussions. Buddhism's Middle Way is to take neither view as true. This is expressed by the fourfold negation (tetralemma): x exists, x does not exist, x neither exists nor does not exist, and x both exists and does not exist. See Edward Conze, *Buddhist Thought in India: Three Phases of Buddhist Philosophy* (Ann Arbor: University of Michigan Press, 1967), 219.

4. Cook, "Gyōji, Continuous Practice," *How to Raise an Ox: Zen Practice as Taught in Master Dōgen's Shōbōgenzō*, 176.

5. "Ordinary coarse tea and plain rice are buddhas' thoughts, ancestors' phrases. Because buddha ancestors prepare tea and rice, tea and rice maintain buddha ancestors. Accordingly, they need no powers other than this tea and rice." Tanahashi, "Everyday Practice," *Treasury of the True Dharma Eye: Zen Master Dōgen's Shōbō Genzō*, vol. 2, 622.

6. Stambaugh writes, "Dōgen blocks any possibility of conceptualizing the taking place of the dwelling in a dharma-situation of being-time: 'The sharp, vital quick itself of dharmas dwelling in their dharma positions, is being-time.' It is interesting to note here that Dōgen chooses a sound to convey, not depict or portray, the dharmas dwelling in their dharma-situations. . . . The sound does not congeal into a picture; we come quite close to pure, unobjectifiable dynam-

ics. Moreover, the 'sharp, vital quick' of dharmas dwelling in their dharma-situations completely obviates the dichotomy of eternalism/nihilism that is to be avoided at all costs by any Buddhist. The lines following emphasize this point: "You mustn't by your own maneuvers make it a nothingness; you mustn't forcible make it a being." Stambaugh also makes the point that onomatopoeic use of language reinforces the impermanent aspect of sound. She writes, "[Sound] . . . is not some thing or a thing, and yet it is by no means nothing. Sound does not persist of itself. . . . A single note by itself makes no (musical) sense. In spite of this lack of constancy (persistence of itself), the notes must maintain their pitch (dharma-position), otherwise we do not have sound, but noise or chaos." Stambaugh, *Impermanence Is Buddha-Nature*, 53.

7. "Sharp, vital quick: *kappatsupatchi*. An onomatopoeic description of the lively movement of a leaping fish, it is often used to describe outstanding Zen activity. Here it stands for what is utterly ungraspable and unclassifiable into distinctions such as nothingness and being, impermanence and permanence." Waddell and Abe, "Uji," *The Heart of Dōgen's Shōbōgenzō*, 53, n32.

8. Kōshō Uchiyama and Thomas Wright, trans., *Refining Your Life: From the Zen Kitchen to Enlightenment* (New York: Weatherhill, 1983), 12. This book is a translation and commentary on Dōgen's *Tenzo Kyōkun* (Instructions for the Cook). It has been republished as *How to Cook Your Life: From the Zen Kitchen to Enlightenment* (Boston: Shambhala Publications, 2005).

CHAPTER 20: GROPING FOR YOUR ORIGINAL FACE

1. This paragraph, an example of where various translators place paragraph breaks, gives us some insight into a translator's understanding of Dōgen's thought process. Most translations end this paragraph with the first line of the next paragraph in Waddell and Abe's translation, "Left entirely to the being-time of the unenlightened, both enlightenment and nirvāṇa would be being-time that was nothing more than an aspect of going-and-coming." Waddell and Abe, "Uji," *The Heart of Dōgen's Shōbōgenzō*, 54.

2. Carl Bielefeldt, trans., "Treasury of the Eye of the True Dharma Book 3 Buddha Nature (*Busshō*)," *Sōtō Zen Journal Dharma Eye: News of Sōtō Zen Buddhism Teachings and Practice*, no. 25 (March 2010), 20. Brackets in original quotation.

3. Waddell and Abe are translating *mitō* (J., not yet arrived) to mean mistaken understanding. The meaning would then become "you don't understand it as something you don't understand." Waddell and Abe, "Uji," *The Heart of Dōgen's Shōbōgenzō*, 53, n33.

4. Waddell and Abe, "Uji," *The Heart of Dōgen's Shōbōgenzō*, 49.

5. Tanahashi, "Expressions," *Treasury of the True Dharma Eye: Zen Master Dōgen's Shōbō Genzō*, vol. 1, 440.

6. Waddell and Abe, "Genjōkōan (Manifesting Suchness)," *The Heart of Dōgen's Shōbōgenzō*, 43.

7. Waddell and Abe, "Genjōkōan (Manifesting Suchness)," *The Heart of Dōgen's Shōbōgenzō*, 43.

8. Unno writes: "Shin Buddhism comes alive for those who live in the valley and in the shadows. It challenges people to discover the ultimate meaning of life in the abyss of the darkness of ignorance. As we respond fully to the challenge, the Shin teaching helps us to negotiate our way through the labyrinth of saṃsāric life. The wonder of this teaching is that liberation is made available to us not because we are wise but *because* we are ignorant, limited, imperfect, and finite. In the language of Pure Land Buddhism, we who are foolish beings (*bonbu*) are transformed into the very opposite by the power of great compassion." Taitetsu Unno, *River of Fire, River of Water* (New York: Doubleday, 1998), 11–12. Dōgen also uses *bonbu*, which Nishijima and Cross translate as "common person." Nishijima and Cross, "Sanskrit Glossary, prthag-jana," *Master Dōgen's Shōbō-genzō*, bk. 1, 340.

Chapter 21: Deva Kings Presencing Here and Now

1. Dōgen considered sequential causality to be something laid on top of the totality of being-time or the moment expressed as now (J. *nikon*) and the moment expressed as passage (J. *kyōryaku*). However, Dōgen does not deny dependent origination. Sequential causality carries the dualistic model of a particular cause which results in a particular outcome. Universal cause and effect is holistic and, as Dōgen expresses it, "entirely worlding the entire world with the whole world" (Waddell and Abe, "Uji," *The Heart of Dōgen's Shōbōgenzō*, 53). From this perspective, in "Uji," Dōgen is not particularly concerned with exploring the issue of dependent origination as a causal condition. His interest is how it reveals itself obliquely through his exploration of the nature of being-time. Often, when faced with Dōgen's strict adherence to describing reality from the position of the absolute's expression in the everyday, we incorrectly think he is suggesting that karma or the results of our actions are not important; e.g., there is no relationship between our actions and the outcome. This is far from the truth of his teachings. To approach the world from the position of the absolute, as expressed in the relative, means that we must respond ethically and morally. To fail to do so is to shirk from our responsibility as beings engaged in the Bodhisattva Way. Dependent origination is interconnected interpenetration expressed.
2. Kim, *Eihei Dōgen: Mystical Realist*, 161.
3. Kim, "Uji, Existence-time," *Flowers of Emptiness: Selections from Dōgen's Shōbōgenzō*, 228.
4. Kim, "Uji, Existence-time," *Flowers of Emptiness: Selections from Dōgen's Shōbōgenzō*, 228.
5. This refers to subjectivism. Subjectivism is the idea that all of our knowledge is limited to that which is experienced by the self.
6. Heine, *Existential and Ontological Dimensions of Time in Heidegger and Dōgen*, 183. Brackets added by this author.
7. Waddell and Abe, "Uji," *The Heart of Dōgen's Shōbōgenzō*, 53.
8. Waddell and Abe, "Uji," *The Heart of Dōgen's Shōbōgenzō*, 53.

9. Kim, *Flowers of Emptiness: Selections from Dōgen's Shōbōgenzō*, 228.
10. Chang, *The Buddhist Teachings of Totality: The Philosophy of Hwa Yen Buddhism*, 162.
11. Tanahashi, "Mountains and Waters Sūtra, Sansui-kyō," *Moon in a Dewdrop: Writings of Zen Master Dōgen*, 102.
12. Cook, "Gyōji, Continuous Practice," *How to Raise an Ox: Zen Practice as Taught in Master Dōgen's Shōbōgenzō*, 176.
13. Cook, "Gyōji, Continuous Practice," *How to Raise an Ox: Zen Practice as Taught in Master Dōgen's Shōbōgenzō*, 176–77.
14. Okumura, *Realizing Genjokoan: The Key to Dōgen's Shōbōgenzō*, 18.
15. Okumura, *Realizing Genjokoan: The Key to Dōgen's Shōbōgenzō*, 20.

CHAPTER 22: PASSAGE OF NO-PASSAGE

1. Heine provides an alternate translation for this passage. I offer it here because Waddell and Abe's translation of *kyōryaku* as "passing seriatim" seems obscure and confusing:

> Don't conceive of this passage as something like the wind and rain moving from east to west. There is nothing in the whole world that is not moving around, nothing that is not advancing or retreating, [nothing that is not in] passage. Passage is like spring in that all the various manifestations of spring themselves are passage. You must realize that there is passage nowhere else than in spring. For example, the passage of spring is necessarily that which passages in-and-through spring. Passage is not [just] spring; however, since it is the passage of spring, passage now completes the Way at the very time spring appears. You must carefully examine the matter backwards and forwards.

Heine, *Existential and Ontological Dimensions of Time in Heidegger and Dōgen*, 159.

2. *Passage* is a translation of the Japanese word *kyōryaku*. Heine translates it as "totalistic passage" ("Glossary," *Existential and Ontological Dimensions of Time in Heidegger and Dōgen*, 191). Kim translates this as "to pass through, to pass by, to experience" and "passage infers the dynamics of the 'intra-epochal' reality of the absolute present (nikon)." (*Flowers of Emptiness: Selections from Dōgen's Shōbōgenzō*, 231, n15). Waddell and Abe, whose translation "seriatim passage" I take issue with, explain it as "the movement of time in its authentic sense as being-time occurs without ever leaving the instant present, as continuous occurrence of 'nows' manifesting themselves discontinuously as independent stages." ("Uji," *The Heart of Dōgen's Shōbōgenzō*, 51, n21). It is this discontinuous or dharma position aspect of a being-time that Waddell and Abe are calling "seriatim." Masao Abe translates *kyōryaku* as "passageless-passage," which I think is the most evocative of these translations. (*A Study of Dōgen: His Philosophy and Religion*, glossary, 246)

3. *Prajñā* is Sanskrit for wisdom, although it holds deeper connotations than our conventional understanding of the word *wisdom*. This word has different nuanced meanings depending upon the school of Buddhism. In this case, Dōgen's use of prajñā includes the actualization of wisdom as a being-time expressed.
4. Nishijima and Cross, "Maka-hannya-haramitsu," *Master Dōgen's Shōbōgenzō*, bk. 1, 29.
5. Nishijima and Cross, "Maka-hannya-haramitsu" *Master Dōgen's Shōbōgenzō*, bk. 1, 29.
6. Heine, *Existential and Ontological Dimensions of Time in Heidegger and Dōgen*, 159.
7. Okumura, *Shōbōgenzō-zuimonki: Sayings of Eihei Dōgen Zenji recorded by Koun Ejō*, 137–38.
8. Okumura, *Shōbōgenzō-zuimonki: Sayings of Eihei Dōgen Zenji recorded by Koun Ejō*, 137–38.
9. Nishijima and Cross, "Udonge, The Udumbara Flower," *Master Dōgen's Shōbōgenzō*, bk. 3, 248–49. Italics and brackets in original.
10. Nishijima and Cross, "Udonge, The Udumbara Flower," *Master Dōgen's Shōbōgenzō* bk. 3, 248–49.
11. Nishijima and Cross, "Bendōwa, A Talk about Pursuing the Truth," *Master Dōgen's Shōbōgenzō*, bk. 1, 10.

CHAPTER 23: HOW LONG DOES ENLIGHTENMENT TAKE?

1. Waddell and Abe note that "There is an allusion to the Buddhist idea that long kalpas of practice are needed before Buddhahood can be attained (or the need of many years of zazen to become a Buddha) which, as ordinarily understood, is an objective, dualistic view inimical to authentic Buddhist practice." "Uji," *The Heart of Dōgen's Shōbōgenzō*, 55, n42
2. A broad overview of Śākyamuni Buddha's teaching, in some schools, is that the goal of practice is to get off the wheel of birth-and-death. The fact of our rebirth indicates that we had been catapulted into our life by karmic clinging from previous lives. The goal of the practitioner is to eradicate all clinging to a fixed self and to stop engaging in actions that leave a trail of karmic residue. This karmic residue creates a desire to keep something, get rid of something, and to perpetuate our views or life. When we stop the perpetuation of unwholesome actions, we eventually, after many, many lifetimes, reached a lifetime or lifetimes in which we are only taking care of, or wearing away, the repercussions of previous lives, but not creating karmic residue. Finally we reach a state in which we are no longer caught by rebirth and are liberated (and not reborn). This path statement has been modified over the years by various schools, although the general outline remains the same. In the case of the Bodhisattva Path, the bodhisattva's karmic clinging is that he/she wants to help other beings and is in this way reborn over and over in order to lead others to realization.

3. Waddell and Abe, "Busshō (Buddha-nature)," *The Heart of Dōgen's Shōbōgenzō*, 62. "Because it is like this, the self and surrounding environment of sentient being-entire being is not in the least involved in the waxing influences of karma, is not bred by illusory causation . . ."
4. Kim, *Eihei Dōgen: Mystical Realist*, 167–68.
5. Kim, *Eihei Dōgen: Mystical Realist*, 220.
6. Dōgen does mention rebirth and the repercussions of cause and effect in some fascicles, in particular "Sanji Go" (Karma in the Three Periods) and "Shinjin Inga" (Identifying with Cause and Effect). These essays are part of what is called the twelve-fascicle edition of the Shōbōgenzō, which were compiled or written in the latter part of his life. These twelve texts are the basis for what is called the Decline Theory (of Dōgen's writing) and is a source of controversy among some Buddhist scholars. For a discussion of the Decline Theory see Steven Heine's book *Did Dōgen Go to China? What He Wrote and When He Wrote It* (New York: Oxford University Press, 2006). The Decline Theory posits that Dōgen rescinded much of his earlier nondual teachings on cause and effect. To my mind, Dōgen never denied that one is responsible for one's actions (karmic repercussions) while simultaneously one is never blocked from fully realizing one's true state at this time.
7. The question of Dōgen's relationship to karmic repercussions has been a controversial topic in the modern era, centered in what is called the Critical Buddhism movement. Critical Buddhism addresses what it views as amoral teachings in Japanese Buddhism. Proponents of Critical Buddhism contend that the teachings of Buddha-nature, in particular, are not Buddhist and thereby discourage us from taking up our social responsibilities. Two Shōbōgenzō fascicles on Hyakujō's Fox Kōan, "Dai Shugyō" (Great Practice) and "Shinjin Inga" (Deep Belief in Cause and Effect), are at the epicenter of this discussion as it concerns Dōgen's teachings. A good place to explore this topic is in *Pruning the Bodhi Tree: The Storm over Critical Buddhism*, where Heine writes an essay that directly addresses the issues surrounding Dōgen's understanding, called "Critical Buddhism and Dōgen's Shōbōgenzō: The Debate over the 75-Fascicle and 12-Fascicle Texts." Hubbard and Swanson, *Pruning the Bodhi Tree: The Storm over Critical Buddhism*, 251–85.
8. Heine, *Existential and Ontological Dimensions of Time in Heidegger and Dōgen*, 131.
9. Waddell and Abe, "Busshō (Buddha-nature)," *The Heart of Dōgen's Shōbōgenzō*, 73.
10. Waddell and Abe, "Bendōwa (Negotiating the Way)," *The Heart of Dōgen's Shōbōgenzō*, 8.
11. Waddell and Abe, "Bendōwa (Negotiating the Way)," *The Heart of Dōgen's Shōbōgenzō*, 19.
12. Tanahashi. "Continuous Practice Part One," *Treasury of the True Dharma Eye: Zen Master Dōgen's Shōbō Genzō*, vol. 1, 333–34.

13. Tanahashi. "Continuous Practice Part One," *Treasury of the True Dharma Eye: Zen Master Dōgen's Shōbō Genzō*, vol. 1, 332.

CHAPTER 24: YAOSHAN BITES THE IRON BULL

1. This case appears in Dōgen's collection of three hundred kōans called the Shinji or Mana Shōbōgenzō. There are some variations of this conversation in earlier Chinese texts, perhaps the basis of Dōgen's case. English translations of the Shinji Shōbōgenzō are Gudo Nishijima, *Master Dōgen's Shinji Shōbōgenzō: 301 Kōan Stories* (Surry: Windbell Publications, 2003), 200, and John Daido Loori, *The True Dharma Eye: Zen Master Dōgen's Three Hundred Kōans* (Boston: Shambhala Press, 2005), 202. Andy Ferguson gives a fuller version of this dialogue in *Zen's Chinese Heritage: The Masters and Their Teachings* (Somerville, MA: Wisdom Publications, 2000), 107.

2. Yaoshan is also quoted at the beginning of the fascicle. "For the time being, I stand astride the highest mountains peaks. For the time being, I move on the deepest depths of the ocean floor."

3. Wuji Dashi is Shitou Xiqian's posthumous name. Shitou is best known to Western Zen students as the author of the "Sandōkai" (Merging of Difference and Unity).

4. Shi't'ou and Mazu are major contributors to the foundation and spread of Zen Buddhism in China.

5. Three vehicles: Arhat (Śrāvaka) Path, Pratyekabuddha Path, and the Bodhisattva (Buddha) Path.

6. Twelve divisions of the sūtras: (1) the Dharma in prose, (2) the Dharma in verse, (3) Buddha's predictions for his disciples, (4) teachings given by the Buddha in verse, (5) Buddha's spontaneous teachings, (6) teaching of the circumstances of sermons and monastic rules, (7) stories about previous lives not lived by the Buddha, (8) teachings begun with the phrase "Thus have I heard," (9) jātaka tales of the Buddha's previous lifetimes, (10) expansion of the Buddha's teaching, (11) stories of the miracles and praise of the Buddha and his disciples, and (12) teachings on the Buddha's teaching. From "Twelve divisions of the scriptures," *The Soka Gakkai Dictionary of Buddhism* (Tokyo: Soka Gakkai International, 2002), http://www.nichirenlibrary.org/en/dic/Content/T/287.

7. Bodhidharma is credited as the founder of Zen in China. He came from India, which is west of China.

8. What it might mean to say "northern school" or "southern school" based upon modern scholarly research is debatable. In this context, Yaoshan is trying to indicate that he does not understand practice from a nonintellectual point of view, and Bodhidharma is credited with teachings that were "outside the scriptures." The story of the controversy between the southern and northern schools is a fascinating and complicated one. Heinrich Dumoulin offers a good introduction to the topic in his series *Zen Buddhism: A History* (New York: Macmillan Publishing, 1988), vol. 1, "India and China," 107–15. A scholarly dis-

cussion of this topic can be found in John McRae, "Shen-hui and the Teaching of Sudden Enlightenment in Early Ch'an Buddhism," in *Sudden and Gradual: Approaches to Enlightenment in Chinese Thought*, ed. Peter Gregory (Honolulu: Kuroda Institute: Studies in East Asian Buddhism 5, University of Hawaii Press, 1987), 227–78, and in John McRae, *The Northern School and the Formation of Early Ch'an Buddhism* (Honolulu: University of Hawaii Press, 1986).

9. Andy Ferguson, *Zen's Chinese Heritage: The Masters and Their Teachings* (Somerville, MA: Wisdom Publications, 2000), 107.

10. In "Shoshi Sairai" (The Meaning of Bodhidharma Coming from India), you can find Dōgen's discussion of the kōan "Xiangyan: Up a Tree" from the Gateless Gate kōan (Mumonkan) collection. This kōan asks the question of what you would do if you were hanging by your teeth from a tree protruding from a cliff and someone asked you, "What is the meaning of Bodhidharma coming from India?" What would you do? If you answered verbally, you would fall to your death. But you must respond to the question. The kōan cited is from the collection usually translated as the Gateless Barrier or the Gateless Gate (J. *Mumonkan*, c. *Wu-men Kuan*). This is case 5. My source is Robert Aitken, trans., "Case 5: Hsiang-yen: Up a Tree," *The Gateless Barrier: The Wu-men Kuan (Mumonkan)* (New York: North Point, 1990), 38. It is also in Dōgen's kōan collection, case 243. See Daido Loori, *The True Dharma Eye: Zen Master Dōgen's Three Hundred Kōans*, 333.

11. See Bielefeldt, "Treasury of the True Dharma Eye *Shōbōgenzō* Book 20, Being-Time *Uji*," *Sōtō Zen Journal Dharma Eye: News of Sōtō Zen Buddhism Teachings and Practice* no. 30 (September 2012), 26, n13. Bielefeldt also comments in his endnote that this sentence can be translated as it would be read in Chinese, "for the time being" (which is what Waddell and Abe have done in our translation), or as Dōgen might have meant it, "being-time." Dōgen's meaning would be rendered as "Being-time makes him raise his eyebrows and blink his eyes."

12. See Bielefeldt, "Treasury of the True Dharma Eye *Shōbōgenzō* Book 20, Being-Time *Uji*," *Sōtō Zen Journal Dharma Eye: News of Sōtō Zen Buddhism Teachings and Practice,* no. 30 (September 2012), 26, n13.

13. The iron bull or ox may be an allusion to the legend of the Chinese Emperor Yu who was said to have created an iron ox that spanned the two sides of the Yellow River acting as flood prevention. Its head was on the southern side of the river and its tail on the northern shore. It symbolized strength and stability. This reference is from Katsuki Sekida, trans., *Two Zen Classics: Mumonkan and Hekiganroku* (New York: Weatherhill, 1977), 251.

CHAPTER 25: A RAISED EYEBROW, A BLINK OF THE EYE

1. Tanahashi, "Only a Buddha and a Buddha," *Treasury of the True Dharma Eye: Zen Master Dōgen's Shōbō Genzō*, v. 2, 880.

2. Waddell and Abe, "Uji," *The Heart of Dōgen's Shōbōgenzō*, 55, n46.
   For those of us who were asleep during English grammar class, a personal pronoun is referring to persons. Examples are: I, you, he, she, it, we, you, or they.

A demonstrative pronoun refers to an object or sometimes a person. Examples are: this, that, these, those.

3. Nishijima and Cross, "Uji, Existence-time," *Master Dōgen's Shōbōgenzō*, bk.1, 115, n46.

4. Waddell and Abe, "Uji," *The Heart of Dōgen's Shōbōgenzō*, 52.

5. Bielefeldt, "Treasury of the True Dharma Eye *Shōbōgenzō* Book 20, Being-Time *Uji*," *Sōtō Zen Journal Dharma Eye: News of Sōtō Zen Buddhism Teachings and Practice*, no. 30 (September 2012), 20. See note 11 of the previous chapter.

6. In Buddhism, the tetralemma is most often associated with Nāgārjuna, the often cited founder of the Madhyamaka School of Buddhist philosophy. He writes in the *Mūlamadhyamakakārikā* (chapter XVIII, verse 8), "Everything is real and is not real, both real and not real, neither real nor not real. This is the Lord Buddha's teaching." Jay Garfield, *The Fundamental Wisdom of the Middle Way: Nāgārjuna's Mūlamadhyamakakārikā* (New York: Oxford University Press, 1995), 49. The tetralemma is also a device used in the Pali Cannon. One example can be found in the *Aggivacchagotta Sutta* "Vacchagotta on Fire." Bhikkhu Ñāṇamoli and Bhikkhu Bodhi, "*Aggivacchagotta Sutta* to Vacchagotta on Fire," *The Middle Length Discourses of the Buddha: A New Translation of the Majjhima Nikāya* (Boston: Wisdom Publications, 1995), 590–94.

7. Stambaugh, *Impermanence Is Buddha-Nature: Dōgen's Understanding of Temporality*, 66.

8. Stambaugh, *Impermanence Is Buddha-Nature: Dōgen's Understanding of Temporality*, 67.

CHAPTER 26: THE MORNING STAR APPEARS

1. Waddell and Abe, "Uji," *The Heart of Dōgen's Shōbōgenzō*, 56.

2. Carl Bielefeldt, "Treasury of the True Dharma Eye *Shōbōgenzō* Book 29, 'Mountains and Waters Sutra,'" *Sōtō Zen Journal Dharma Eye: News of Sōtō Zen Buddhism Teachings and Practice*, no. 9 (October 2001), 12. Brackets added by this author.

3. Waddell and Abe, "Uji," *The Heart of Dōgen's Shōbōgenzō*, 49.

4. Waddell and Abe, "Uji," *The Heart of Dōgen's Shōbōgenzō*, 49.

5. Waddell and Abe, "Uji," *The Heart of Dōgen's Shōbōgenzō*, 50.

6. Waddell and Abe, "Uji," *The Heart of Dōgen's Shōbōgenzō*, 54.

7. Tanahashi, "Only a Buddha with a Buddha," *Treasury of the True Dharma Eye: Zen Master Dōgen's Shōbō Genzō*, vol. 2, 880.

8. Tanahashi, "Only a Buddha with a Buddha," *Treasury of the True Dharma Eye: Zen Master Dōgen's Shōbō Genzō*, vol. 2, 880.

9. Francis Cook, trans., "*Ganzei*: Eye-Pupil," *Sounds of the Valley Streams: Enlightenment in Dōgen's Zen: Translations of Nine Essays from Shōbōgenzō* (Albany: State University of New York Press, 1989), 83–84. Brackets in original quotation.

10. Cook, *Sounds of the Valley Streams*, 83. Brackets in original quotation.

11. Cook, *Sounds of the Valley Streams*, 84.

12. "The first patriarch was Mahākāśyapa. Once, the World-honored One held up a flower and blinked. Kāśyapa smiled. The World-honored One said, 'I have the Treasury of the Eye of the True Dharma and Wondrous Mind of Nirvāṇa, and I transmit it to Mahākāśyapa.'" Francis Cook, trans., *The Record of Transmitting the Light: Zen Master Keizan's Denkōroku* (Los Angeles: Center Publications, 1991), 30.
13. Tanahashi, "Guidelines for Studying the Way, *Gakudō Yōjin-shū*," *Moon in a Dewdrop: Writings of Zen Master Dōgen*, 38.
14. Nishijima and Cross, "Menju, The Face-to-Face Transmission," *Master Dōgen's Shōbōgenzō*, bk. 3, 156. Brackets in original citation.
15. Tanahashi, "Face-to-Face Transmission," *Treasury of the True Dharma Eye*, vol. 2, 572.

CHAPTER 27: THE MIND IS A DONKEY, THE WORD IS A HORSE

1. Line one: *A* (mind) equals *X* (realization) but *B* (word) does not equal *X* (realization). Line two: *B* (word) equals *X* (realization) but *A* (mind) does not equal *X* (realization). Line three: Both *A* (mind) and *B* (word) equal *X* (realization). Line four: Neither *A* (mind) nor *B* (word) equal *X* (realization).
2. From the Chinese text *Lien-teng hui-yao*, a transmission history, compiled in 1183 by Hui-weng Wu-ming. A complete translation of Guixing's verses includes a commentarial line:

   For the time being, the word reaches but the mind does not.
   You mistakenly interact with shadows using discriminations.
   For the time being, the mind reaches but the world does not.
   You are like the blind who grope the elephant, each "seeing"
       a different being.
   For the time being, the mind and word both reach.
   You break the empty space and the radiant extends 10 directions.
   For the time being, neither mind nor word reach.
   People without eyes run around and suddenly fall into a deep hole.

   This translation is from unpublished notes by the author from a class on "Uji," taught by Shohaku Okumura at Zuiōji Monastery in October 2004. The added commentarial lines seem to indicate various stages of practice or delusion.
3. Thomas Cleary translates mind (J. *i*) as "intent" and Nishijima and Cross as "will." Thomas Cleary, "Being Time (*Uji*)," *Shōbōgenzō: Zen Essays by Dōgen* (Honolulu: University of Hawaii Press, 1986), 108, and Nishijima and Cross, "Uji, Existence-time," *Master Dōgen's Shōbōgenzō*, bk. 1, 116. Mind and intention/will are part of the five skandhas: form, feelings, perception, intention, and consciousness. These are the five components of an individual person. Heine translates mind (J. *i*) as "*I* means both intention and meaning as well as attention, care, and thought, implying that which is prior to what is said and what any saying actually conveys; it also signifies disposition, will(ing), etc. *I* has been

used in Chinese Buddhist texts as a translation of *manas* (thought)." Heine, *Existential and Ontological Dimensions of Time in Heidegger and Dōgen*, 184, n36. For the most part I have interpreted this as "intention."

4. Tanahashi, "Body-and-Mind Study of the Way," *Treasury of the True Dharma Eye: Zen Master Dōgen's Shōbō Genzō*, vol. 1, 426.
5. Waddell and Abe, "Uji," *The Heart of Dōgen's Shōbōgenzō*, 49.
6. Hee-Jin Kim, *Dōgen on Meditation and Thinking: A Reflection on His View of Zen*, 70.
7. Waddell and Abe, "Uji," *The Heart of Dōgen's Shōbōgenzō*, 56.
8. Tanahashi, "Painting of a Rice Cake," *Treasury of the True Dharma Eye: Zen Master Dōgen's Shōbō Genzō*, vol. 1, 444.
9. Waddell and Abe, "Busshō (Buddha-nature)," *The Heart of Dōgen's Shōbōgenzō*, 67.
10. Waddell and Abe, "Busshō (Buddha-nature)," *The Heart of Dōgen's Shōbōgenzō*, 73.
11. Case 156 of the Shōbōgenzō Shinji, from John Daido Loori, *The True Dharma Eye: Zen Master Dōgen's Three Hundred Kōans*, 210.
12. Daido Loori, *The True Dharma Eye: Zen Master Dōgen's Three Hundred Kōans*, 210–11.
13. In "Shoaku Makusa" (Not Doing Wrongs), "Not committing and good doing are donkey business not having gone away and horse business coming in." Nishijima and Cross, "Shoaku-makusa, Not Doing Wrongs," *Master Dōgen's Shōbōgenzō*, bk. 1, 105. Dōgen defines "not committing" as "accordance with things" (103) and "good doing" as "the universe itself." ("The realization of *good doing* is the Universe itself, but it is beyond arising and vanishing, and it is beyond causes and conditions."), bk. 1, 105. Another example in "Hokke Ten Hokke" (The Flower of Dharma Turns the Flower of Dharma) is "Though the former turning [being turned by the Flower of Dharma] is, even now, without cease, we, reversely, are naturally turning the Flower of Dharma. Though we have not finished donkey business, horse business will still come in." Nishijima and Cross, "Hokke Ten Hokke, The Flower of Dharma Turns the Flower of Dharma," *Master Dōgen's Shōbōgenzō*, bk. 1, 215. This is also covered in *Sanjūshichi Bon Bodai Bumpō* (Thirty-Seven Elements of Bodhi): "While we have not yet ceased expending the self on a word of total transformation, we meet a trader who buys the self as a totally transformed mind. Donkey business is unfinished, but some horse business comes in." Nishijima and Cross, "Sanjūshichi Bon Bodai Bunpō, Thirty-Seven Elements of Bodhi," *Master Dōgen's Shōbōgenzō*, bk. 4, 13. As we can see in all of these examples, each one is a case of transformation's passage from one state to another without sequential demarcation.
14. Nishijima, *Master Dōgen's Shinji Shōbōgenzō*, 207.
15. Waddell and Abe, "Uji," *The Heart of Dōgen's Shōbōgenzō*, 57, n58. Brackets in the original. The kōan is also quoted in Dōgen's *Shōbōgenzō* fascicle "Kajō" (Everyday Life).
16. Nishijima and Cross, "Kajō, Everyday Life," *Master Dōgen's Shōbōgenzō*, bk.

3, 226. Italics in this quotation are added by Nishijima and Cross to indicate that Dōgen wrote a section using Chinese characters. The Shōbōgenzō is written in Japanese in combination with Chinese characters. See the "Notes on the Translation," p. xi of the volume cited above. These same notes can be found at the beginning of any of the books of Nishijima and Cross's translation of Shōbōgenzō.

CHAPTER 28: ENCOUNTERS

1. Kim writes that obstruction "does not imply, as its ordinary meaning would imply, a dualism of obstructor and obstructed. For Dōgen, this would refer to 'self-obstruction,' which means perfect singularity and freedom. Hence, when reaching is said to be obstructed by itself, this means that reaching totally exerts itself and is radically singular and free." Kim, "Uji, Existence-time," *Flowers of Emptiness: Selections from Dōgen's Shōbōgenzō*, 233, n3.5.

2. I found the clearest explanation of this concept in Joan Stambaugh's book *Impermanence Is Buddha-Nature: Dōgen's Understanding of Temporality*, 76–77, 86–88, and 93–104.

3. Kim writes of Dōgen's grammatical methodology, "Any noun can be converted into a verb form, and we can say, for example: 'Eating eats eating, and thereby eating realizes itself'. . . . Similarly, 'Dōgen dōgen-s Dōgen, and thereby Dōgen realizes himself,' and so forth. In this way, the subject and the predicate interpenetrate one another in *activity*. . . . Paradoxically, obstruction in Dōgen's thought meant total freedom in the non-obstruction of self-obstruction." Kim, *Eihei Dōgen: Mystical Realist*, 289–90, n169.

4. Waddell and Abe, "Genjōkōan (Manifesting Suchness)," *The Heart of Dōgen's Shōbōgenzō*, 42.

5. Waddell and Abe, "Genjōkōan (Manifesting Suchness)," *The Heart of Dōgen's Shōbōgenzō*, 41.

6. Waddell and Abe, "Genjōkōan (Manifesting Suchness)," *The Heart of Dōgen's Shōbōgenzō*, 41.

7. Nishijima and Cross, "Katto, The Complicated," *Master Dōgen's Shōbōgenzō*, bk. 3, 36.

8. Tanahashi, "Painting of a Rice Cake," *Treasury of the True Dharma Eye: Zen Master Dōgen's Shōbō Genzō*, vol. 1, 444.

9. A dialogue between Masters Sansheng Huiran and Xinghua Cunjiang originally from the *Lien-teng hui-yao*. See Waddell and Abe, "Uji," *The Heart of Dōgen's Shōbōgenzō*, 57, n64.

10. Gudo Nishijima, *Master Dōgen's Shinji Shōbōgenzō: 301 Kōan Stories*, 124.

11. Loori, "Case 92, Teaching and Not Teaching," *The True Dharma Eye: Zen Master Dōgen's Three Hundred Kōans*, 123.

12. "A silver bowl filled with snow; a heron hidden in the moon." Sōtō Zen Text Project, trans., "Precious Mirror Samadhi," *Sōtō School Scriptures for Daily Services and Practice* (Tokyo: Sōtōshu Shumucho, 2001), 33.

13. Waddell and Abe, "Uji," *The Heart of Dōgen's Shōbōgenzō*, 55.

CHAPTER 29: ULTIMATE ATTAINMENT IN BEING-TIME

1. "These four Zen phrases all indicate ultimate attainment in being-time. Manifesting suchness, or immediately present (*genjō-kōan*); the key to higher attainment (*kōjō kanrei*); body of total emancipation (*dattai*); one with this and apart for this (*sokushi rishi*)." Waddell and Abe, "Uji," *The Heart of Dōgen's Shōbōgenzō*, 58, n66.
2. A reminder of the meaning of mind (J. *i*). Also see note 1 chapter 27 of this book. Heine defines mind as referring to will or volition, as well as thought. Either way, we can make a connection between mind and the aggregates making up the whole person.
3. Nishijima and Cross, "Bendōwa, A Talk about Pursuing the Truth," *Master Dōgen's Shōbōgenzō*, bk. 1, 12. Brackets in original quotation.
4. Kim, *Eihei Dōgen: Mystical Realist*, 76.
5. Kim, "Genjō-kōan, The Realization-Kōan," *Flowers of Emptiness: Selections from Dōgen's Shōbōgenzō*, 55, n1.
6. Kim, "Genjō-kōan, The Realization-Kōan," *Flowers of Emptiness: Selections from Dōgen's Shōbōgenzō*, 55, n1.
7. "Inmost request" is a phrase attributed to Shunryū Suzuki Roshi.
8. Heine, *The Zen Poetry of Dōgen: Verses from the Mountain of Eternal Peace*, 132.
9. Carl Bielefeldt defines *kōjō kanrei* this way: "The term *kanreisu* refers to the pivots at the top and bottom of a door frame, on which the door turns; hence, the pivotal point of something." Bielefeldt, "Treasury of the True Dharma Eye *Shōbōgenzō* Book 20, Being-Time *Uji*," *Sōtō Zen Journal Dharma Eye: News of Sōtō Zen Buddhism Teachings and Practice*, no. 30 (September 2012), 27, n16, "The higher pivot."
10. "What has been called 'the sūtras' is the whole Universe in the ten directions itself; there is no time or place that is not the sūtra." Nishijima and Cross, "Bukkyo, The Buddhist Sutras," *Master Dōgen's Shōbōgenzō*, bk. 3, 102.
11. Cook, "Bukkōjō-ji, Beyond Buddha," *Sounds of the Valley Streams: Enlightenment in Dōgen's Zen Translation of Nine Essays from Shōbōgenzō*, 108.
12. Nishijima and Cross, "Butsu-kōj-no-ji, The Matter of the Ascendant State of Buddha," *Master Dōgen's Shōbōgenzō*, bk. 2, 107–18. This difficult fascicle explores the teaching on the ascendant state of a buddha by several Zen ancestors. The buddha in the ascendant state is a nonbuddha having gone beyond labels. Going beyond is not about the potential or results, revelation or concealment, or speaking and listening. This person beyond buddha has "dropped off the face and eyes of a buddha and it has dropped off the body-and-mind of a buddha." Nishijima and Cross, "Butsu-kōjō-no-ji, The Matter of the Ascendant State of Buddha," *Master Dōgen's Shōbōgenzō*, bk. 2, 111. The implication is that the highest attainment or total emancipation is going to look something like that of ordinary everyday life transformed through reaching and not-reaching. It is just this being-time as appropriate action.

13. Originally attributed to Bodhidharma, but dated much later in the Tang dynasty. Dumoulin, *Zen Buddhism: A History, India and China,* 85.
14. Tanahashi, "Intimate Language," *Treasury of the True Dharma Eye: Zen Master Dōgen's Shōbō Genzō,* vol. 2, 533.
15. Tanahashi, "Intimate Language," *Treasury of the True Dharma Eye: Zen Master Dōgen's Shōbō Genzō,* vol. 2, 534. Italics in original quotation.
16. *Dattai* in Japanese has the meaning of the body cast off or body of total emancipation. Nishijima and Cross translate this as "laying bare the substance." One has gotten free of or shed something. *Dattai* is *datsu,* "to be free of" and *tai,* "body, substance, the concrete reality." Nishijima and Cross, "Uji, Existence-Time," *Master Dōgen's Shōbōgenzō,* bk. 1, 117, n62.
17. Waddell and Abe, "Genjōkōan (Manifesting Suchness)," 41.
18. Heine, *Existential and Ontological Dimensions of Time in Heidegger and Dōgen,* 100.
19. J. *sokushi rishi.* In a footnote Waddell and Abe point out that "immediate present ultimate Dharma," "higher attainment," "total emancipation," and "you are one with this and apart from this" are four aspects of realization. Waddell and Abe, "Uji," *The Heart of Dōgen's Shōbōgenzō,* 58, n66.
20. Tanahashi, "Glossary: splattered with mud, wet with water," *Moon in a Dewdrop: Writings of Zen Master Dōgen,* 335.
21. Leighton and Okumura, "Mazu's Shout Poisoned with Kindness," *Dōgen's Extensive Record: A Translation of the Eihei Kōroku* (Somerville, MA: Wisdom Publications, 2004), 593. This kōan is also case 54 of Daido Loori's *The True Dharma Eye: Zen Master Dōgen's Three Hundred Kōans,* 72, and case 54 of Gudo Nishijima's *Master Dōgen's Shinji Shōbōgenzō: 301 Zen Stories,* 76. It is referred to in the Blue Cliff Record, case 11 (see Thomas and J. C. Cleary, trans., *The Blue Cliff Record* (Boston: Shambhala, 1977), commentary beginning on p. 73). It also appears as case 190 "Baizhang Goes to See Mazu" in Thomas Kirchner's *Entangling Vines: Zen Kōans of the Shūmon Kattōshū* (Kyoto: Tenryu-ji Institute for Philosophy and Religion, 2004), 98–99.
22. "Such examples as [Jinhua] Juzhi's one finger, Hunagbo's sixty hits, Baizhang's whisk, Linji's shout, Dongshan [Shouchu]'s three pounds of sesame, and Yunmen's dried shit stick are not caught upon the stages from living beings to Buddha, and they already transcend the boundaries of delusions and enlightenment." Leighton and Okumura, "Verification, Practice, and Expounding Are One and the Same," *Dōgen's Extensive Record: A Translation of the Eihei Kōroku,* 519. Brackets in original.
23. Leighton and Okumura, "Verification, Practice, and Expounding Are One and the Same," *Dōgen's Extensive Record: A Translation of the Eihei Kōroku,* 519.
24. Leighton and Okumura, "Verification, Practice, and Expounding Are One and the Same," *Dōgen's Extensive Record: A Translation of the Eihei Kōroku,* 520.

CHAPTER 30: IS THERE SOMETHING MORE?

1. Waddell and Abe, "Uji," *The Heart of Dōgen's Shōbōgenzō,* 58.

2. "The word *half* in this quotation may be understood in a sense analogous to the word *partial* above." Waddell and Abe, "Uji," *The Heart of Dōgen's Shōbōgenzō*, 58, n69. "Partial above" refers to "partial exhaustive penetration" on p. 53 (n31) of the same text.

3. Nishijima and Cross comment in a footnote that the word Dōgen uses for half is *han*. This is the same word used earlier in "Uji" that Waddell and Abe translate as a partial being time (see note above). Dōgen's use of the half in a phrase can be understood as "something concrete, individual, or real, as opposed to the ideal." Nishijima and Cross, "Uji, Existence-Time," *Master Dōgen's Shōbōgenzō* bk. 1, 113, n29.

4. There are many references to half a person in the Shōbōgenzō and Eihei Kōroku. One of the most illustrative is Dharma Hall Discourse #215 in the Eihei Kōroku. Dōgen says, "If someone asked, 'What is the place where there is only half a person?' I would simply tell him: The seven [ancient] buddhas could not avoid staying in the monks' hall, opening up their quilts at night, and folding them up in the morning. Moreover, they could not avoid searching for a phrase to express the way." Leighton and Okumura, "The Place of Half a Person Dharma Hall Discourse no. 215," *Dōgen's Extensive Record: A Translation of the Eihei Kōroku*, 224.

5. Nishijima and Cross, "Sanjūshichi Bon Bodai Bunpō, Thirty-Seven Elements of Bodhi," *Master Dōgen's Shōbōgenzō*, bk. 4, 6.

6. "Half reaching," "partial exertion," "wrong," and "mistakes" can be understood to have the same meaning. Waddell and Abe, "Uji," *The Heart of Dōgen's Shōbōgenzō*, 58, n69.

7. Loori, "Case 284 Tianping's Three Wrongs," *The True Dharma Eye: Zen Master Dōgen's Three Hundred Kōans*, 386. This is case 98 of the *Blue Cliff Record*.

8. Nishijima, *Master Dōgen's Shinji Shōbōgenzō: 301 Kōan Stories*, 357; Thomas Cleary, *Secrets of the Blue Cliff Record: Zen Comments by Hakuin and Tenkei* (Boston: Shambhala Publications, 2000), 341; Thomas and J. C. Cleary, trans., *The Blue Cliff Record*, 539; and Loori, *The True Dharma Eye: Zen Master Dōgen's Three Hundred Kōans*, 386.

9. Yuanwu Keqin (1063–1135) was one of the two commentators of the cases presented in the *Blue Cliff Record*. The other is Xuedou Chongxian (980–1052), who compiled the collection.

10. Thomas and Cleary, "Case 98, T'ien P'ing's Travels on Foot," *The Blue Cliff Record*, 544–45.

11. Loori, "Case 284, Tianping's Three Wrongs," *The True Dharma Eye: Zen Master Dōgen's Three Hundred Kōans*, 387.

12. Waddell and Abe, "Uji," *The Heart of Dōgen's Shōbōgenzō*, 53, n32.

13. Tanahashi, "Seeing the Buddha," *Treasury of the True Dharma Eye: Zen Master Dōgen's Shōbō Genzō*, vol. 2, 597.

14. Tanahashi, "Seeing the Buddha," *Treasury of the True Dharma Eye: Zen Master Dōgen's Shōbō Genzō*, vol. 2, 597–98.

15. Nishijima and Cross, "Bendōwa, A Talk about Pursuing the Truth," *Master Dōgen's Shōbōgenzō*, bk. 1, 19–20. Brackets in original citation.

16. Dōgen wrote: "When I was at Mount Tiantong, a monk called Lu . . . was serving as tenzo [Head of Kitchen]. One day . . . I noticed Lu drying mushrooms in the sun . . . he had no hat on his head. The sun's rays beat down so harshly that the tiles along the walk burned one's feet. Lu worked hard and was covered with sweat. I could not help but feel the work was too much of a strain for him. His back was a bow drawn taut, his long eyebrows were crane white. I approached and asked his age . . . he was sixty-eight. Then I went on to ask him why he never used any assistants. He answered, 'Other people are not me.' 'You are right,' I said; 'I can see that your work is the activity of the Buddhadharma, but why are you working so hard in this scorching sun?' He replied, 'If I do not do it now, when else can I do it?' There was nothing else for me to say. As I walked on along that passageway, I began to sense inwardly the true significance of the role of tenzo." Dōgen, through his interactions with Lu in China, realized how practice went beyond the activities of study and zazen. This monk embodied the full expression of responding to a moment's need. Uchiyama and Wright, *Refining Your Life: From the Zen Kitchen to Enlightenment*, 9–10.

17. Tanahashi, "Texts in Relation to Dōgen's Life and Translation Credits," *Treasury of the True Dharma Eye*, vol. 1, lx.

18. Kaṣāya is another name for an okesa, an outer stole signifying a monk's ordination. A smaller robe (also signifying lay ordination) is called a *rakusu*. The robe is placed upon one's head during the recitation of the verse. After chanting the participant puts on their okesa or rakusu. This ritual is still performed by lay and ordained persons in modern Sōtō Zen temples at the end of morning zazen practice.

19. Tanahashi, "Power of the Robe," *Treasury of the True Dharma Eye: Zen Master Dōgen's Shōbō Genzō*, vol. 1, 134.

20. Sōtō Zen Text Project, *Sōtō School Scriptures for Daily Services and Practice*, 72.

21. Nishijima and Cross, "Kesa-kudoku, Merit of the Kasāya," *Master Dōgen's Shōbōgenzō*, bk. 1, 146.

Index

actualizing, 145, 176, 204, 250n7
and being-time, 54, 127–29, 195
Dōgen and, 152, 170, 180–81, 182
expression of, 104, 143, 212, 239n2
Mu-, 123–24, 247n14
practice and, 69, 183–84
See also Dōgen fascicles, "Busshō"

C

Caodong. See Sōtō School
cause and effect, 115–16, 121, 175,
    252n1
Dōgen and, 42, 182, 255n6
Ch'ang-ch'ing Hui'lêng. See Changq-
    ing Huileng
Ch'ing-yüan Hsing-ssu. See Qin-
    gyuan Xingsi
Changqing Huileng, 207, 233
Chao-chou Ts'ung-shen. See
    Zhaozhou Congshen
Chikan. See Setchō Chikan
Chōkei Eryō. See Changqing Huileng
coming and going, 76–78, 85, 97,
    158–60, 166, 241n10, 241n12
    living and dying, 79, 80, 241n11,
    241n13
    time and, 29, 98, 156, 245n1. See also
        going and coming
    unobstructed, 162, 163
compassion, 14, 41, 70, 119, 187
    to actualize, 55, 84, 105, 198
    dharma and, 78, 231
    skill and, 45, 66, 106, 125
    power of, 252n8
    and practice, 218
Congyi of Tianping. See Tianping
    Congui
continuous practice, 112, 119, 140,
    154, 167–68, 174, 197, 204, 207,
    222. See also Dōgen fascicle,
    "Gyōji" (Continuous Practice);
    gyōji; practice-realization
Cook, Francis, 148, 149
Cunjiang. See Xinghua Cunjiang

D

Dai-i. See Nanyue Huairang
Daiman Kōnin. See Daman Hongren
Dainin Katagiri Roshi. See Katagiri
    Roshi, Dainin
Daman Hongren (fifth ancestor), 123,
    233
dancing, 133–34
Daoxin, 123
Daoyuan: Jingde chuandeng lu (Jingde
    era Record of the Transmission of
    the Lamp), series of stories com-
    piled by, 36
delusion, 55, 76, 104–6, 126, 220–22
    and enlightenment, 42, 44–45,
        86–90, 96–97, 263n22
    Hee-Jin Kim and, 244n1
    intoxicants that cause, 240n7
    and the particular, 54, 211, 228
    and passage to realization, 135, 164,
        172, 218
    past, present, future, and, 86, 100, 103
    and realization, 64, 67, 68, 84, 104,
        117, 129
    stages of practice and, 259n2
    and thinking, 71, 159, 164
    and the vermilion palace, 242n2
    See also three-headed demon, the
Dharma Hall Discourse (at Eiheiji
    Monastery), 131, 132
dharma position, 47, 50, 115–16, 124,
    142, 210
    as all being-time, 38–43, 95, 120,
        156, 182
    and being-time, 29, 45, 196, 204,
        250–51n6
    dharmas and, 28, 131–32, 134–37,
        150, 155
    independent, 105, 174, 205, 212–13,
        217
    jū-hōi, 35, 36, 37
    and practice, 48, 69, 76, 220
Dōgen fascicles
"Bendōwa" (Wholehearted Practice
    of the Way), 20, 54, 143, 230; and

kyōryaku translated as, 42, 237n15,
245n1, 253n2
past, 40, 96, 100, 105, 222, 247n17
experience of, 93–94, 114
experiences, 105, 161, 167, 191
flying, 27, 107, 108, 110
and present, 27, 118–19, 121, 169,
190, 243n2
and/or future, 40, 81, 98, 125, 156,
159, 172–73
practice and, 46, 160
past, present, and future, 20, 68, 92,
124, 127
all buddhas of, 61, 82, 196
and delusion, 86–87, 100, 103
dharma positions and, 38–39
ideas about, 91, 101
sequence of, 55–56, 99, 123
practice, 47, 67–69, 116–17, 197, 217,
218
and Buddha Way, practice of, 30,
180
delusion and stages of, 259n2
dharma position and, 48, 69, 76, 220
effort in, 15, 62, 77, 139, 148, 152
enlightenment and, 86–88, 100, 148,
153, 169, 184
"Genjōkōan" and, 63, 73, 161
"Gyōji" and, 139, 144, 151, 153,
169–70, 183–84
kōan and daily, 149, 171
-realization, 41, 146, 169–71, 184,
218
See also continuous practice;
practice-realization
practice-realization, 18, 76, 122, 140,
168, 201
actualization of, 94, 153
and being-time, 22, 206, 220, 222
and buddha-nature, 143, 145
confidence in, 146–47, 149
and continuous practice, 41, 146,
169–71, 184, 218
Dōgen and, 67–71, 124, 144, 180,
232
enacted, 205, 229

fully presencing, 21, 125
is right now, 7, 100, 128, 184
life as, 56, 78, 125
Master Gutei's student and, 177, 178
shōjō no shu, 36
shushō-ittō, 47
time of, 157–58
precepts, bodhisattva, 64, 106, 192,
240n7
presencing, 41, 62, 79, 101, 244n1
actualized, 245n1
of all things, 63, 239n4
and being-time, 29, 45, 158, 164, 195,
239n1
and dharma positions, 115, 136–37,
196, 214
eternal, 93
everything is, 120, 139, 166
fully, 112, 181
immediate, 29, 163, 189
inclusive, 135
and a moment, 8–9, 38, 61, 146, 150,
160
now, 182
our particular, 70
and reality, 19, 126
total, 125
zazen and, 20–21
present moment, the, 62, 81–83, 111,
114, 137–38, 152
and being-time, 227
engaging, 40, 58
the eternal now, 93
experiencing, 89, 91–93, 100–101,
120
and expression, 164, 200
image of, as a circle, 105
past and future and, 91, 158–59
and practice, 47, 68, 117
realization and, 67, 160–61
responding skillfully in, 73, 121, 212

Q
Qingyuan Xingsi, 27, 118, 123–24,
190, 234

About the Author

SHINSHU ROBERTS is a Sōtō Zen priest and Dharma successor of Sojun Weitsman. Her writing has appeared in several anthologies, including *Seeds of Virtue, Seeds of Change: A Collection of Zen Teachings, The Hidden Lamp: Stories from Twenty-five Centuries of Awakened Women*, and *Receiving the Marrow: Teachings on Dogen by Soto Zen Women Priests*. She is co-founder of Ocean Gate Zen Center in Capitola, CA, where she lives.

What to Read Next from Wisdom Publications

Realizing Genjōkōan
The Key to Dōgen's Shōbōgenzō
Shohaku Okumura
Foreword by Taigen Dan Leighton

"A stunning commentary. Like all masterful commentaries, this one finds in the few short lines of the text the entire span of the Buddhist teachings."—*Buddhadharma: The Practitioner's Quarterly*

Engaging Dōgen's Zen
Tetsuzen Jason Wirth, Kanpu Bret Davis, and Shudo Brian Schroeder

"A rich and invaluable collection reflecting Dogen's unique wisdom."
—Roshi Joan Halifax, Abbot, Upaya Zen Center

Dōgen's Extensive Record
A Translation of the Eihei Kōroku
Eihei Dōgen, Taigen Dan Leighton, Shohaku Okumura
Foreword by Tenshin Reb Anderson

"Taigen and Shohaku are national treasures."
—Norman Fischer, author of *Sailing Home*

About Wisdom Publications

Wisdom Publications is the leading publisher of classic and contemporary Buddhist books and practical works on mindfulness. To learn more about us or to explore our other books, please visit our website at wisdomexperience.org or contact us at the address below.

Wisdom Publications
199 Elm Street
Somerville, MA 02144 USA

We are a 501(c)(3) organization, and donations in support of our mission are tax deductible.

Wisdom Publications is affiliated with the Foundation for the Preservation of the Mahayana Tradition (FPMT).